Ancient Peoples and Places

THE MINOANS

General Editor

DR GLYN DANIEL

ABOUT THE AUTHOR

Sinclair Hood was educated at Harrow School and Magdalen College, Oxford. After the war he took a diploma in European Prehistoric Archaeology at London under Dr Kathleen Kenyon and Professor V. Gordon Childe. Since 1947 he has been connected with the British School of Archaeology in Athens as student, Assistant Director (1949–51), and Director (1954–62). He took part in excavations with Dr Kenyon at Jericho, Sir Leonard Woolley at Atchana, and Professor Alan Wace at Mycenae, and from 1950–61 conducted excavations at Knossos in Crete, the Minoan Bronze Age civilisation of which has always been a special interest. Publications include The Home of the Heroes: the Aegean before the Greeks.

THE MINOANS

CRETE IN THE BRONZE AGE

Sinclair Hood

120 PHOTOGRAPHS
126 LINE DRAWINGS
5 MAPS
1 CHRONOLOGICAL TABLE

T&H
THAMES AND HUDSON

THIS IS VOLUME SEVENTY-FIVE IN THE SERIES

Ancient Peoples and Places

GENERAL EDITOR: DR GLYN DANIEL

First published in Great Britain in 1971 by Thames and Hudson Ltd, London

Filmset by Keyspools Ltd, Golborne, Lancs and printed in Great Britain by Camelot Press Ltd, Southampton.
Not to be imported for sale into the U.S.A.
ISBN 0 500 02073 6

CONTENTS

Chronological Table

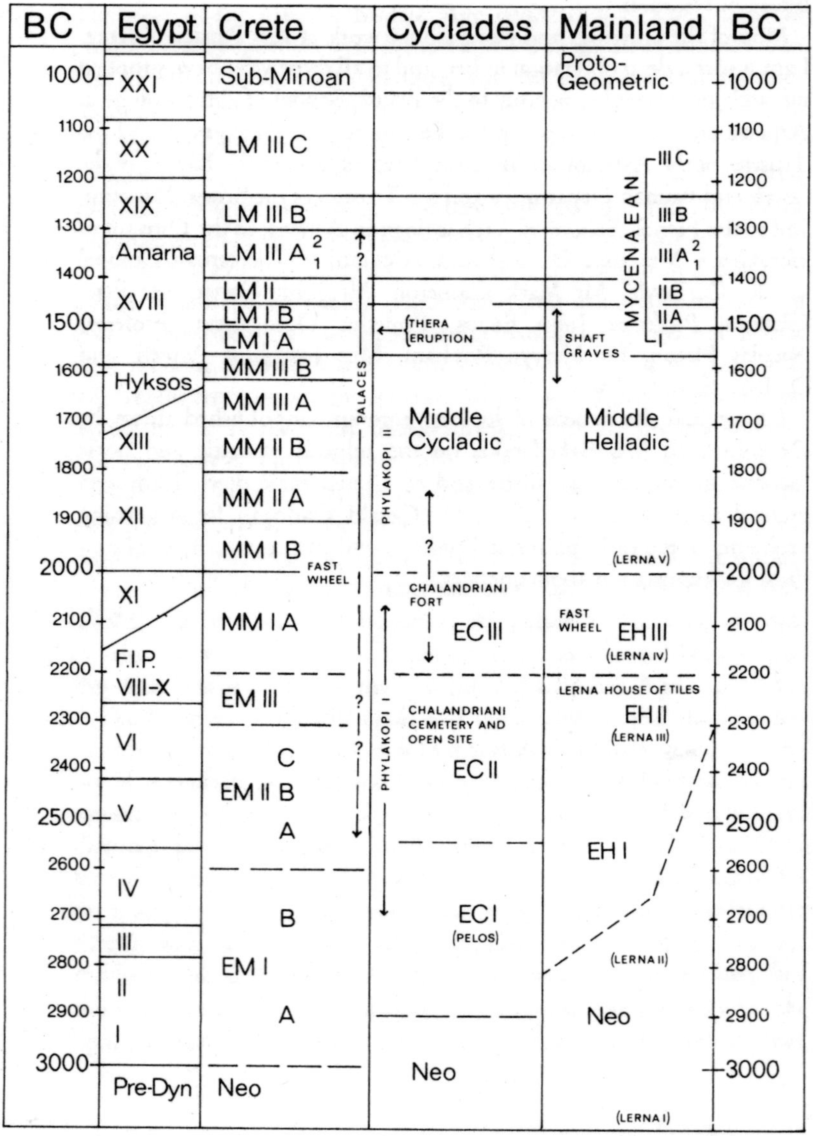

Preface

The story of the Minoan Bronze Age civilization of Crete is to an unique extent connected with the work of one man, Sir Arthur Evans.[1] His travels in Crete began in 1894, and his excavations at Knossos continued at intervals from 1900 until 1936 shortly before his death. The results of these excavations and his remarkable survey of the Minoan civilization, which is still and will long remain the standard and authoritative work on it, were published between 1926 and 1935 in the four massive and richly illustrated volumes of his *Palace of Minos*.

In 1911 Richard Seager, the American archaeologist and friend of Evans, wrote: 'In the history of archaeology no discoveries have raised greater controversy or proved more fascinating to the general public than those of Minoan Crete.'[2] The controversy at least remains, and still largely centres upon the question which was of paramount interest in the time of Evans and Seager; namely, when did the first Greeks, that is, people of Greek speech, settle in Crete? The range of opinion is wide; that Greeks were always there in the island,[3] that they came after the destruction of the earlier Bronze Age palaces *c.* 1700 BC, or, more reasonably, after the disaster which wrecked Crete in the middle of the fifteenth century BC. Alternatively it can be argued that they arrived after the final destruction of the palace at Knossos, the date of which is itself a matter of controversy; or, as I myself believe, that they only reached Crete in the twilight of the Bronze Age *c.* 1200 BC.

The basic work for this book was done while I held the Geddes-Harrower Professorship of Greek Art and Archaeology in the University of Aberdeen in 1968, and I am most grateful for the stimulus and opportunity this gave me. Much is owing to various friends who have discussed parts of the book with me, and especially to Dr William Brice for advice and help about Cretan writing, and to Mr Mark Cameron for the most generous way in which he has placed his unique knowledge of Cretan wall painting at my service together with some of his own unpublished photographs. The sections concerned have much benefited from the criticism of these friends, although the responsibility for the opinions expressed remains my own. Dr Peter Warren kindly read through the section on the early settlement at Mirtos which he has excavated, and discussed problems of the Early Minoan period with me. I am much obliged to him, and to Dr Keith Branigan, who kindly lent me the typescript of his book on the 'Foundations of Palatial Crete' before publication.

Most of the drawings and plans are the work of Mrs Patricia Clarke. I am under a deep obligation to her, and to all those who have supplied me with photographs, notably to the British School of Archaeology at Athens, and to the Keeper of the Department of Antiquities and the Trustees of the Ashmolean Museum, Oxford; also to the Keeper of the Greek and Roman Department and the Trustees of the British Museum, and to the French School of Archaeology in Athens; to the Director of Herakleion Museum, Dr Stylianos Alexiou; to Lieutenant-Colonel C. R. C. Boyle, Mr Mark Cameron, Mr John Carter, Mr Peter Clayton, Professor John Evans, Professor Doro Levi, Professor Nicolas Platon, Dr Mervyn Popham, Miss Josephine Powell, and Dr John Sakellarakis.

I have had the benefit of looking through unpublished theses by Dr John and Mrs Sakellarakis on the subjects of cattle and horse sacrifice in Bronze Age Crete and of Cretan male dress. I am very grateful to them, as well as to Mr Gerald Cadogan for discussing problems of the early palace at Phaistos with me, and to Miss Honor Frost for information about anchors.

M.S.F.H.

Chronological Table

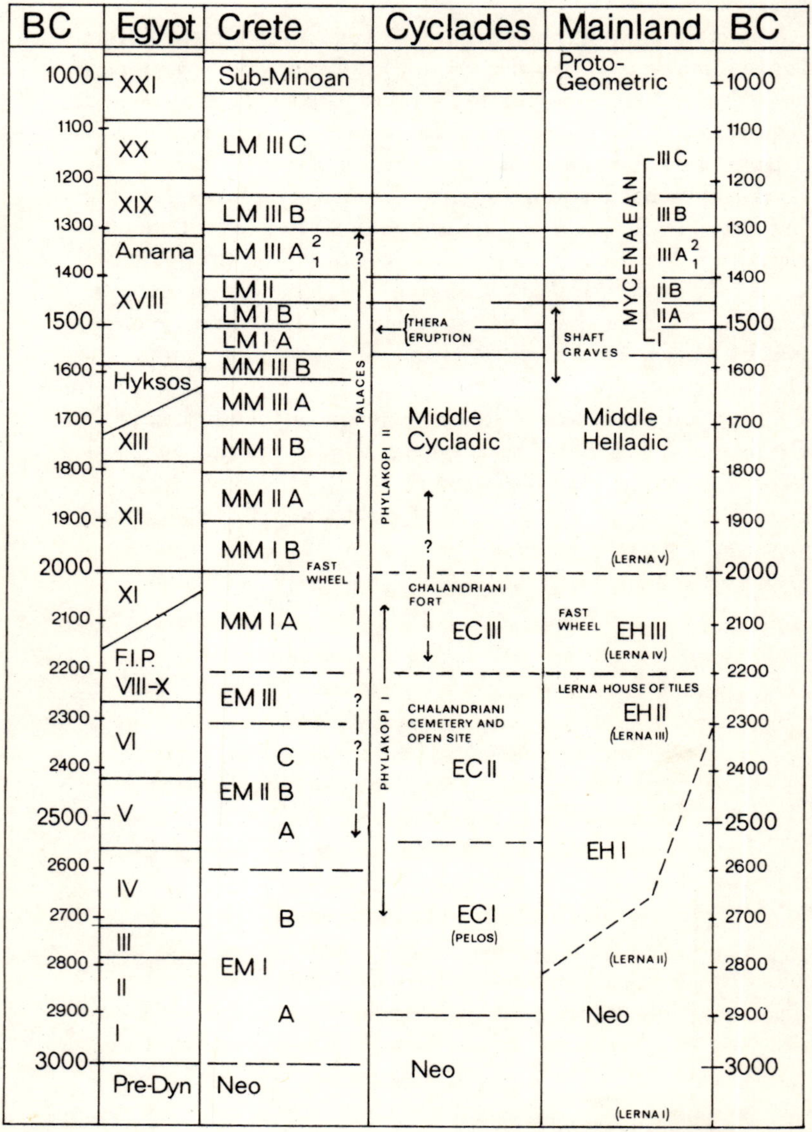

Introduction

'The Mediterren Queene', or 'Queene of the Isles Mediterrene': this is how William Lithgow, one of the earliest of modern travellers to visit Crete, described it in 1609. But he was thinking of the position of the island and of its great natural beauty, together with the advantages of a fertile soil and benevolent climate which it enjoys. For Crete is not as large as either Sicily, Sardinia or Corsica; and although longer than Cyprus it is smaller in area.

Crete is today the southernmost province of modern Greece, and the southeastern tip of Europe, lying nearer to the equator than Malta or the rock of Gibraltar. In early times it would have been virtually the first desirable land for settlement encountered by adventurous sea-voyagers from the coasts of North Africa, Syria or Anatolia. It is *Fig. 1* therefore not altogether surprising that the first high civilization on European soil should have arisen in Crete. That civilization, in many of its features Oriental, and almost certainly the creation of people reaching the island at some point from the East, is nevertheless very different in character from the contemporary civilizations of Egypt and Mesopotamia. The eye of discernment or of faith can distinguish something peculiarly European in it, something which was inherited by the civilization of Classical Greece and ultimately by our own.

The Bronze Age which saw the rise and fall of this civilization in Crete lasted nearly 2,000 years, from somewhere *c.* 3000 to *c.* 1000 BC. The end of the Bronze Age, when iron was beginning to replace bronze for making tools and weapons throughout the Near East, happened to coincide in Crete with the end of a long period of decline accompanied by warfare and invasion from beyond the seas. The last of the invaders who overran Crete in the twilight of the Bronze Age were the Dorian Greeks.

From then onwards Crete was a part of the new Greek world of the Iron Age. Indeed the island was one of the main artistic and cultural centres of Greece in Geometric and Archaic times from the ninth to seventh centuries BC. But later, during the Classical period, it was something of a backwater divided between a large number of ever-warring city states. At last in 67 BC it was occupied by the Romans under Metellus and became a province of their empire. After more than eight hundred years of comparative peace and prosperity under Roman and Byzantine rule Crete was overrun by the Arabs *c.* AD 825. Reconquered by the Byzantines in AD 961 the island was eventually acquired by Venice at the time of the Fourth Crusade in AD 1204. After nearly half a millennium of Venetian rule it was captured by the Turks at the end of the seventeenth century. They held it until 1898 when, after a series of revolts, the Cretans became independent. A decade later, in 1909, the island was united with Greece.

By the end of the Middle Ages travellers from the West had already begun to interest themselves in the antiquities of Crete. One of the earliest of these was a Florentine priest, Buondelmonte, who was in the island in 1422 and saw much that has since vanished. During the nineteenth century the sites of many of the Greek and Roman cities were successfully identified by two Englishmen, Robert Pashley, fellow of Trinity College, Cambridge, who was in Crete in 1834 soon after the Greek War of Independence, and Captain (later Admiral) Spratt, commanding H.M.S. Spitfire, engaged in making Admiralty charts of the waters round Crete in the 1850's. At the end of the nineteenth century many more ancient sites were noted and described by Evans, and by Italian colleagues such as Federigo Halbherr and Antonio Taramelli. It was during this period after Schliemann's discovery of the royal Shaft Graves at Mycenae on the Greek mainland in 1876 that the Late Bronze Age (or 'Mycenaean' as they were then called) antiquities and settlements of Crete began to attract notice.

But until Crete became independent of Turkish rule, no archaeological excavation on any large scale could be undertaken there. As a consequence little was known before 1900 about the earlier Bronze Age civilization of Crete. In March of that year Evans began his historic excavations at Knossos, the chief Bronze Age site in the island.[1] Other British expeditions undertook the excavation of Zakro and Palaikastro in the far east of Crete. At the same time American archaeologists, notably Richard Seager, the friend of Evans, and Harriet Boyd, excavated Gournia, Vasiliki and Mochlos on the Gulf of Mirabello; while an Italian team began to uncover the palace at Phaistos in the Mesara plain in the south.

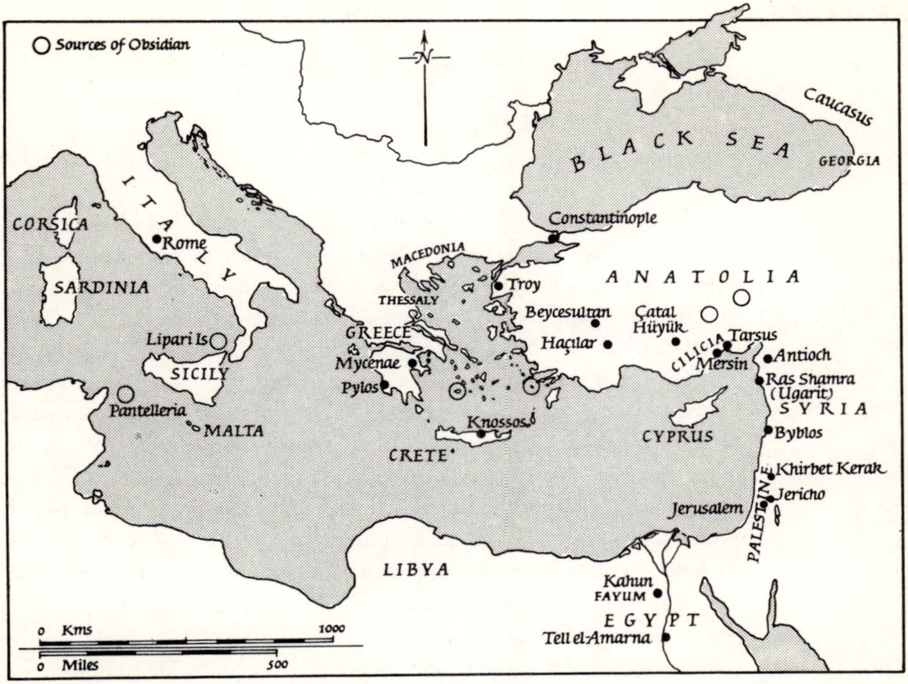

Fig. 1 The Eastern Mediterranean

The exploration of a third great palace, at Mallia along the coast east of Knossos, was begun by Joseph Hazzidakis in 1915 and continued by a French expedition after the First World War. Meanwhile Hazzidakis undertook other important excavations, notably at Tylissos, west of Knossos; and Stephen Xanthoudides from 1904 onwards explored a number of early circular tombs round the edge of the Mesara plain. A line of able Greek Antiquities Officers, Spyridon Marinatos, Nicolas Platon, and Stylianos Alexiou, and their assistants, have continued this work of excavation. In 1962 Platon discovered, and has since cleared, a fourth important palace at Zakro in eastern Crete.

Exploration and the recording of sites somewhat lapsed after the initial spurt at the end of the nineteenth century, but was continued by John Pendlebury in the 1930's, and by others since the Second World War, notably by Paul Faure with special reference to the island's caves. The building of roads and military bases, together with the intensification of agriculture by the use of bulldozers and mechanical deep ploughs, has during the last few years led to a spate of chance discoveries and the inevitable destruction of much that had survived until now.

Knossos had been an important city during later Greek and Roman times. It was a focus of ancient legend; the home of king Minos, and a presumed site of the labyrinth built by the wonder-craftsman Daedalus to imprison the minotaur, offspring of Minos's own wife, the 'lewd and luxurious Pasiphae', as Lithgow calls her, 'who doted on a white bull'. The Bronze Age palace had been identified there over twenty years before Evans began to excavate it in 1900. The first small soundings in the palace were made in 1878 by the local British Consul with the appropriate name of Minos Kalokairinos; a large storage jar which he unearthed being now in the British Museum. In 1886 Schliemann visited Knossos and negotiated to acquire the palace site. The agreed price for the land is said to have included compensation for 2,500 olive trees; but Schliemann on counting the trees found there were only 889, and the negotiations came to an end.

It was assumed that the Bronze Age palace at Knossos would be like those which Schliemann had already uncovered at Mycenae and Tiryns on the Greek mainland. But soon after he began work on it Evans realized that this palace at Knossos was much larger than any known 'Mycenaean' one, and entirely different in plan. At the same time it became clear that the Bronze Age civilization of Crete was not only older than the 'Mycenaean' civilization of the Greek mainland, but was in some ways ancestral to it.

Evans therefore decided to call the Bronze Age civilization of Crete by a separate name, and chose 'Minoan' after Minos, that legendary king of Knossos whom Theseus had thwarted, escaping with his daughter Ariadne after he had killed the minotaur. This choice has been criticised on the grounds that it is inappropriate to name a civilization after a single king. But Evans was of the opinion—and he may have been right—that Minos was not the name of a king, but a royal title, like Pharaoh in Egypt; the name Minoan for the Bronze Age civilization of Crete corresponded to Pharaonic for the Egyptian.

CHAPTER I

Crete: The Island

Crete[1] extends some 150 miles from west to east, although its greatest effective width in the centre is only about 35 miles; while the neck by Rethimno in the west is less than 12 miles, and that near Hierapetra in the east less than 8 miles across. The island is mountainous, and this must always have affected the character of the people who lived in it. The three main ranges are Dikte in the east; Ida in the centre with the highest peak 8,060 ft above sea level; and the White Mountains in the west with their bare whitish summits only a few feet lower than Ida.

The Cretan mountains are basically composed of grey limestone; but earlier deposits of brown, grey and greenish schists, quartzites and shales, are exposed in many parts of the island. A soft white rock, described as marly limestone and known to the modern Cretans as *kouskouras*, covers large areas round the coasts; especially in the north, where the chief settlements were situated in ancient times. There is much of this *kouskouras* round Knossos and Phaistos, and as it was soft and easy to cut the Bronze Age people chose exposures of it to dig their tombs.

The strata or layers of deposit in the limestone of the Cretan mountains in general slope down from south-west to north-east; with the result that on the south coast of the island the mountains tend to drop sheer into the sea, while the largest areas of comparatively low-lying and cultivable ground, as well as the best harbours, are in the north. Most of the important settlements of the Bronze Age were therefore in the north, as are the chief towns and ports of Crete today. The difficulties of the south coast and its lack of good harbours are well illustrated by the description of St Paul's voyage in the Acts of the Apostles. *Fig. 2*

The main areas of land good for agriculture and settlement in the north of the island are round Siteia, the Gulf of Mirabello, the bay of Mallia, with an important Bronze Age city and palace; and above all the hinterland of modern Herakleion which was controlled by Knossos in ancient times. In the west there is the country behind Rethimno, and that round Suda Bay and Khania which sent William Lithgow into

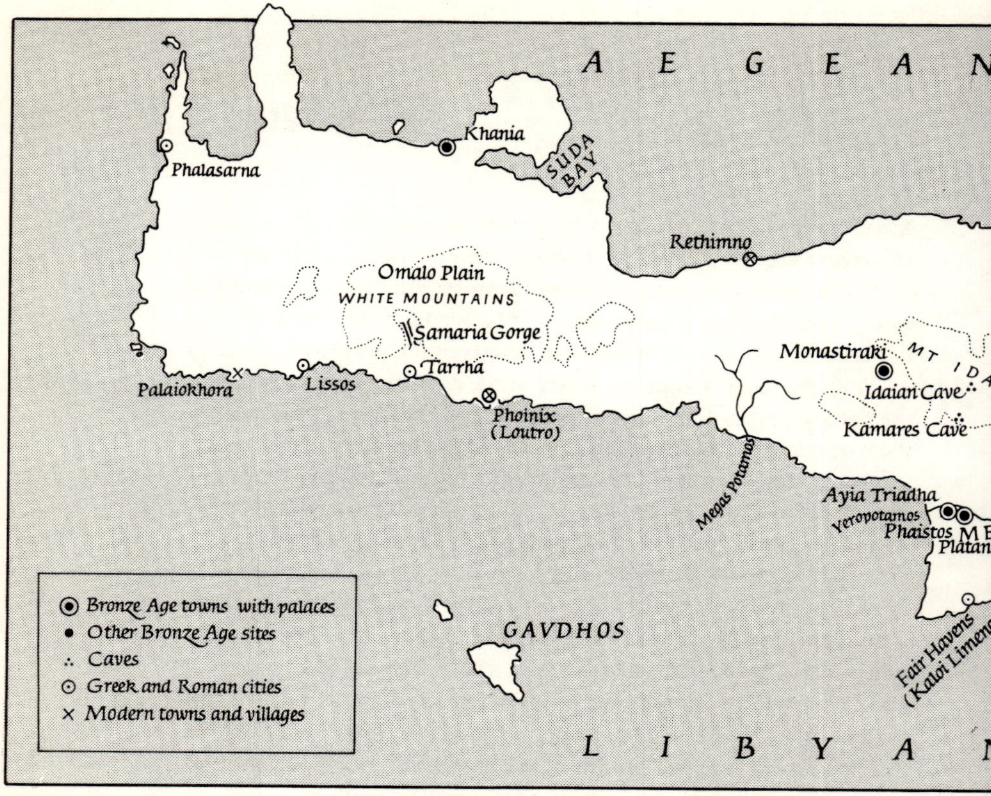

Fig. 2 Crete, showing Bronze Age sites

raptures when he saw it in 1609: 'For beauty, pleasure and profit, it may easily be surnamed the garden of the whole Universe, being the goodliest plot, the Diamond sparke, and the Honny-spot of all Candy'—that is of Candia which was the medieval name for Crete.

But the largest actual plain in Crete, the Mesara, lies, inconsistently, in the south. This runs for some thirty miles from west to east between the foothills of Ida to the north and the Asterousi Mountains which divide it from the Libyan sea. At the west end of the Mesara plain near the coast was the Bronze Age city of Phaistos with its palace, second only in size and splendour to that of Knossos, and by it Ayia Triadha which appears to have been its harbour town, although now far inland owing to the silt brought down by the Yeropotamos. In

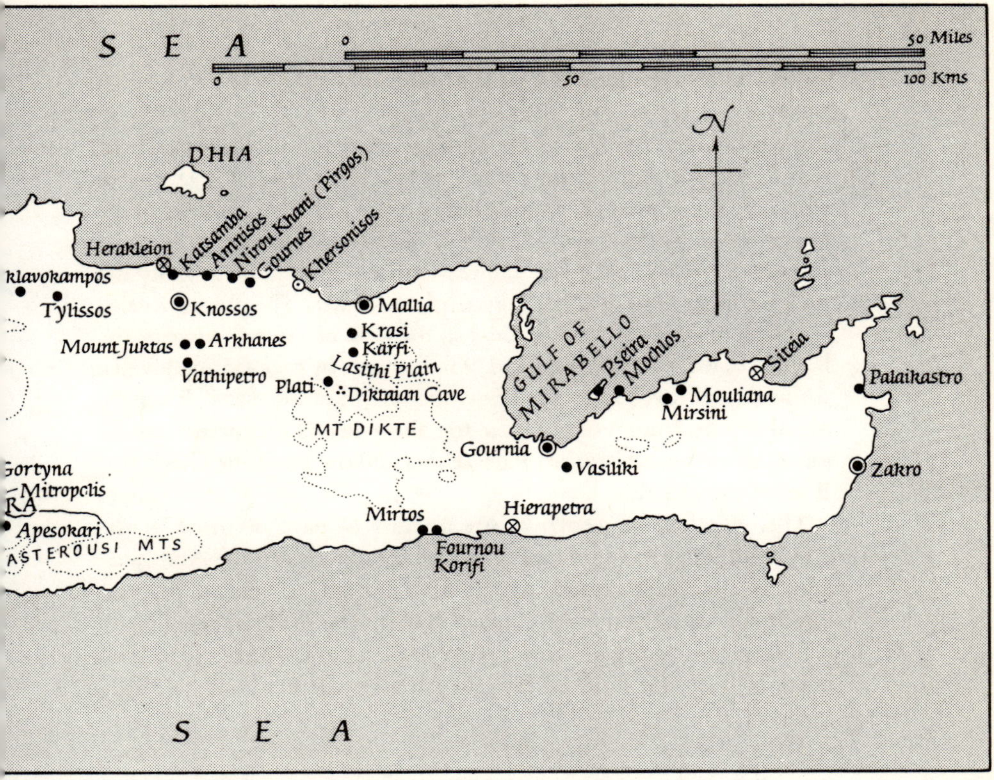

later times Gortyna succeeded Phaistos as the chief city of the plain, and eventually became the leading Greek city of Crete and capital of the Roman province of Crete and Cyrene (the modern Libya). Although the Mesara is potentially fertile it now lacks water.

The Mediterranean is virtually tideless, and in many places round its shores submerged settlements, houses and harbour installations show that the sea level has risen since ancient times.[2] This rise in sea level appears to reflect a substantial increase in the waters throughout the oceans of the world consequent upon the gradual melting of the polar ice caps. Many of the Bronze Age settlements along the coasts in the centre and east of Crete are now wholly or partly submerged below the sea or exposed on the shore. The sea level along the north coast here appears to be some three or four feet higher now than it was in Roman times.

In contrast to this the whole of the western end of Crete has been raised upwards at some quite recent date.[3] The ancient Greek city of Phalasarna, for instance, on the north-west coast had an inner harbour joined to the sea by a rock-cut canal. Today the bottom of the canal is many feet above sea level, and the harbour only shows as a dry depression in summer or a shallow marsh in winter. The old sea level is visible in the cliffs of western Crete in the form of a notch worn by the lapping of the waves, and a band of holes made by rock-boring bivalve shell-fish that dwelt at or just below the surface of the water. It can be traced at a maximum height of 26 feet above that of the present day on the south-west coast between Palaiokhora and the site of the Greek and Roman city of Lissos.

This elevation of western Crete appears to have occurred in the early Middle Ages, and it may not have begun until after the Arab conquest in the ninth century AD. It was evidently a gradual process, spread over many years. For Captain Spratt, who made a careful study of it during his Admiralty survey work in the 1850's, detected successive stages of it on the sheltered cliffs which form the north side of Suda bay.

The rise of the land in western Crete is only one aspect of a factor which has had an important bearing on the history of the island. For Crete lies in a very unstable part of the Mediterranean basin, and is subject to frequent earthquakes which have left their imprint in the archaeological record. Earthquakes were certainly responsible for many of the great destructions which overtook the Bronze Age palaces and cities.

Much of Crete has what is known as a karst landscape; the limestone over large parts of the island being riven by deep, narrow gorges, and riddled with caves. Over a thousand caves of all shapes and sizes have been recorded, and there are still more to discover. These caves have been used throughout the ages, as dwellings, burial places, and sanctuaries. In times of danger they are convenient hiding places and refuges, and were so employed by the Christians of Crete during their revolts against the Turks and by British agents when the island was occupied by the Germans in the Second World War.[4]

The gorges are especially impressive where they have sliced through the mountains that rise steeply from the sea on the south coast. The longest and scenically the most spectacular is that of Samaria which penetrates the heart of the White Mountains to reach the sea by the ancient Greek city of Tarrha. In winter a stream flows through the gorge; but during the dry months of summer the stream bed affords an easy passage from the coast into a valley from which there is access to the upland plain of Omalo.

These upland plains are another distinctive feature of the Cretan landscape. They occupy large sinks or basins formed by a tilting inwards of the limestone strata, and are drained by caves or swallow holes. There are traces of Bronze Age occupation round the Omalo, but it may have been occupied and cultivated only during the summer months as is the case today. The largest of these upland plains is that of Lasithi at the foot of Mount Dikte. It is exceedingly fertile, and watered during the summer by wells from which the water is pumped to the surface with the help of numerous windmills. The Lasithi plain is ringed with villages occupied throughout the year, although conditions are hard in winter. In the Bronze Age there were numerous settlements round the plain, and on its southern edge near the modern village of Plati lay an important town with what may have been a palace.[5] A cave used as a sanctuary in the mountains behind neighbouring Psychro has as good a claim as any to be the Diktaian cave, the birthplace of Zeus according to later Greek tradition. The Idaian cave, where he was hidden and reared, overlooks another upland plain, that of Nidha, in Mount Ida.

CLIMATE

The climate of Crete today is probably not very different from what it was in the Bronze Age. The winters are sunny and mild; snow hardly ever falls in the coastal regions, although it does in the mountains; and in the folds of Ida pockets of it last throughout the summer. Crete is in the latitude of the Atlas Mountains and Morocco, and the summers are hot; but the heat is normally tempered by cool sea-winds.

Rain comes at intervals throughout the winter, but the heaviest rains are in the spring and autumn, the former and latter rains of the Bible. The months between May and August are virtually rainless, and lack of water during the summer is one of the great problems of modern Crete as it is of most parts of Greece. There are still plenty of springs; but in the Bronze Age water was almost certainly more abundant. At Knossos, for instance, several of the springs which supplied the ancient city are now dry.

This decline in the water supply does not appear to reflect a change of climate since ancient times. It is rather due to erosion consequent upon the destruction of the forests which once clothed the lower slopes of the mountains.[6] The trees kept the soil in place; but this soil which helped to retain the ground water has now been washed away by the winter rains, so that there is no longer a reserve to feed the streams and springs during the drought of summer.

There are no navigable rivers in Crete. All, as Lithgow says, are 'shallow and discommodious for shipping, in respect of their short courses and rocky passages'. But a few streams fed by perennial springs flow all the year round. Many, however, during the rainless summer months, become dry pebble beds which then serve as paths.

When the first human settlers arrived in Crete they may have found large parts of the island heavily wooded with oak, chestnut, pine and cypress. There was plenty of timber available during the Bronze Age, to judge from the extensive use of it in building then. Crete was still celebrated for its timber in Roman times, and Lithgow in 1609 described Mount Ida as 'over-clad even to the top with cypre trees'. But the cypress trees, which were being cut for building ships for the Venetian navy in the century before Lithgow's visit, hardly survive today except in the remoter parts of the White Mountains. The deforestation of Crete is due in the first instance to the cutting down of trees, not only for building ships and houses, but also, and more ruinously perhaps, for burning to make charcoal. At the same time the trees are unable to reproduce themselves owing to the ubiquitous goats which eat the seedlings.

FAUNA

The wild goats, or *agrimia*, which survive in the mountains of western Crete today are probably feral, that is to say, descendants of domestic goats introduced to the island in early times.[7] But the island's first settlers may have been confronted by deer of various kinds, as well as by

Fig. 3 Scorpion and rogalidha on early Cretan seals

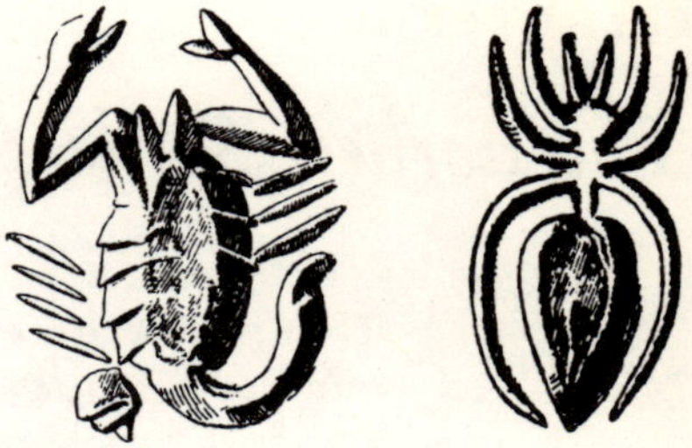

the more dangerous wild boar and lions, depicted on a variety of seals. Plates 41, 42

Poisonous snakes are not much in evidence in Crete, but there are vipers, as Lithgow discovered. 'It is sayd by some Historians that no venemous animall can live in this isle: but I saw the contrary: For I killed on a Sunday morning, hard by the sea side, and within two miles of Rethimos, two serpents and a viper'.

Scorpions thrive in Crete as in other parts of the Mediterranean area. But more dangerous in the opinion of Cretans, ancient and modern, are rogalidhas, small, tarantula-like spiders, which bite.[8] As with the tarantula, the traditional cure for a rogalidha bite was to dance. *Fig. 3*

CHAPTER II

The Earliest Settlers

Fig. 4

There is no evidence that hunters of the Old Stone Age (Palaeolithic) ever reached Crete. An implement of red chert from Lasithi has a superficial resemblance to a Palaeolithic one, but is likely to be of Neolithic or Bronze Age date.[1] During the last Ice Age (Glaciation) of the Pleistocene, however, when much of the water from the oceans of the world was locked up in the great polar ice caps and expanded glaciers, the level of the Mediterranean was considerably lower than it is now; the island of Kythera was apparently joined to the Greek mainland, and the straits separating it from Crete may have been quite narrow. There is no reason why hunters from the Peloponnese should not have crossed to Crete, swimming or drifting on logs or rafts in pursuit of game or adventure.

But at the moment the earliest certain traces of man in Crete are assignable to the Neolithic or New Stone Age. These traces were left by peasant farmers with a settled way of life, cultivating crops and breeding domestic animals, cows, sheep and goats. The first of the Neolithic farmers were clearly immigrants who reached Crete from beyond the sea, bringing with them some of their domestic animals and seed for their crops. By the beginning of the Bronze Age they appear to have spread into every part of Crete, including the remote islet of Gaudhos to the south-west. Some of them lived in caves, whether all the year round or when shepherding their flocks during the summer months. They also had villages, which might be situated on the tops of low hills. Some of these villages were near the coast,[2] but many were inland as at Knossos, where a knoll was chosen for settlement overlooking the junction of two streams in a sheltered valley more than three miles from the sea. The Bronze Age palace was eventually built above the accumulated debris of the Neolithic village here.

This Neolithic settlement at Knossos is an artificial mound of accumulated occupation debris, like the great mounds (*hüyüks*) of Turkey and the *tells* of the Near East.[3] As houses went out of use or were destroyed, their ruins were levelled and new houses were built above them. The walls of the houses were largely of mud brick, and their roofs

Fig. 4 Chert tool from Lasithi, actual size

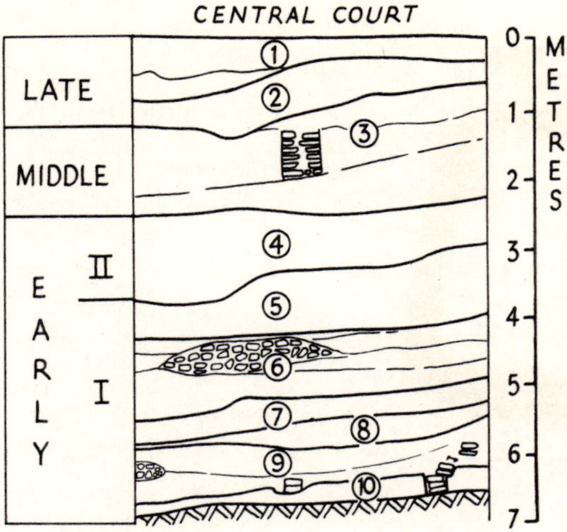

Fig. 5 Section of the Neolithic levels at Knossos

were probably flat with a thick layer of clay over branches supported by wooden rafters as was usual in later times in Crete. The ruins of such houses, even if only one storey high, might leave quite a thick deposit.

In the course of centuries the debris of the Neolithic settlement at Knossos reached a height of some 23 feet above the original surface of the knoll where the first inhabitants had erected their huts. Recent excavations have detected ten successive building levels which can be divided between four stages, two of Early, and one each of Middle and Late Neolithic; these stages being distinguished by changes of fashion in the shapes and style of decoration of pottery. *Fig. 5*

In the lowest level 10, however, no pottery has been found, and very little in level 9 above it. The absence of pottery from level 10 could be accidental, since only a small area of it was opened. Level 10 may represent a long period of time, many years if not centuries; for if the Carbon 14 dates are to be trusted, these ten Neolithic occupation levels at Knossos would span a period of 3,000 years or more, an average of 300 years a level.

A stage when people were engaged in agriculture, but had not yet begun to make pottery, has been recognized at the bottom of many early settlement mounds throughout the Near East, including a number in Thessaly in the north of Greece.[4] The earliest level 10 at Knossos may

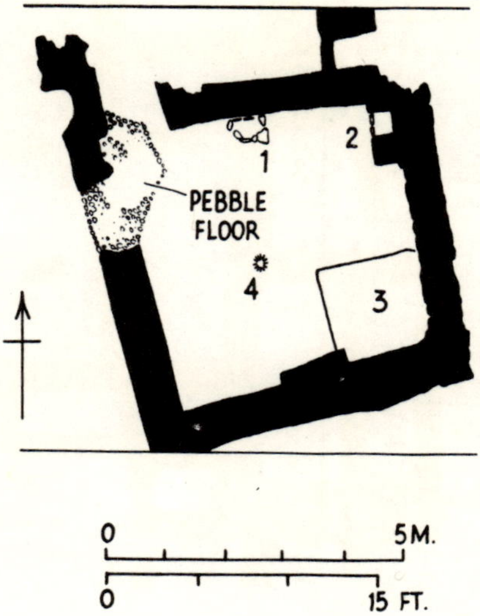

1, 2 BINS

3 BED PLATFORM

4 FIRE-HOLE

Fig. 6 Middle Neolithic house at Knossos

therefore reflect a similar Pre-pottery or Non-pottery phase of agricultural settlement in Crete.

The Neolithic pottery of Crete was all made by hand. It was in general dark-surfaced; but even in the Early Neolithic at Knossos some vessels had light-coloured surfaces, shades of yellow or red. The finer vases, those that may have been used for eating and drinking as opposed to large storage vessels, were invariably burnished or polished. Some of the vases were decorated; with incisions or punctuations which might be filled with white paste, or with applied ribs or knobs. During the Middle Neolithic period the surfaces of the finest vases were rippled by means of a very thorough burnish. Until a few years ago this Middle Neolithic rippled ware was only known from Knossos; but it has now been found in other parts of Crete, at Mitropolis near Gortyna in the Mesara plain and in a cave near Khania.

The first settlers at Knossos may have lived in huts built of wood. These have left no trace apart from holes dug for posts. But in level 9, when pottery is first attested, houses were being constructed with walls of mud or mud brick. Moreover some of the bricks used for building houses in level 9 appear to have been deliberately hardened by

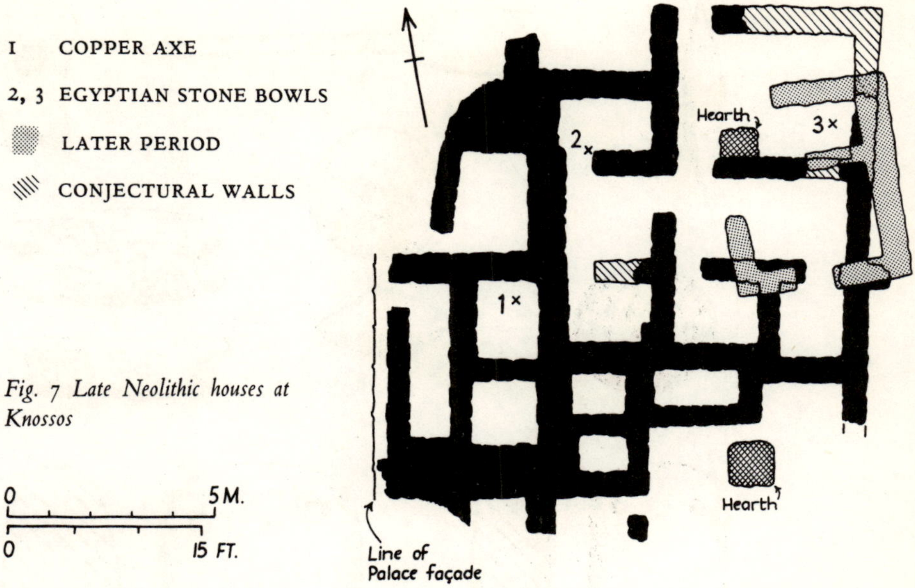

Fig. 7 Late Neolithic houses at Knossos

firing them. In the later Neolithic levels at Knossos, and throughout the Bronze Age there and elsewhere in Crete, the bricks used in building were merely dried in the sun and never deliberately fired. It looks as if the Neolithic settlers, whether the original immigrants of level 10 or a new group introducing the use of pottery at the beginning of level 9, may have brought with them a tradition of using fire-hardened bricks, only to abandon it in their new home.

Houses in level 9 at Knossos were already, it seems, rectangular-roomed. Their walls were of mud or mud brick without any stone foundations. But in the later Neolithic levels the mud brick walls were normally built upon a stone foundation or socle. This system of building, with the lower part of the wall of stone, the upper part of mud or mud brick, remained standard throughout the Cretan Bronze Age and into Greek and Roman times.

A room of the Middle Neolithic level 3 at Knossos was about 15 feet square with a door in the north-west corner.[5] A bin or cubby-hole built of stone slabs against the north wall, to the left on entering, contained a clay pot. A similar bin in the north-east corner held a large storage jar. There was a wide, shallow projection in the middle of the south *Fig. 6*

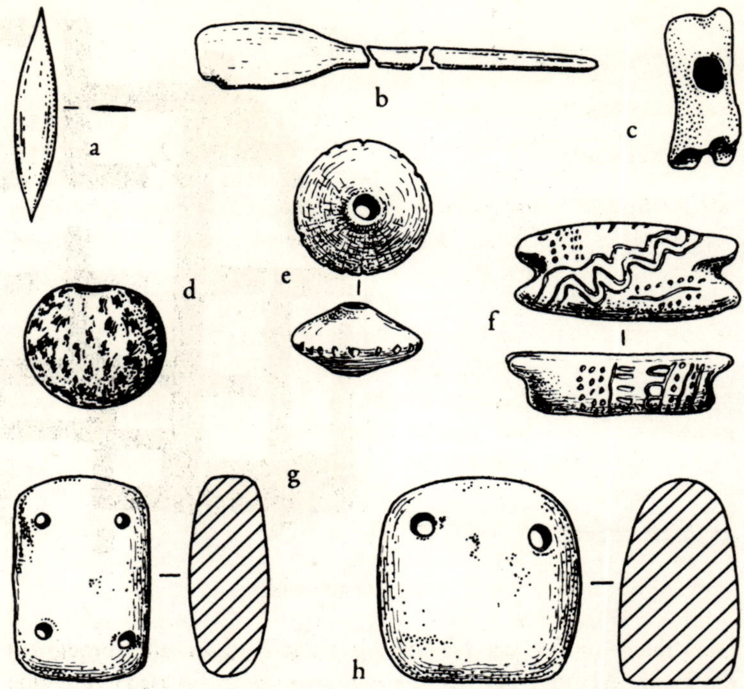

Fig. 8 a, *Neolithic bone arrow-head;* b, *spatula;* c, *whistle;* d, *stone mace-head;* e, *clay spindle-whorl;* f, *shuttle;* g, *and* h, *loom weights. All from Knossos, 1 : 3*

wall; and a low platform by it in the corner furthest away from the door may have been used as a bed. Similar low sleeping platforms are occasionally found in the Bronze Age palaces and houses of Crete. The walls of the room had evidently been coated with a smooth clay plaster. The floor was of beaten earth, and a sunk hearth or fire-hole in the middle of it may have been used for cooking in rainy weather and for warmth in winter. But most of the cooking was probably done, as it is today, out-of-doors.

Fig. 7

Houses by the end of the Neolithic period might be quite elaborate in plan. Two rooms in Late Neolithic houses at Knossos had square fireplaces in the middle or set against a wall. Fixed hearths of this kind are unusual in Bronze Age Crete, but they have been noted in houses of the Middle Minoan period at Mallia.

The Neolithic people of Crete had tools of stone and bone. They shaped pebbles, by grinding, into axes or chisels. Sharp chips or blades of flint and chert, rock crystal and obsidian, may have served as knives or razors; or, mounted in wood hafts, as sickles. The obsidian was mostly brought from the island of Melos, but some of it apparently came from far away in Central Anatolia.[6] The Neolithic Cretans almost certainly had bows and arrows, and leaf-shaped points cut from the rib bones of animals may have served as arrow-heads. But arrow-heads of stone or obsidian have not been recognized, although they abound in the Neolithic of the Cycladic islands and occur on the Greek mainland. The Cretans alone it seems among the Neolithic peoples of Greece sometimes armed their wooden clubs with perforated stone heads. Maces of this kind were standard weapons throughout the Near East in early times.

The Neolithic inhabitants of Crete spun and wove cloth. They made clay shuttles for winding thread, and clay spindle whorls and loom weights. Bone implements (spatulae) resembling flat spoons, found in the lowest Non-pottery level 10 at Knossos, were probably employed to scrape flour from the surface of the saddle-shaped querns on which corn was ground. There is even some evidence for Neolithic music in Crete. Pierced toe bones (phalanges) of animals from the Middle Neolithic level 3 at Knossos may have been used as whistles. Little figurines of clay or stone, usually female but sometimes male, do not appear to represent gods and goddesses. Many were perhaps dolls, although some may have been employed in sympathetic magic or initiation ceremonies.[7] *Fig. 8*

Caves were used for burials. The Neolithic settlers appear to have passed beyond the stage of burying their dead inside their houses before they arrived in Crete. In the lowest Non-pottery level 10 at Knossos seven burials were found during the recent excavations; but they were all of young children. It was a widespread custom in early times to bury children under the floors of houses, but in Crete during the rest of the Neolithic period and throughout the Bronze Age even children were normally taken outside the settlement for burial.

When and from what region did the Neolithic settlers reach Crete? There are eight Carbon 14 dates for the Knossian Neolithic; the earliest for the Non-pottery level 10 of 6100 BC, the latest of 3730 BC for level 4.[8] The first of these dates roughly corresponds to those obtained for the

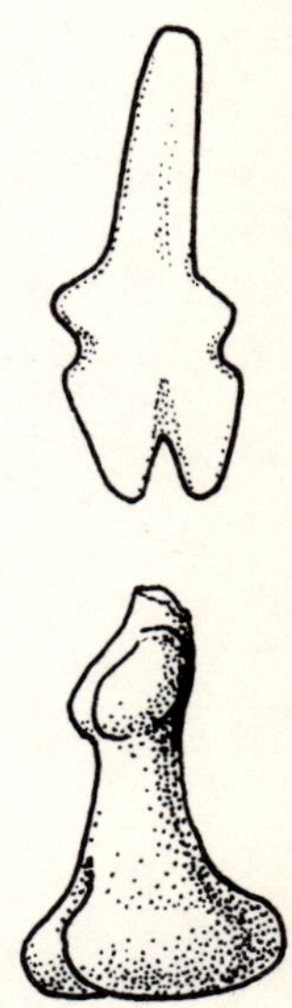

Fig. 9 Neolithic figurines of stone (above) and clay

lower levels of the great Neolithic town of Çatal Hüyük in Central Anatolia.

Curious in the light of these early Carbon 14 dates is the relatively advanced and sophisticated character of the Neolithic civilization of Crete. At Knossos even in the Non-pottery level 10 the adult dead were no longer buried inside their houses as they were at Çatal Hüyük. Moreover the earliest Neolithic pottery, when it appears in level 9, is of an evolved type which looks as if it was the heir of a long tradition.

One day it should be possible to find convincing parallels for this earliest Neolithic pottery of Crete in some other part of the Near East, which would show that the people who made it came from there. But all that can be said for the moment is that the Neolithic people of Crete arrived by sea, apparently from the East; perhaps from western Anatolia, which is near to Crete, or from the coastal plain of Cilicia, or even from the shores of Syria-Palestine.[9]

CHAPTER III

The Beginning of the Bronze Age

The transition from the Neolithic to the Minoan Bronze Age is defined in terms of radical changes in pottery fashions. These changes may reflect the presence of immigrants or invaders from overseas: there are signs of widespread dislocation and upheaval throughout Crete at the end of the Neolithic period, *c.* 3000 BC. Many people seem to have taken refuge in the caves of the island then, as in other troubled periods of Cretan history, and some of the earliest Bronze Age settlements are on high defensible hills.[1]

If invaders reached Crete at this time from some area with a more advanced technology, they might have introduced the art of metal-working to inaugurate a true Bronze Age. But supplies of copper were available in many parts of the island, and may have been exploited before the end of the Neolithic period.[2] A flat axe of copper was lying on the floor of one of the Late Neolithic houses at Knossos;[3] although it could have been an import like the Egyptian stone bowls also found there. *Fig. 10* *Fig. 7*

Until a few years ago little was known about the earliest phase of the Minoan Bronze Age. It was even possible to argue that most of the pottery assigned by Evans to the Early Bronze Age really dated from the time when the great palaces were built at Knossos and Phaistos *c.* 2000 BC.[4] But in 1958 an ancient well was discovered in the north-east quarter of the palace site at Knossos. The well had been filled with debris and pottery after a fire destroyed part of the settlement at the very beginning of the Bronze Age, the phase which Evans defined as Early Minoan I.

This earliest Minoan pottery differs in many respects from that of the latest Neolithic. New vase-shapes include bowls on high pedestals, the smaller doubtless used as drinking cups, the larger as food vessels. At the same time there is a change of fashion in the style of vase decoration; the white-filled incisions or rippling of Neolithic pottery being replaced by 'pattern burnish', where the instrument with which the vase is burnished or polished is used to decorate it, either by burnishing with a different strength, or by making a design in burnish on a smoothed *Fig. 14*

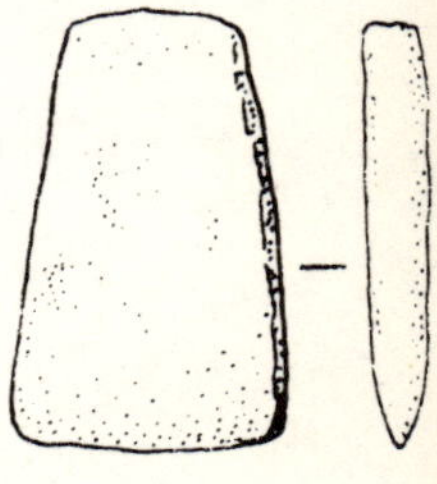

Fig. 10 Copper axe, half-size

Fig. 11 Libyan with side-lock in front of ear

matt surface. At the beginning of the Cretan Bronze Age most of the fine table-ware was decorated in this way, the surfaces of the vases being normally dark grey to black, though sometimes deliberately fired light brown or red. Pottery with pattern burnish is known as Pirgos ware, after a site on the coast of Knossos where there was an important Early Bronze Age settlement and burial cave.

Bowls on high pedestals and with pattern burnish were already it seems coming into fashion at Knossos before the end of the Neolithic there.[5] But spouted jugs for pouring liquids are not attested in Crete until the beginning of the Minoan Bronze Age. Many then have yellowish surfaces with a new type of decoration in red, brown or black paint. Pottery decorated in this way is known as Ayios Onouphrios ware after a spot below the hill of Phaistos where a group of early vases was recovered, apparently from a tomb, at the end of the last century.

Plate 7

Spouted jugs are found in western Anatolia from the time of the First City of Troy if not earlier, and it has been argued that this useful type of vase was either copied by Cretans from Anatolian models in clay or metal or introduced to Crete by Anatolian immigrants. It is open to question, however, whether jugs of this kind were used in western Anatolia earlier than in Crete; the chronological equations between Crete and Anatolia during this period being still very uncertain. Moreover, the early Cretan jugs, with their rounded bottoms and yellow surfaces, look as if they had been copied directly from vessels made out of gourds of the kind that still grow in Crete; and their simple painted decoration appears to be skeuomorphic, derived from the string nets or slings in which gourd vessels were carried.

Another homeland from which immigrants might have reached Crete at the beginning of the Bronze Age is the south-eastern corner of the Mediterranean.

Evans long ago drew attention to aspects of the Minoan civilization which he thought must be derived from Libya; and he therefore suggested that the Bronze Age of Crete began with the arrival of refugees escaping from the western part of the Delta region when this was conquered by Mena, who according to tradition united the north of Egypt to the Kingdom of the South, thus becoming the founder of the First Egyptian Dynasty somewhere about 3000 BC.[6]

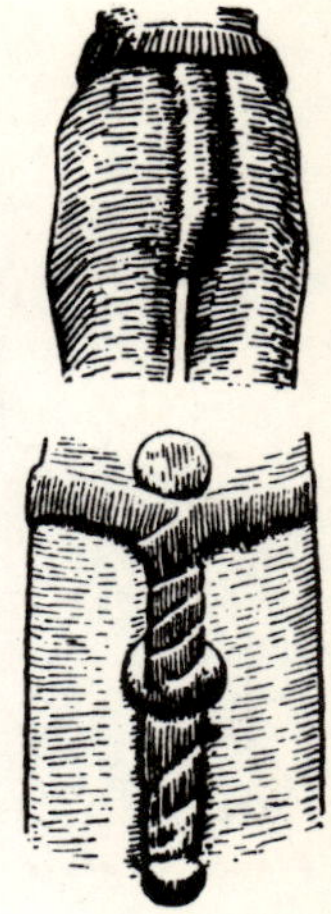

Fig. 12 Early Cretan and Predynastic Egyptian cod-pieces

The most important of these elements which Evans referred to Libya were the cod-piece traditionally worn as part of their dress by Cretan men, their custom of leaving locks of hair hanging down in front of their ears, and the early circular tombs of Crete. The Cretan cod-piece was originally straight and narrow like that worn by the people of Libya in later times. But a similar type appears on Predynastic figurines and was retained as part of military dress in Egypt. In Crete and Libya therefore the cod-piece may represent the survival of a fashion once general throughout a wide region that included Egypt and adjacent areas such as Syria and Palestine. Conservatism of this kind is a key to many aspects of the Minoan civilization of Crete, where beliefs and customs originally prevalent elsewhere in the Near East tended to linger.

EARLY CIRCULAR TOMBS

Their numerous circular tombs are among the most striking monuments left by the early inhabitants of Crete.[7] These tombs were communal, used for burials by a clan or extended family over many generations, even centuries. The Libyans also built circular tombs; but they are not strictly comparable with the early Cretan ones, and those which have been explored appear to be much later in date. The Cretan circular tombs are thickly concentrated in the region of the Mesara plain, and along the coast to the south of it. This is one reason why Evans thought that they might be of Libyan origin. But such tombs have been found in the north round Knossos, and one has been excavated near Mirsini on the north-east coast. *Fig. 13*

These circular tombs of Crete were either built above ground, or had their floors sunk only a few feet below it. None have survived with a roof, and it is therefore arguable that they had flat roofs or were open-air enclosures; but they may have been domed, like the tholos or bee-hive tombs widespread throughout Greece in the Late Bronze Age. The walls of the early Cretan tombs lean inwards, and tend to be immensely thick in relation to the diameter of the chamber, as if to support the thrust of a dome. The domed vault was normally perhaps built of stone bonded with clay. But the largest tombs such as Platanos A (with a chamber about 43 feet across) may have been vaulted in mud-brick like circular houses in the early settlement at Khirokitia *Fig. 126*

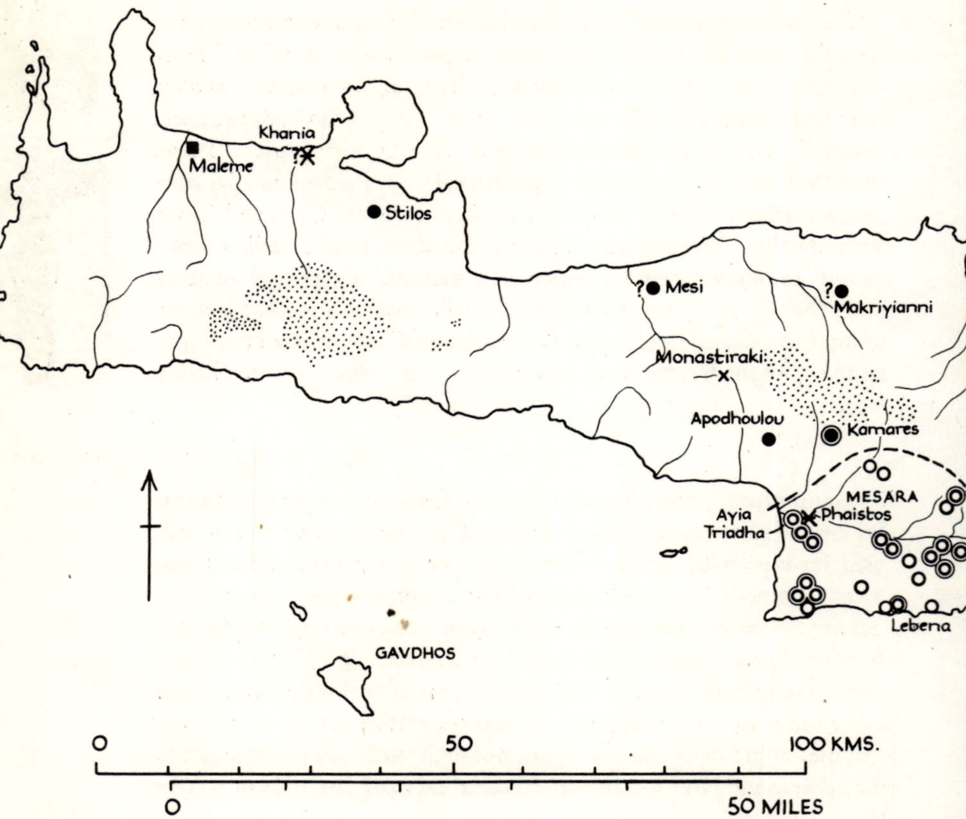

in Cyprus, which according to the Carbon 14 dates flourished about 5800 BC, contemporary with the beginning of the Cretan Neolithic.[8] At Khirokitia as in many other parts of the Near East in the earliest times the dead were buried inside the houses in which they had lived.

People have always tended to build tombs to resemble houses. But in Crete it seems houses normally had rectangular rooms even during the Neolithic period. The dead, however, are conservative, and these early round tombs of Crete may represent a primitive type of house retained for their use after the living had abandoned it.[9] Similarly, although shrines in Bronze Age Crete were for the most part rectangular,

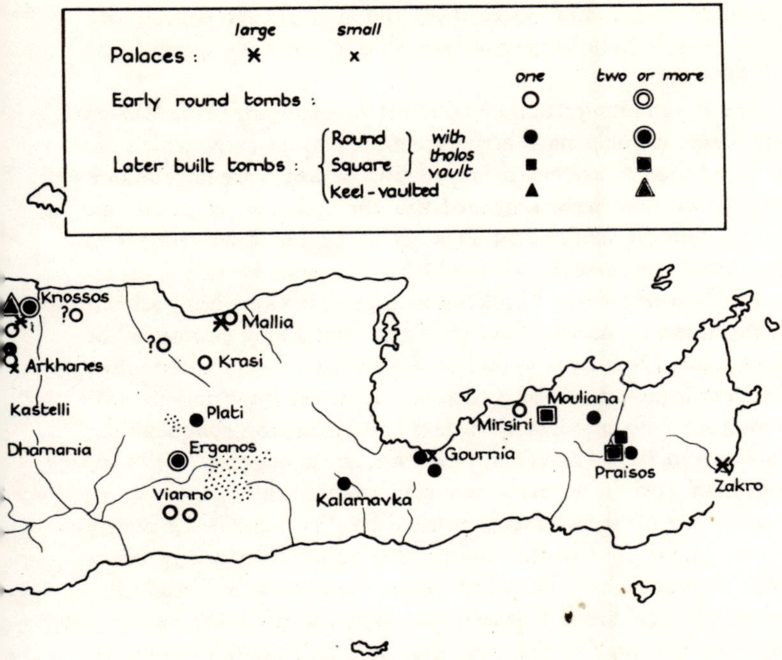

Fig. 13 Crete, showing early circular tombs and later built tombs

roomed, some appear to have been circular as in Egypt.[10] Clay models of round buildings go back to Early Minoan times, and a few, dating from the very end of the Bronze Age and later, have goddesses inside them.[11] A section of wall that might have belonged to a circular shrine was noted on the highest point of the early settlement of Fournou Korifi in southern Crete.

The custom of collective burial in circular tombs was evidently brought to Crete by immigrants or invaders from some region where round huts had once been traditional, and they may have arrived at the beginning of the Minoan Bronze Age, since there is no evidence for the existence of such tombs before then. But it is always possible that circular tombs of some kind were established in a part of Crete earlier in Neolithic times.

If there was an immigration into Crete at the beginning of the Minoan Bronze Age, it might have been precipitated by an event which has been called the first exercise in imperialism of which we have record. Evans, as we have seen, suggested that the conquests of Mena, the legendary founder of the First Dynasty in Egypt, drove refugees to Crete from the region of the western Delta. The name Mena is only preserved in the works of later Greek historians, no such king being known from the historical records of ancient Egypt. But a king Narmer of the First Egyptian Dynasty, who may or may not have been the conqueror of the Delta region, is now attested as having carried his victorious arms into southern Palestine. It is not certain how lasting this conquest was; but towns were sacked and destroyed by fire, and at one place, Tell Gat, an Egyptian garrison seems to have been established.[12]

Various resemblances have been noted between some of the pottery that was in use in Palestine during the period immediately before Narmer's conquest, and the earliest Bronze Age pottery of Crete.[13] But these resemblances are of a general character; and while the people of Palestine at this time buried their dead in clan or family vaults, no tombs exactly like the early circular ones of Crete have yet been recognized there.

CHAPTER IV

Pottery and Chronology

THE MINOAN SYSTEM OF PERIODS

In the same way that he arranged the sequence of Neolithic pottery found at Knossos into three periods, Early, Middle and Late, Sir Arthur Evans divided that of the succeeding Bronze Age into Early, Middle and Late Minoan. Each of these three main periods he divided again into three, making nine in all. But some of these nine periods it was found could be subdivided on the basis of observable differences in the pottery made during the earlier and later parts of them. An early phase A, and a later B, were therefore distinguished in several instances. Since Evans died in 1941 at the ripe age of 90 the last of his nine periods, Late Minoan III, has been still further subdivided into Late Minoan III A, B 1 and B 2; but late Minoan III B 1 and 2 are now usually called Late Minoan III B and C.

For the Minoan Bronze Age therefore, covering some two thousand years, sixteen or more periods are distinguishable from each other in terms of pottery, and to some extent of other classes of object made. This gives an average length of over a century for each period; but many of the later ones were clearly shorter in duration, the earlier ones longer.

There are difficulties, however, in applying this system of periods devised by Evans. It was based in the first instance on changes of fashion in the pottery of Knossos. But even at Knossos, which appears to have been the chief site of the island throughout the Minoan Bronze Age, it is often difficult to decide the period to which a single vase, or even a deposit of vases, belongs. It can be still more difficult when dealing with pottery from a provincial site. Although the civilization of Crete throughout the Bronze Age was basically homogeneous, local differences and divergences of fashion existed in the pottery as they did in other aspects of life such as burial customs. Pottery workshops specializing in the production of fine decorated vases appear to have been attached to the great palaces at Knossos and Phaistos, their products being largely confined to the palaces themselves and the towns which surrounded them. Thus pottery of some periods (such as Late Minoan

II), clearly defined at Knossos, is difficult to recognize elsewhere in Crete. Hence a degree of uncertainty exists as to how the sequence of changes in pottery fashion in other parts of Crete correlates with that at Knossos. This has led to confusion, and the system of periods defined by Evans has been the subject of much criticism. It has been argued that some of his divisions, like Early Minoan III, were not really separate periods of time at all. But excavations at Knossos in 1957–61 have shown that all of the periods defined by Evans are distinguishable there in true succession.[1]

Evans took major shifts of fashion in the style of decoration of the fine table-ware as marking the divisions between his three main periods. Thus Early Minoan decoration was characteristically in dark paint on a light ground. During Middle Minoan times the fashion was for decoration in white and red paint on a dark-washed surface; finally, Late Minoan taste swung back in favour of designs in dark on light. But these shifts of fashion were gradual, and do not appear to have coincided with any major events of Cretan history. An alternative system of periods for the Cretan Bronze Age has therefore been suggested with divisions based, not upon changes in the pottery, but upon major events in the history of the great palaces.[2] The palaces at Knossos and Phaistos appear to have been built during the period which Evans called Middle Minoan I. The earlier part of the Bronze Age before their foundation is therefore named Prepalatial. Both palaces were destroyed it seems *c.* 1700 BC and afterwards rebuilt. What lies before this destruction is called the period of the First or Early Palaces, or Protopalatial; and what comes after it, the period of the Second or Later Palaces, or Neopalatial. The period after the final destruction of the palace at Knossos in the fourteenth century BC is named Post-palatial. But the nomenclature of this Palatial system of periods is cumbersome; and the assumptions upon which it is based are not altogether certain. For instance, at the moment there is a wide range of disagreement about the date of the final destruction of the palace at Knossos. It is therefore convenient to retain the system of periods defined by Evans together with his names for them.

cf. Appendix

Early Minoan I. The pottery of the earliest phase (A) has already been described. Since much of it is dark-surfaced and burnished like the finer Neolithic wares, it is often called Subneolithic. But new vase-shapes, notably bowls on high pedestals and spouted jugs, are now in evidence, and the fashion for incised designs has been replaced by 'pattern burnish'. Some of the vases are decorated in red, brown or black paint, on a light surface, a style unknown to the Cretan Neolithic, but which continued in use throughout the Bronze Age and into later Greek times. Plate 7

A later phase (B) of Early Minoan I is not yet well defined. Thin-waisted, often solid pedestals are now in evidence at Knossos, while the fashion for pattern burnish is on the wane. Thickened anti-splash rims begin to appear on bowls. Most of the vases from the burial cave at Pirgos, near Nirou Khani on the north coast, are probably assignable to this phase and to Early Minoan II. *Fig. 14*

Early Minoan II. In the earliest phase (A) vases with dark grey burnished surfaces still dominate as table-ware at Knossos, but 'pattern burnish' has become rare. Bowls are regularly given thickened anti-splash rims. Such rims are also characteristic of the latest Chalcolithic (Kum Tepe I B) phase of western Anatolia, immediately before the Early Bronze Age of Troy I there.

In phase B anti-splash-rim bowls continue in general use at Knossos; these and many other types of vase now being light-surfaced with decoration normally in red, but also in brown or black paint. Designs are still apt to be linear and comparatively simple in character, but include concentric loops which hang from the rims of cups and goblets and may be ultimately derived through Cilicia or Syria from the repertory of the Ubaid horizon of early Predynastic date (before *c.* 3500 BC) in Mesopotamia.

Vases with dark over-all washes continue the tradition of the grey burnished wares of Early Minoan I. These washed surfaces are sometimes mottled in shades of black, red and brown; and while such mottling may have resulted at first from an imperfect control of the firing, it was often in the end deliberately induced by artificial means. Mottled ware is known by the name of the site, Vasiliki, where Seager first discovered it in 1906. It was very popular in the east of Crete and may have been invented there, although Vasiliki ware, apparently of local manufacture, has been found not only at Knossos, but even at Khania in the far west of the island. Plate 6

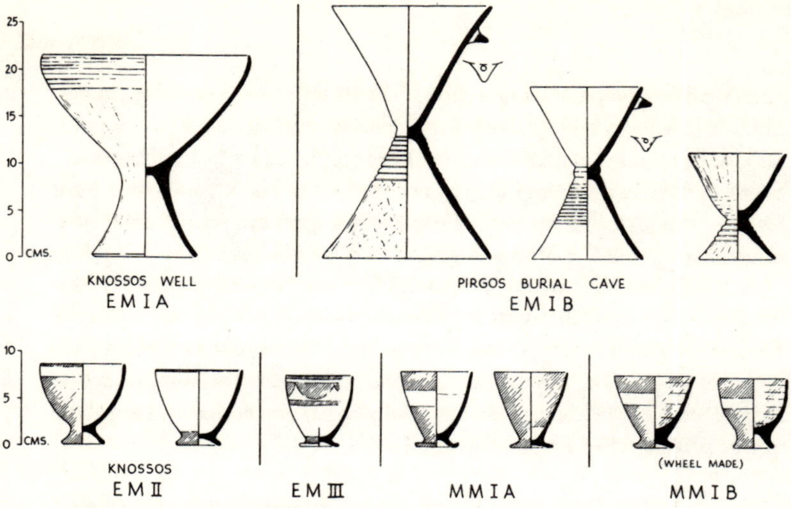

Fig. 14 Development of the Minoan goblet

Fig. 14

Plate 6

A shape of vase current throughout Crete during this period is a small high-footed goblet descended from the large pedestalled drinking bowls fashionable at the beginning of Early Minoan I, and ancestral to the 'egg-cup' goblets so abundant at Knossos in Early Minoan III and later. A tendency towards exaggeratedly long spouts may reflect Egyptian fashions, since long-spouted vessels of metal and stone were in vogue in Egypt during the Pyramid Age of the Old Kingdom, overlapping with Early Minoan II in Crete.

From the beginning of Early Minoan II if not earlier, a few dark-surfaced vases at Knossos were being decorated in creamy white paint. The effect was somewhat similar to that of the white-filled incisions of Cretan Neolithic pottery, but was obtained by applying white paint directly to the surface of the vase. This fashion for decoration in white ('light on dark') became increasingly strong at Knossos until by the last phase (C) of Early Minoan II it predominated there. But now and in all subsequent periods, all the while that the 'light on dark' style of decoration was in fashion, many vases continued to have light surfaces with decoration in dark, usually brown or black paint.

Early Minoan III. This period as defined by Evans at Knossos does not appear to have been a long one, and the pottery assignable to it has much in common with that of Middle Minoan IA. Dark-washed vases, however, are decorated in white paint without the use of red.

Middle Minoan I A. Evans made the line of division between Early and Middle Minoan the point when decoration in two colours, a shade of red as well as white, began to be fashionable at Knossos. Pottery so decorated is known as Kamares ware after a sacred cave on Mount Ida where it was first noted about 1890. Dark burnished pottery decorated with red, or occasionally with red and white paint, has been found at Phaistos in southern Crete in deposits that appear to be Early Minoan or even Late Neolithic.[3] The fashion for decoration in red and white paint may therefore have originated in the south of Crete and only spread later to the north. It reached the east later still; and some if not the bulk of the abundant pottery there with white-painted decoration conventionally assigned to Early Minoan III must be contemporary with Middle Minoan I at Knossos.

On the other hand the spiral, which was to become a favourite element of design with Cretan artists, may have been first exploited in the east of the island, where spirals were being painted in white on clay vases by Early Minoan III and carved in relief on stone bowls in Early Minoan II, it seems. A curious system of decoration very fashionable during Middle Minoan I A was barbotine, with prickles or serrated ridges in relief in many different variations. This type of decoration, usually combined with paint, and often applied with more exuberance than taste, appears to have been most at home in southern Crete.

While the finest vases at Knossos during this period were of polychrome ware, with designs in red and white, many had decoration in white alone. This is true of most of the little 'egg-cup' goblets, which abound at Knossos and elsewhere in northern Crete but were not made in the south or east. An important technical innovation which may have reached Crete now is the fast potter's wheel. This had been employed for clay vases in Egypt since the Pyramid Age, and long before then in Mesopotamia. In Crete the first tentative efforts with the fast wheel may go back to Middle Minoan I A, but it was not in common use until Middle Minoan I B. Even then, however, and until the beginning of the Late Minoan period, the larger vases were usually made by hand. *Fig. 14*

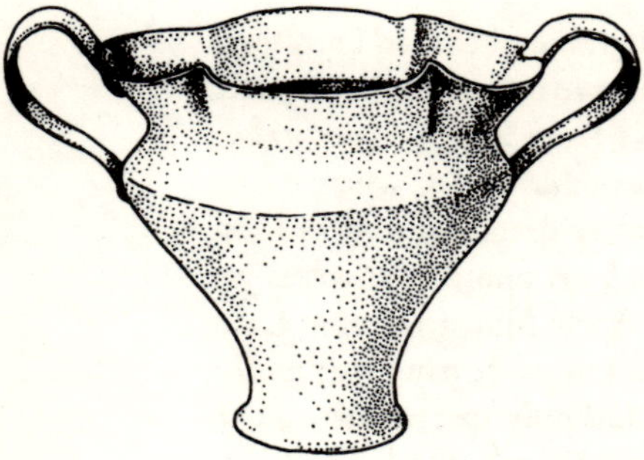

Fig. 15 Silver cup and clay imitation of a metal vase from a tomb at Gournia

Middle Minoan I B. The first great palaces appear to have been built at Knossos and Phaistos early in Middle Minoan times. Their construction may reflect the increasing wealth and power of the native rulers of Crete rather than conquest from abroad. Another symptom of prosperity is the

Fig. 15 way in which clay vases now imitate the shapes and even the style of decoration of metal ones. From Middle Minoan I A onwards most of the smaller vases and especially the drinking cups appear to be deliberate copies of metal originals. There is even an attempt to reproduce the thinness of metal, culminating in the remarkable 'egg-shell' ware made

Fig. 16 Silver cups from Tod

in the palace workshops at Knossos and Phaistos in Middle Minoan I B—II.

In Crete itself few metal vases of this period have survived. But a treasure of over 150 silver cups, with one of gold, which may all be of Cretan manufacture, has been found at Tod in Upper (South) Egypt.[4] The cups, which had been buried in copper boxes in the foundations of a temple there during the reign of the Pharaoh Amenemhet II (*c.* 1938–1904 BC), are not Egyptian; and with their bold, simple decoration, they are reminiscent of metal-imitating clay cups made in Crete during Middle Minoan I B. In the boxes with them were Mesopotamian cylinder seals of precious lapis lazuli, together with unworked lumps of lapis, brought from distant Afghanistan. Silver was more valuable than gold in Egypt at this time, and this group of silver cups and lapis lazuli may have been tribute from some Syrian prince, the ruler perhaps of the great port of Byblos, then subject to Egypt. But the cups might still have been made in Crete and exported to Syria. A silver jar and a cup decorated with spirals in relief, which were found inside the stone coffin of one of the the later rulers of Byblos, appear to be Cretan; and a clay goblet imported from Crete to Byblos is assignable to Middle Minoan I B, the very period during which the Tod cups, if they are Cretan, may have been made. *Fig. 16*

By the end of Middle Minoan I B some of the finer pottery at Knossos and Phaistos is being decorated in three colours, white and two shades of red, and a fourth colour, yellow, is sometimes added. Designs are still for the most part abstract, but figures, human or divine, are occasionally painted on vases from Middle Minoan I B onwards. *Fig. 17*

Middle Minoan II.[5] The Kamares tradition of dark-surfaced pottery with designs in shades of red and white now reaches its highest perfection. The washes are often a brilliant shiny black, rivalling the so-called black glaze of Classical Athens. The most remarkable products of this period are the cups of metal-imitating egg-shell ware, which may have been confined to the palace workshops of Knossos and Phaistos. With their elaborately fluted and embossed shapes they give some idea of what the gold and silver cups of the time must have been like. Most of the fine ware, including cups and jars of various kinds, had ornate painted decoration. Cups with rounded sides and everted rims were very *Fig. 18*

Fig. 17 White-painted figure on vase from Phaistos

Fig. 18 Middle Minoan II jar from Phaistos, with polychrome decoration. The red parts of the design are indicated by shading

Fig. 19 fashionable, this shape being a favourite with the makers of egg-shell ware. Another shape of drinking cup that becomes increasingly popular is named after the famous pair of gold cups found in 1889 in a bee-hive

Plate 51 tomb at Vafio on the Greek mainland.

Spiral designs now begin to be much in evidence on clay vases at Knossos as well as elsewhere in Crete. A limited repertory of motifs taken from nature includes stylized palm trees and octopuses.[6] While most of the finer vases have designs in white, or in white and shades of red, on a dark wash, there are hybrids combining this 'light on dark' with 'dark on light' decoration. Many of the larger vases continue to be decorated as before in 'dark on light'.

Fig. 19 Middle Minoan cup shapes

Fig. 20 Middle Minoan III stone jar with shell inlays

Middle Minoan III A. After this high-water mark in Middle Minoan II the quality of the pottery begins to decline, although, under the influence perhaps of contemporary fresco painting, the first attemps at a truly naturalistic style of vase decoration appear at this time. But the manufacture of fine egg-shell ware ceases, and the washes that coat the vases tend to be dull shades of black, purple-brown or red, instead of the brilliant shiny black characteristic of Middle Minoan II. Plate 5

Decoration in relief is sometimes very elaborate, with bold spirals and motifs such as scallop shells copied from nature. But painted decoration is now less in evidence on the fine ware, and at Knossos at any rate there is a taste for cups of metallic shapes with plain dark washes or decorated with white spots. Some of the stone vases made at Knossos at this time were inlaid with spots of white shell. This taste for white-spotted decoration may have been inspired in the first instance by an attractive pumice-flecked obsidian imported from the island of Yiali near Kos for making vases and seals. *Fig. 20*

The deterioration in the quality of the pottery produced at centres like Knossos and Phaistos is not simply part of a general decline of civilization. The 'light on dark' painted decoration of Middle Minoan II was highly fugitive, and the egg-shell ware fragile. The delicate clay vases of that time were not very practical, and the demand for them may have ceased as metal ones became more available. Perhaps the highly competent artists who made them were redeployed to other crafts, such as working in gold and silver, engraving gems and moulding faience.

Fig. 21 Jug with peas or vetches from Palaikastro

Middle Minoan III B. At the end of the Middle Minoan period the 'light on dark' style of decoration begins to go out of fashion, and the earlier practice of decorating vases of fine ware in dark paint on a light ground is revived. At first this 'dark on light' decoration is largely confined to Tortoise Shell Ripple, as Evans called it: vertical stripes in red, brown or black, on a yellow or orange ground (see Plate 10).

The stripes are usually somewhat ragged or have their edges smudged by polishing the slipped surface of the vase while it was still wet. The idea may have been to imitate the shimmering flutes of gold and silver vessels. This novel system of decoration is already coming into vogue at Knossos during the earlier phase (A) of Middle Minoan III. In Middle Minoan III B it is very common and a few vases then are decorated in *Fig. 21* 'dark on light' with spirals or designs taken from nature, although until the beginning of the Late Minoan period this type of decoration is normally executed in 'light on dark'.

Late Minoan I A. While the 'light on dark' style of decoration is still current at the beginning of Late Minoan I at Knossos, and lingers in fashion in eastern Crete, designs in 'dark on light' are now usual. Tortoise Shell Ripple is less in evidence, and there is a developing taste for reeds or flowers, while many vases are adorned with spirals. Plate 4 The more elaborate vases often have polychrome decoration; but with this new-style polychrome ware the designs are in red and black on a light surface, and white paint is only used for details. This use of red paint in addition to black goes out of fashion in Late Minoan I B, although both then and later details are often added to the decoration in white.

Late Minoan I B. The shapes of the finer vases continue to imitate Plate 13 metal as they had since Middle Minoan times, and occasionally the painted decoration itself appears to be copied from metal-work. While Plate 8 many vases are still adorned with designs of reeds or flowers, some boast 'Marine Style' decoration, with extraordinarily life-like octopuses and other sea creatures such as dolphins, argonauts, starfish and conch shells set against a background of rock and seaweed. This Marine Style pottery may have been produced by the palace workshops of Knossos, the designs being taken from wall paintings or relief vases of stone or

Fig. 22 Late Minoan I B flower combining papyrus and lily

Figs. 23, 24 Libation vase with Marine Style decoration from Pseira and argonaut on a Marine Style vase from Knossos

metal. Marine Style vessels, mostly of a ritual character, were sent to every part of Crete, and even reached the Greek mainland.

In contrast to the fine products of the palace workshops, the mass of the decorated pottery made at Knossos and elsewhere in Crete during this period represents a decline from the more universally high standards of Late Minoan I A. This dichotomy in the pottery may reflect some malaise in Cretan society on the eve of the disasters which overwhelmed it *c.* 1450 BC.

Late Minoan II. Pottery assignable to this period is virtually confined to the region of Knossos. New vase shapes, apparently of mainland origin, come into fashion there now; notably the squat alabastron, and stemmed drinking cups of various kinds (see Plate 14). Decoration largely derived from the old Plant and Marine Styles, but with the addition of birds and flowers that may be copied from contemporary wall paintings, tends to be stiff and formal in character. But large and ornate 'Palace Style' jars are often impressive in a grandiose way. Plate 15

Late Minoan III. The style of vase decoration which originated at Knossos during Late Minoan II has spread throughout Crete by the earliest phase (A) of this period. Abstract designs are fashionable, and the tendencies towards stylization of motifs taken from nature become increasingly pronounced, until by Late Minoan III C their natural origins are often difficult to detect. *Fig. 25*

Fig. 25 Late Minoan IIIC spouted tankard with stylized octopus from the Diktaian Cave

DATING THE CRETAN BRONZE AGE

The dating of the Cretan Bronze Age depends upon correlations with Egypt, and to a lesser extent with Mesopotamia, Syria, Cyprus and Anatolia. Written records make it possible to reconstruct a sequence of actual dates in Egypt with some degree of accuracy back to the beginning of the Twelfth Dynasty *c.* 2000 BC. Back to the time of the establishment of the First Dynasty *c.* 3000 BC, dates can be calculated within a couple of centuries either way.

Pottery of Cretan manufacture has been found in Egypt, and Egyptian objects such as scarabs and stone vases in Crete. Fragments of stone bowls made in Egypt at the time of the Old Kingdom or before were recovered in Late Neolithic houses at Knossos. A number of seal-stones and trinkets, notably foot-shaped amulets, resembling those current in Egypt at the end of the Old Kingdom and in the First Intermediary Period, have been found in the collective tombs of Crete in contexts vaguely assignable to the end of Early Minoan or beginning of Middle Minoan times.

Plate 9

Important for Middle Minoan dating are fragments of Cretan vases from Kahun in the Fayum of Egypt. A kind of boom town was built here to house workmen and officials employed on the construction of a pyramid for one of the great kings of the Twelfth Dynasty, Senusret II, who reigned *c.* 1906–1888 BC. Soon after the pyramid was built the town at Kahun was virtually abandoned, or inhabited by a population of squatters, who are unlikely to have imported fine decorated pottery from abroad. The Cretan vases were therefore presumably brought to the town during the period when the pyramid was under construction, although this has been disputed.

Evans believed that much of this pottery from Kahun was Middle Minoan II A in character. But some of the fragments he assigned to the succeeding phase, Middle Minoan II B, on the grounds that they came from vases decorated with rosettes having pointed petals of a type fashionable then. But pointed petals and spiky leaves of one kind or another are already in evidence on vases of Middle Minoan I B at Knossos. This Cretan pottery from Kahun may be a homogeneous group on the borders of Middle Minoan I B and Middle Minoan II, indicating a date for the end of Middle Minoan I B *c.* 1900 BC or not much later.

But the Minoan sequence of periods is closely linked to the Bronze Age of Cyprus by Cretan imports there. A Middle Minoan I A vase has been found in an Early Cypriot III tomb, which suggests that the two periods must be roughly contemporary. On one theory the Cypriote Middle Bronze Age was a comparatively short phase lasting a couple of centuries *c.* 1800–1600 BC. If these dates are right, Middle Minoan I A could hardly have begun before *c.* 2000 BC, and the Cretan pottery from Kahun, dating from Middle Minoan I B at earliest, would necessarily belong to a period after the reign of Senusret II.[7]

The latest pottery from an early circular tomb at Lebena and a tomb at Gournes just east of Knossos with Egyptian scarabs of Twelfth Dynasty date is reported as Middle Minoan I A, but some of the vases from the Lebena tomb appear to be wheel-made and may date from Middle Minoan I B. Three Twelfth Dynasty scarabs and a Mesopotamian cylinder seal of the period of Hammurabi, founder of the First Dynasty of Babylon, were recovered from the smaller of the circular tombs (Tholos B) at Platanos. Since the latest clay vases from this tomb are assigned to Middle Minoan I B, it has been inferred that Middle Minoan I B in Crete cannot have begun before the reign of Hammurabi. But the dates of the scarabs and the cylinder seal are disputed, and in any case the tomb was probably still being used for burials after the end of Middle Minoan I B.[8] Comparatively few clay vases were found in it, many fewer than the number of burials, and the later burials may not have had vases with them. Plate 101

Another scarab from a Middle Minoan II deposit in the city at Knossos has been variously assigned to the late Twelfth or Thirteenth Dynasty, or to the succeeding Hyksos period (1730–1580 BC). An alabaster lid inscribed with the name of Khian, one of the most important of the Hyksos rulers of Egypt, was found in the palace at Knossos in a deposit assigned by Evans to Middle Minoan III A.[9] But Khian's position in the sequence of Hyksos kings is not yet clearly established, and the date of the deposit with the lid has been challenged. Plate 12

Pictures of tributaries or envoys who appear to be Cretans were painted on the walls of several tombs of high Egyptian officials during the early part of the Eighteenth Dynasty (*c.* 1580 BC onwards). The style of their dress and the character of the objects which they are carrying as gifts to the Pharaoh suggest that the Late Minoan I B period of

Crete may have been roughly contemporaneous with the long reign of Thotmes III (1504–1450 BC). Late Minoan I B vases have been recovered from Egyptian tombs of his time, although an alabaster jar inscribed with his name was found in a tomb at Katsamba by the Bronze Age harbour-town of Knossos with burials assignable to the beginning of Late Minoan III A.

Plate 11

A reliable dating point is the mass of Aegean pottery found at Tell el-Amarna, site of the ephemeral capital of Ikhnaton, and imported into Egypt during his reign (*c.* 1372–1354 BC). But this was all of it apparently Mycenaean brought from the mainland of Greece, and it is not altogether clear what styles of pottery were being produced in Crete then.

CHAPTER V

Happenings and Events

REFUGEES AND INVADERS

The Minoan Bronze Age may have been inaugurated by people from some part of the eastern Mediterranean who brought with them, besides metallurgy, new styles of pottery and the custom of burial in domed circular tombs. It is always possible that other immigrants from the East made their homes in Crete during the centuries which followed. If the wars and movements of peoples which affected many of the lands round the eastern shores of the Mediterranean during the course of the third millennium drove refugees overseas, the large and fertile island, with a climate and ecology not very different from those of their homelands, was an inviting goal for them.[1] Crete was perhaps the New World of this time, and the stimulus provided by a mixture of peoples with different traditions and backgrounds may have been responsible for the unique flowering of civilization there during the period of the great palaces from *c.* 2000 BC onwards.

About the middle of the third millennium barbarous invaders erupting from the north, apparently from what is now Georgia on the south side of the Caucasus mountains, overran Syria and Palestine. These invaders made a primitive type of burnished pottery, known from the Palestinian site where it was first discovered as Khirbet Kerak ware. They came to settle, and established themselves not only in the interior of Syria but at coastal sites like Ras Shamra. Syrian refugees might have found their way to Crete then. Some features of Early Minoan II pottery are reminiscent of Syrian pottery of the phase (Amuq G) which immediately preceded the Khirbet Kerak invasion. Moreover it was in Early Minoan II that seals appear to have been first made in Crete, and some of the earliest Cretan seals are not unlike Syrian seals.

Other refugees from the East might have reached Crete in Early Minoan III times, coinciding with the First Intermediary Period of Egypt, when the Nile valley appears to have been overrun by invaders from Syria or Palestine. The idea of writing could have spread to Crete then or in Early Minoan II. But the adoption of seal usage and writing in Crete was not necessarily due to immigration or invasion from abroad.

It might simply reflect the spread of Oriental ideas through commercial and other contacts.

On one theory the great palaces at Knossos and Phaistos owed their foundation to dynasts from abroad who subdued Crete at the beginning of the Middle Minoan period. But there may have been palaces in Crete back in Early Minoan times, and the large building assigned to Early Minoan II at Vasiliki has been reasonably interpreted as one. On the whole therefore the construction of the great palaces at Knossos and Phaistos seems more likely to reflect the increasing prosperity of Crete during the Middle Minoan period than foreign invasion.

A study of the skeletons of the early inhabitants of Crete could one day throw decisive light on the question of immigration into the island. A French anthropologist, R. P. Charles, has concluded that Crete was exposed to immigration on a considerable scale during Early Minoan I and again in Early Minoan II-III. He believes, however, that the immigrants came, not from the East, but from the mainland of Greece, in the first instance from the Peloponnese, and later in Early Minoan II-III from Attica![2]

It has indeed been suggested that some aspects of Cretan life at the end of the Early Minoan period may reflect an influx of refugees from the Argolid when the flourishing Early Helladic II civilization there was overwhelmed by invaders from the north or east.[3] Clay seal impressions from deposits of the end of Early Helladic II at Lerna and elsewhere have designs reminiscent of those on Cretan seals assigned to Early Minoan III-Middle Minoan I A. It might be inferred that these impressions were made by Cretan seals. But if Early Helladic II is taken as ending about the same time as Early Minoan II, the Lerna seal impressions must be earlier than the Cretan seals with similar designs. This would imply that these impressions were not made by Cretan seals, but by native wooden seals (which have all perished!), and that the designs on these were ancestral to the comparable ones on Cretan seals of stone and ivory. But the assumption that Early Helladic II exactly corresponds to Early Minoan II is disputable. If, as seems probable, the Early Helladic II period in the Argolid overlaps with Early Minoan III or the beginning of Middle Minoan I, the comparable seals in Crete will be as early as, or earlier than, the seal impressions from Lerna. In that case the Lerna sealings might have been stamped

Fig. 26

Fig. 26 Seal designs from Lerna (Greece) and Platanos compared

by seals of Cretan origin. The spiders that appear on some of the Lerna sealings and (along with scorpions or lions!) on early Cretan seals, may be the dreaded rogalidhas, unknown it seems on the mainland.[4]

Colonists from the Cycladic islands may have settled along parts of the north coast of Crete during the Early Minoan period. Some Early Minoan pottery resembles that of the Cyclades; but a few bottles of Early Cycladic type from the burial cave at Pirgos may be imports, like a couple of Early Helladic II sauceboat-shaped drinking cups found in a cave near Khania in western Crete.

END OF THE EARLY PALACES C. 1700 BC

The city and palace at Knossos seem to have suffered extensive damage, perhaps more than once, during the course of the Middle Minoan II period. Within the same period the palace at Phaistos was apparently damaged by earthquake, but was afterwards restored and some time later destroyed by fire. The destruction here was exceedingly thorough. The ruins of the old palace were levelled, and a new palace with a different plan and a slightly different alignment was built on top of them.[5] What may have been a small palace at Monastiraki west of Mt Ida was also destroyed by fire during this period.[6] These destructions may not all have occurred at the same time, nor resulted from the same causes, whatever these were—earthquakes, or wars between the different states of Crete, or foreign invaders.

It has been suggested that Greeks first settled in Crete after the destruction of the palaces at Knossos and Phaistos at the end of Middle Minoan II *c.* 1700 BC. A more plausible theory brings Luwians from southern Anatolia.[7] The Luwians were a people of mixed origin having a language with Indo-European elements in it, related to Hittite, and ancestral to Lycian which was still spoken by the people of south-west Anatolia in Roman times. The palace at Beycesultan, which may have belonged to one of the Luwian rulers, has been suggested as a possible model for the later Cretan palaces. But the comparison is not very close, and in any case it looks as if the earlier palaces at Knossos, Phaistos and Mallia, were similar in plan to the later ones.[8] Since these earlier Cretan palaces were founded *c.* 2000 BC, they would ante-date the building of the palace at Beycesultan on any theory of Anatolian chronology, which is itself open to discussion.[9] For the moment, therefore, it would seem that neither the archaeological evidence, nor the information to be derived from a study of the skeletons of Bronze Age Cretans, support the idea of an immigration into Crete during Middle Minoan times.

MERIDIAN (C. 1700–1450 BC)

The two and a half centuries covered by the end of the Middle Minoan and the beginning of the Late Minoan periods are the most flourishing of the Cretan Bronze Age. The best of the fresco paintings that adorned the palaces and great houses, and most of the finest surviving creations of Minoan artists in other fields, date from then. Everywhere in Crete there are traces of settlements occupied at this time. The island was densely inhabited, and may have begun to suffer from over-population. With the later Greeks the usual remedy for this was a colony overseas. At the end of the Early Minoan period, well before 2000 BC, a colony of Cretans was established on the island of Kythera between the western tip of Crete and the Peloponnese. Greek legends refer to other Cretan colonies on various islands in the Aegean, and traces of such colonies have been recognized on the volcanic island of Thera, and on Melos, Kea and Rhodes. These colonies abroad were mostly, it seems, founded about the end of the Middle or the beginning of the Late Minoan period *c.* 1650–1500 BC. There was also a colony of Cretans at Miletus on the south-western coast of Anatolia.[10] According to later Greek tradition the original colonists here came from Milatos, and this may have been the name of the Bronze Age city at Mallia.[11]

Fig. 27

Cretans may even have settled on the mainland of Greece during this time of expansion overseas. For the people of the mainland now came increasingly under the influence of the Minoan civilization. Cretan fashions in pottery, in weapons, in dress and in religion, were copied or adapted on the Greek mainland. This process of Minoanization is vividly reflected in the contents of the royal shaft graves at Mycenae. The later burials in these were accompanied by a mass of gold and silver cups, signet rings, jewellery and weapons, either imported from Crete or made by Cretan artists, or by artists trained in a Cretan tradition. But the kings buried in these shaft graves were clearly not Cretans. Were they, however, tributary to Crete? The legend of Theseus with the annual troop of young men and women extorted by Minos from Athens

Fig. 27 The Aegean, showing possible Minoan colonies

may be a memory of a time when parts of the Greek mainland were subject to Knossos. But there is no hint in legend that Mycenae was ever tributary in this manner.

THE ERUPTION OF THERA C. 1500 BC

In Late Minoan I A about the end of the sixteenth century BC the volcanic island of Thera exploded in eruption, burying the Cretan settlements there beneath huge deposits of pumice (*tephra* or volcanic ash). The settlements appear to have been wrecked by an earthquake shortly before the eruption, and most of the inhabitants evidently had time to escape into the open, if not from the island, taking their most valuable possessions with them.[12] The discharge of pumice occurred in three distinct stages. Weathering of the surface of the pumice ejected in the first of these has been interpreted as indicating a gap of time, some twenty-five years or more, between it and the second. But there is no sign of soil formation, and recent study of the evidence suggests that all three stages of the eruption may have been over within the space of a few weeks or months as in the comparable explosive eruption of Krakatoa, an island lying between Java and Sumatra, in AD 1883.[13] The eruption on Thera must have begun soon after the earthquake which wrecked the settlements; otherwise the inhabitants would have had time to repair the damage to their houses and resume normal life in them. After the eruption the void left by the discharge of pumice collapsed to form the existing sea-filled crater (*caldera*). The inrush of water into this would have caused huge waves (*tsunamis*) to spread and sweep down upon the neighbouring coasts. From a single large island Thera became a group of three seperate islands of irregular shape, now increased to five through renewed volcanic activity in the middle of the *caldera* in Roman and recent times.

This eruption, one of the most stupendous in history, evidently wrought some havoc in Crete. The thriving towns and settlements along the north coast, only seventy miles distant from Thera across the open sea, may have suffered the effects of blast from the eruption as well as being swamped by *tsunamis* after it. Cores extracted by boring from the sea-bed show where the deposit of ash from the eruption lies thickest. Since this maximum deposit extends to the south-east of Thera it can be inferred that the wind blew from the north-west at the time of the eruption, suggesting that it took place in summer. It has been estimated that this north-west wind laid a blanket of volcanic ash at least four inches thick over the whole of the populous eastern tip of Crete. The ash, charged perhaps with noxious minerals, may have killed vegetation and for a time at least made cultivation of the ground impossible in this part of the island.

What traces of this cataclysm are there in the archaeological record in Crete? Most of the important settlements in the east of the island were excavated over fifty years ago before there was any awareness of it. A detailed account of levels of the relevant period is so far only available for Palaikastro. Here it seems the town was destroyed in Late Minoan I A, and some of the houses were never repaired afterwards; the walls of the new houses eventually built on top of their ruins are on a different alignment. There are hints of disasters about this time at other sites in the east of Crete, such as Zakro, Pseira and Mochlos. But whether destruction was caused by earthquakes in the first instance, or by blast from the eruption or *tsunamis* after it, is not clear. Knossos was extensively damaged by earthquakes about the time of the eruption in Late Minoan I A and also it seems somewhat earlier in Middle Minoan III B. Other sites nearby appear to have suffered earthquake shock in Late Minoan I A. Pottery from the pillar room of the country house at Vathipetro is assignable to Late Minoan I A and must reflect damage then, but it looks as if the house was repaired and eventually destroyed by fire in Late Minoan I B.[14]

Apart from the damage by earthquakes and great waves, the noise of the eruption and the darkness lasting perhaps days on end while the light of the sun was obscured by clouds of ash, must have filled the people of Crete with terror and despair. Poisonous vapours causing sickness may have added to the horror. The most urgent duty in these afflictions was to appease the gods and implore their aid. In 1901 a vast deposit of Late Minoan I A pottery was recovered from one of a pair of votive pits on a hill above the town at Zakro. The pottery seems to be homogeneous in character, as if the pits had been filled with offerings on a single occasion. Was this an attempt on a public scale to appease the anger of the gods so manifest in the cataclysm? Other votive deposits of the time may have been inspired by the terror of these happenings. In the large house by the shore at Nirou Khani a group of votive cups with lumps of pumice in them was found below the threshold of a door leading to a room used as a shrine. Perhaps the cups were placed there when the house was repaired after damage by great pumice-bearing *tsunamis*.[15]

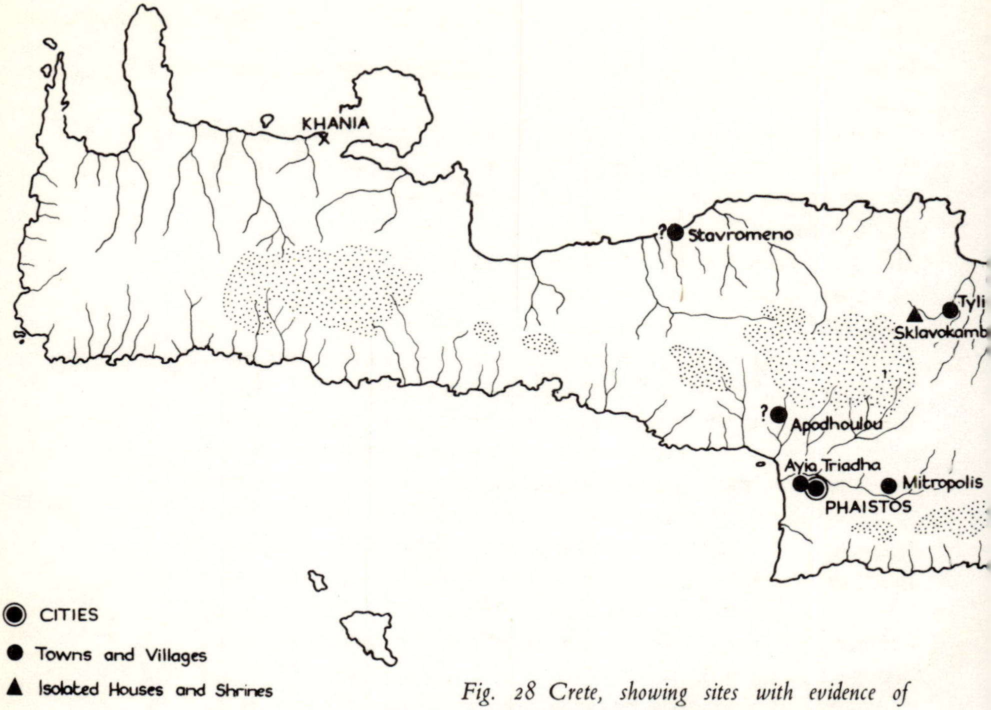

Fig. 28 Crete, showing sites with evidence of destruction in Late Minoan I B, c. 1450 BC

DISASTER C. 1450 BC

Crete survived the shock of the eruption. Damage to towns and palaces and country houses was repaired. The last of the burials in the Mycenae shaft graves may date from now; but at Mycenae and elsewhere on the Greek mainland this is the age of the great stone-built tholos tombs housing the royal and princely dead. These tombs were perhaps copied from the early Cretan circular tombs some of which still survived in use. But while the early Cretan tombs were built above ground, tholos tombs were usually sunk in a deep cutting, sometimes where it was flat, but more often taking advantage of a slope. A mound of earth like a barrow was invarably, it seems, heaped over the top of the tomb, which was approached down a long open passage known as a *dromos*. Mound-covered tholos tombs may have been developed about the beginning of the sixteenth century BC—whether by Cretan immigrants of by natives of the area—in the south-western tip of the Peloponnese

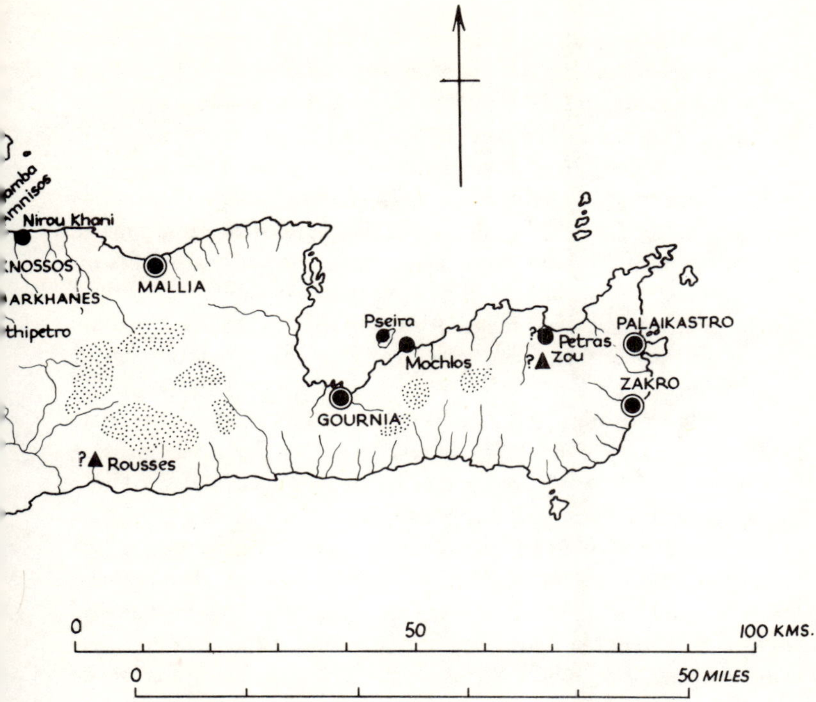

in Messenia. Tholos tombs are most thickly concentrated in this region, and the custom of burial in artificial mounds had long been established here. Moreover it is here that the earliest tholos tombs have been discovered, and some of these appear to have been built above ground like the early Cretan circular tombs.[16]

During this period after the eruption of Thera Cretan influence was at its zenith in the Aegean islands and on the mainland. In Crete itself, however, there are symptoms that all was not well. The contrast between the exquisite pottery of the Palace workshops and the shoddy mass-produced wares of the time has already been noted. Changes in burial customs hint at a loosening of clan ties. Wars of conquest and rule of empire may have corrupted a society which increasing wealth divided. The causes and degree of malaise can only be guessed. At all events this period of outward prosperity ended in disaster.

In Late Minoan I B, a generation or so after the eruption of Thera, Crete appears to have been desolated by war.[17] All the flourishing towns in the east, centre and south of the island were destroyed, and some including Zakro, Mochlos and Pseira, were never reoccupied. Most places were ravaged by fire, although the bodies of people killed have only been recognized in any numbers at Mochlos. At Gournia a few houses were afterwards built on the edge of the destroyed town using squared stone taken from the ruins of the palace there. Similarly at Mallia the town was reoccupied although the palace site was abandoned. Only at the capital, Knossos, the damage seems to have been limited.[18] Perhaps the city and palace there were spared by conquerors anxious to make use of them.

Fig. 28

The early excavators in Crete like Seager were in no doubt as to the war-like nature of these destructions. In the last few years, however, the eruption of Thera has been widely blamed for them. But apart from the fact that the eruption now appears to have taken place a generation or so earlier, it is difficult to envisage a natural catastrophe which ravaged so many coastal sites by fire and caused their abandonment while it spared the capital at Knossos. The way in which inland country mansions like those at Vathipetro and Sklavokampos were destroyed and never rebuilt seems to imply a complete overthrow of the existing social order as a result of invasion and conquest.

Changes in Crete after the disaster suggest the presence of conquerors from the Greek mainland, which does not appear to have suffered at this time. The largest of the new houses built at Gournia, and a palace that arose on the ruins of the old one at Ayia Triadha, the port of Phaistos, may have been planned according to mainland ideas.[19] New pottery shapes found at Knossos during the Late Minoan II period also look as if they were derived from the mainland, while the contemporary 'Palace Style' is so different in spirit from what went before it that it could reflect the presence of foreign conquerors even if it was not actually introduced by them.

A new type of tomb carved deep in the rock and approached by a long narrow passage (dromos) with inward sloping sides is first attested at Knossos in Late Minoan II and may have been evolved there under the influence of Egyptian or Cypriote models. The despatch of captive architects and artists to the mainland after the conquest could have

Fig. 29

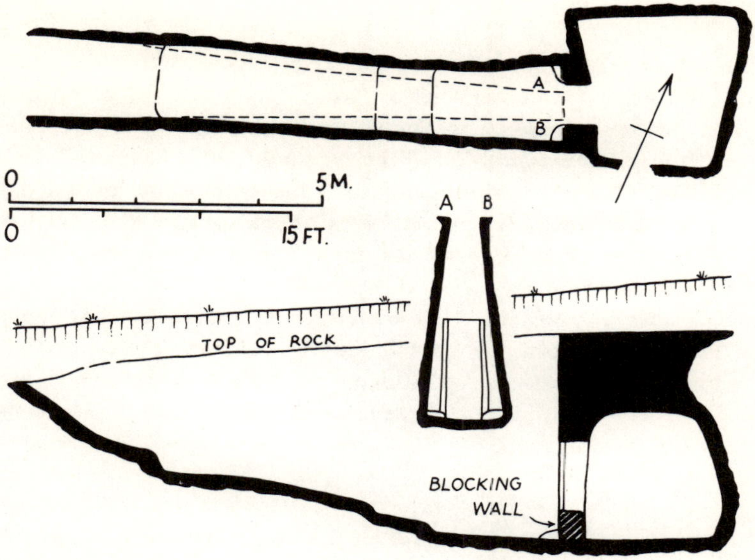

Fig. 29 Late Minoan II rock-cut tomb at Ayios Ioannis near Knossos

been responsible for the rapid spread of this type of tomb and of other Cretan fashions there. The underground tholos tomb for royal burials was probably introduced from the mainland to Crete now. That on the Kefala ridge at Knossos has been assigned to an earlier period; but *Fig. 131* the Palace Style jars of which fragments were recovered in it suggest that it was first used for burials in Late Minoan II times.

Graves of warriors accompanied by whole armouries of superb Plates 94, 95 weapons are found during Late Minoan II in the region of Knossos and also on the Greek mainland. While none of these warrior graves at Knossos can be assigned to a period before the conquest, it is just possible that the conquerors were of colonial or mixed origin, descendants of Cretans who had carved territories for themselves on the mainland. Against this view is the very prevalent assumption that the conquerors spoke and wrote a different language from the Cretans, and that this was Greek.

The palaces in the east of Crete were not rebuilt. That at Knossos survived and was apparently modified to adapt it to foreign tastes and ritual. The Throne Room for instance seems to have been inserted at this time. There may have been another centre of power in the south, where a new palace was built at Ayia Triadha, and that at Phaistos was reoccupied, although whether as a palace or not is uncertain. Perhaps there was a third palatial centre in the west at Khania, which may even have escaped the conquest of the rest of Crete. But the fine decorated pottery here and throughout Crete during Late Minoan III A reflects Knossian fashions and may imply centralized government from a capital at Knossos.

Disaster also seems to have overtaken the colonies overseas at the end of Late Minoan I B, when the settlement at Kastri on Kythera was abandoned, and that at Ayia Irini on Kea was destroyed by fire; a few years after the harrowing of Crete to judge from the evolved style of the pottery found in them.[20]

THE LAST PALACE AT KNOSSOS

The centre and east of Crete if not the whole island may have been under the direct rule of Knossos after the disaster of *c.* 1450 BC. Warrior graves, and military scenes painted on the walls of the palace there, imply the presence of a new and war-like dynasty as Evans saw. Great vases decorated in the 'Palace Style' suggest the wealth and splendour of the capital and the decline of taste.

This era of chill military grandeur at Knossos ended in catastrophe. The palace was destroyed by fire and not rebuilt. When this happened has been a matter of dispute since 1960; but it was probably about 1375–50 BC rather than later (see Appendix).

The final destruction of the palace at Knossos, whatever its date, is likely to have been the work of enemies. The warrior graves and princely tombs in the Knossian region all appear to belong to a period before the destruction. It looks as if the destroyers came from abroad, and were probably once again from the mainland of Greece. They may have ravaged Crete and afterwards subjected it to their rule.

There is evidence that the so-called Palace of Kadmos at Thebes on the mainland was destroyed about the same time as that at Knossos. Possibly both these great centres, one in the north and the other in the south, fell victims to the aggrandisement of Mycenae, which during the thirteenth century BC appears to have been the capital of an empire in control of most of the Aegean area.

CHAPTER VI

Building and Wall-Painting

EARLY VILLAGES

The houses and settlements of Crete at the beginning of the Bronze Age were not, it seems, very different architecturally from those of the end of the Neolithic. An early settlement was excavated in 1967–68 at Fournou Korifi east of Mirtos on the south coast.[1] The settlers had occupied a steep hill overlooking the sea on the western edge of a little coastal plain through which a stream ran. The one-storeyed houses had small rectangular rooms like the Late Neolithic houses at Knossos. *Fig. 7* Their walls were built of rubble, the rough, undressed stones being held together with earth or clay. The upper parts of the walls were sometimes of mud brick. Plaster, some of it painted red or brown, appears to have coated the walls; but floors were of beaten earth. Roofs were evidently flat.

The houses were packed together with only one or two narrow stepped paths between them. The walls of the houses on the edge of the village may have presented an unbroken face without windows. In this face at the end of one of the paths there was a doorway which could be closed with a wooden gate. What must have been a shrine had an altar on which appears to have stood a clay vase in the shape of a woman, evidently a goddess, holding a jug. A curved section of wall on the highest point of the hill may have belonged to another shrine, circular in shape; but apparently built after the settlement had been destroyed by fire and abandoned.[2] The destruction of the settlement is assigned to Early Minoan II.

On a hill at Vasiliki on the isthmus of Hierapetra some fourteen miles north-east of Fournou Korifi another Early Minoan settlement was explored by Seager in 1906–8. Here a building of substantial construction and almost certainly more than one storey high may have been a palace.[3] Some of its walls were held together by an interlacing framework of upright and horizontal timbers, a system regularly employed for the larger buildings throughout the Bronze Age in Crete. Like the settlement at Fournou Korifi this building at Vasiliki was destroyed by fire, but the hilltop was afterwards re-occupied.

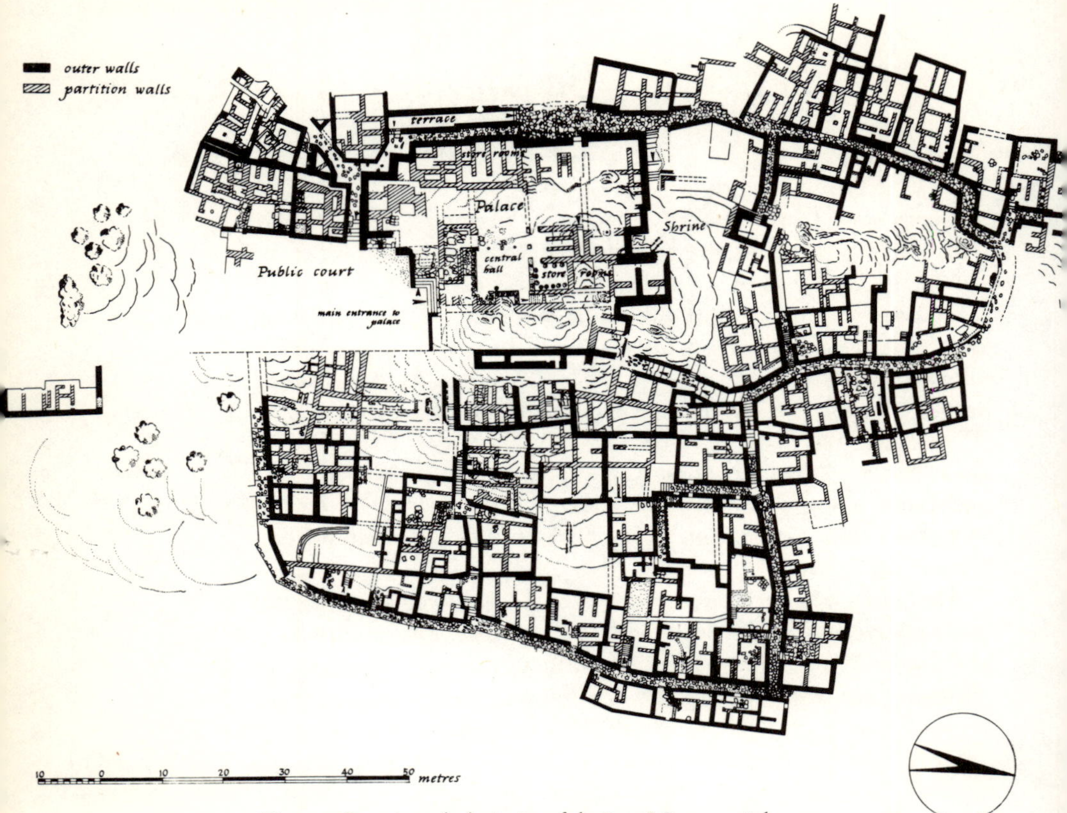

Fig. 30 Gournia at the beginning of the Late Minoan period

Fig. 30 The chief centre of the region, however, was now at Gournia on the coast just over four miles to the north-west of Vasiliki. The Bronze Age town here was first noted by Evans, but was rediscovered by an American expedition which excavated it in 1901–4. It is still the only Bronze Age town of any size that has been completely exposed by excavation in Crete. Paved streets and paths and stairways wind between the houses. The town is dominated by a palace with a large open square on the south. North of the palace is a little temple with a path leading to it from the main street. The houses at Gournia were quite small, with five or six rooms on the ground floor, but some with staircases may have had an upper storey.

In the villages and out in the countryside most of the houses were probably single-storeyed as they still are in many parts of Crete. A bungalow house of this kind was excavated in 1965 at Ayia Varvara on the outskirts of the Bronze Age city of Mallia.[4] This house was a rectangle some 30 feet across from north to south, and rather longer from east to west. The entrance in the north-east corner seems to have led into an open court (1). Apart from this the house had six main rooms. The largest (3) was evidently the living room, and may have been where the men of the house slept; but it also appears to have been used for cooking and eating. Against the wall by the door leading from 1 was an irregular pile of stones (A) enclosing two cooking pots. A stone base (B) in the centre of the room had evidently supported a wooden post or column, while a thin section of the outside wall may indicate the position of a window. *Fig. 31*

Another door in the south-west corner of 3 led to a further range of rooms of uncertain use; but 8 appears to have been a small open well to admit light and air, such 'light wells' being a regular feature of the palaces and houses in the towns. Some wooden steps in the south-east corner of 3 may have given access to a third door leading into the women's quarters (2, 4). These evidently took the form of one large

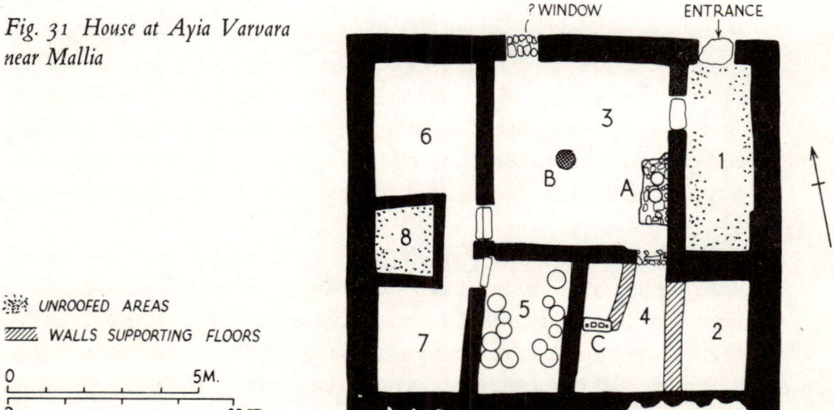

Fig. 31 House at Ayia Varvara near Mallia

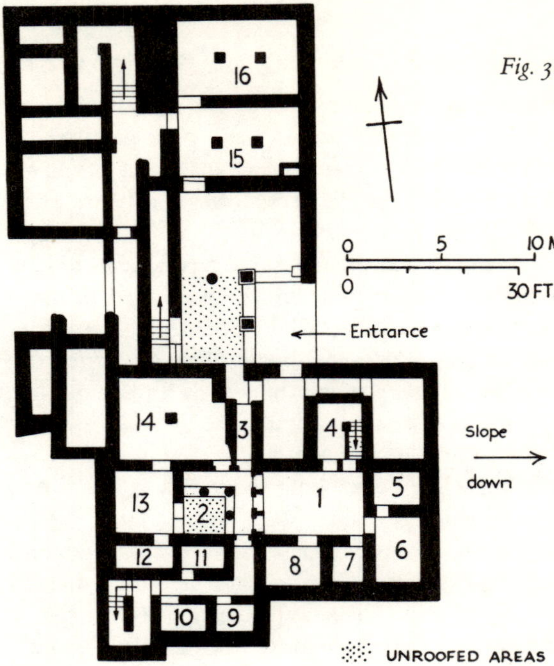

Fig. 32 Tylissos House A

room with a wooden floor supported by a low cross wall which helped to raise it about 15 inches above the surface of the ground. A stone against the middle of the west wall (C) may have been the base of a wooden loom—many clay loom weights were found in this area. The room (5) beyond was for storage. In it were clay jars, some containing seeds of vetch and grain. Stone weights for fishing-nets were also kept here. This simple one-storeyed house is probably typical of many that were scattered throughout the countryside of Crete during the first half of the second millennium. It was destroyed by fire at the time of the disasters of *c.* 1450 BC.

Fig. 32 House A at Tylissos, which was also destroyed then, is a good example of a large contemporary town house.[5] It was at least two storeys high with three staircases. The main entrance was in the middle of the east side, down the slope into which the house was built. The northern part to the right on entering was the service quarter, the southern being residential. The main living-room (1) opened through three doors on to a colonnade which flanked a little open court or light well (2). From here a narrow passage (3) led to the main entrance. On the north side of the living-room was a sunk bathroom (4). Evans called rooms of this kind with steps leading down into them Lustral Basins. There is one attached to the so-called Throne Room at Knossos, and in the palaces they no doubt had ritual functions. But elsewhere they may have been ordinary bathrooms, the tubs containing the water being of clay or maybe of metal, in size and shape much like Victorian hip-baths. Plate 21

A drain in 8 on the south side of the living-room suggests that it was a lavatory. Lavatories, usually set against outside walls in this way, are a regular feature of Cretan palaces and houses. Other small rooms (5–7) opening from the living-room may have been used as sleeping-places by the men of the house. The block of rooms (9–11) in the south-west corner of the house was probably the women's quarters with a private staircase leading to their share of the upper floor. Room 14 with a square pillar in it was apparently a private chapel or house shrine, like similar pillar rooms at Knossos. But the rooms leading from it—13 with a window opening on to the light well (2), and 12—were used for storage. Three huge bronze cauldrons were found in 13, and a bronze ingot and clay tablets in 12. Food, however, was evidently kept in the large pillared rooms (15, 16) at the north end of the house. These contained a number of storage jars, and on the floor above there appears to have been a dining-hall. This convenient arrangement of dining-hall above food stores and kitchens is repeated in the great palaces, notably in that at Zakro at the eastern end of Crete.

THE GREAT PALACES: ZAKRO, KNOSSOS, PHAISTOS

Zakro. Like the house at Ayia Varvara and House A at Tylissos the palace at Zakro was destroyed by fire *c.* 1450 BC. In the main essentials of its plan it resembles the three larger palaces at Knossos, Phaistos and Mallia. The long rectangular central courts of these palaces are orientated roughly from north to south, either with a view to catching the winter sun, or for ritual reasons. A little square stone surround in the north-west corner of that at Zakro may have been the base of an altar. *Fig. 33*

A large room (1) at the north end of the court was evidently the kitchen with a dining hall above it. Many animal bones were found here, and the rooms (I-VIII) to the left had been used for storing food along

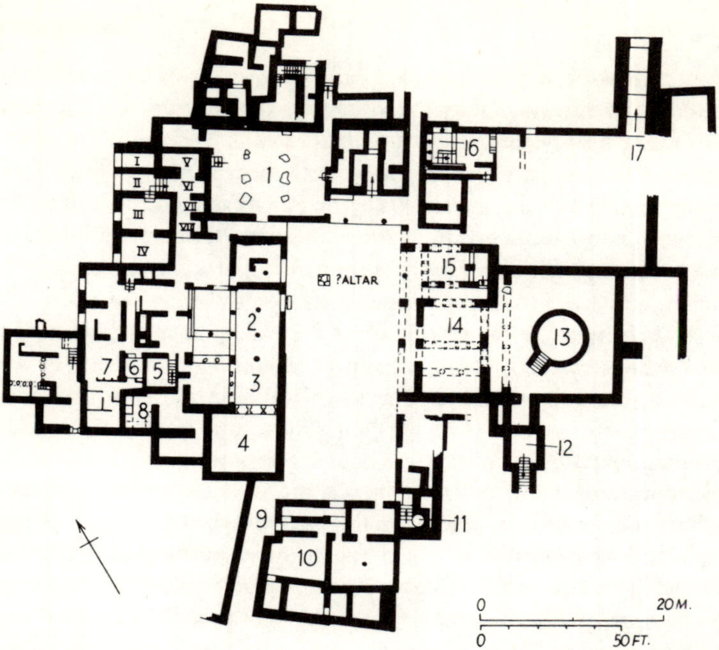

Fig. 33 Plan of the palace at Zakro

with olive oil and wine. The main state apartments (2–4) occupied the west side of the central court. Behind them was a series of rooms used for ritual purposes, including a shrine (6) with a large Lustral Basin (5) next to it. A remarkable group of cult vases was recovered from this area, notably from 8 where they had been stored in bins separated by partitions of mud brick. In room 7 on the west side of the shrine (6) inscribed clay tablets had been kept in wooden boxes of which the bronze hinges had survived. On the upper floor above this west wing of the palace there appear to have been store rooms containing bronze tools and weapons together with bronze ingots and elephant's tusks. All these escaped the rapacity of plunderers when the palace caught fire.

The actual living quarters of the royal family (14–15) were on the east side of the central court as at Knossos. A sunk Lustral Basin (16) may have been the bathroom connected with these. Steps in the south-east corner of the central court led down to a well (11) which appears to have been used for offerings in the last days of the palace.

From it came many small clay vases, one of them full of olives which the water had preserved. The royal suite (14) opened on to a colonnade flanking one side of a large open court. In the middle of this court was a circular well or spring chamber (13) which may have had a roof supported by columns round its edge. The rectangular spring chamber (12) was only, it seems, approachable from outside the palace. One main entrance into the palace has been identified on the north (17). Another (9) on the south seems to have led directly into the central court. A two-storey block (10) by this was used for stacking pottery, and the skilled craftsmen working in ivory, faience and stone, seem to have been established here.

Knossos. The palace at Knossos may have been the model for those at Phaistos, Mallia and Zakro, although there is no question of slavish imitation. The huge pillared hall (1) beyond the north end of the central court at Knossos appears to have had a dining-room above it like the kitchen at Zakro. Much of the area east and south of this pillared hall has been destroyed by erosion and quarrying for stone in later times. But quantities of cooking pots were found in the North-east Magazines. *Fig. 34* Plate 16

The west wing of the palace was traversed by a long corridor (11) with narrow store-rooms (12) opening from it. Stone-lined boxes or cists let into the floors of these rooms and of the corridor were used for storage together with large jars (pithoi). At one time some of the cists had been lined with lead to house clothes and valuables. But after the earthquake in Middle Minoan III B *c.* 1550 BC they were reduced in size, and at the time of the final destruction of the palace most of them and of the storage jars were being used as containers for olive oil. The capacity of these magazines has been estimated as over 240,000 gallons.[6] Plate 37

The ground floor of this part of the palace between the long corridor and the central court was occupied by cult rooms of one kind or another, the most famous of these being the Throne Room (5) with its attached Lustral Basin (6). The façade of a triple shrine of the type known from many representations appears to have overlooked the central court to the south of this. Behind this shrine façade (8) was a room with cists sunk into the floor (9) in which were kept the idols and other objects used in ritual here. From two large cists filled after the earth- Plate 27

Plates 63, 81

quake *c.* 1550 BC came a remarkable series of little faience statues together with clay vases and other cult furniture. When the palace was restored these two deep cists were replaced by three others, smaller and shallower. Doors from one of the rooms behind the triple shrine façade led to a couple of pillar rooms (10).

The main state apartments, which shared the ground floor of the west wing at Zakro with cult rooms, appear to have been on a *piano nobile* above them at Knossos. This upper floor was reached by two imposing flights of steps, one (7) from the central court just south of the Throne Room, the other (16) approached through a wide doorway (15) with a columned porch each side of it, reminiscent of the monumental gates (Propylaia) of later Greece. This doorway stood at the end of a wide passage (14), named by Evans the Corridor of the Procession because its walls were painted with life-size figures of men taking part in some religious procession or rite. The corridor led along the south

Fig. 34 The Palace of Minos at Knossos at the time of its final destruction in the fourteenth century BC. This plan incorporates various features that have in the past been assigned to a reoccupation of the site after the final destruction of the Palace (see Appendix)

1 *Pillared hall*
2 *North-east Magazines*
3 *North entrance passage*
4 *North-west Lustral Basin*
5 *Throne Room*
6 *Lustral Basin*
7 *Stairway to upper floor*
8 *Triple shrine façade*
9 *Room with cists in floor (Temple Repositories)*
10 *Pillar rooms*
11 *Corridor of the West Magazines*
12 *West Magazines*
13 *West Entrance*
14 *Corridor of the Procession*
15 *Monumental doorway*
16 *Stairway to upper floor*
17 *Grand Staircase to Residential Quarters*
18 *East-west corridor*
19 *Light Well, Hall of the Double Axes*
20 *Anteroom, Hall of the Double Axes*
21 *Main living-room of the Hall of the Double Axes*
22 *Private staircase*
23 *Bedroom*
24 *Bathroom or sleeping place*
25 *Service room*
26 *Lavatory*
27 *Treasure chamber*
28 *Colonade*
29 *Terrace*
30 *Store of lapis lacedaemonius (Spartan basalt)*
31 *Schoolroom*
32 *East Entrance*
33 *Shrine of the Double Axes*
34 *Loom-weight basement of the earlier palace*
35 *Court of the Stone Spout*

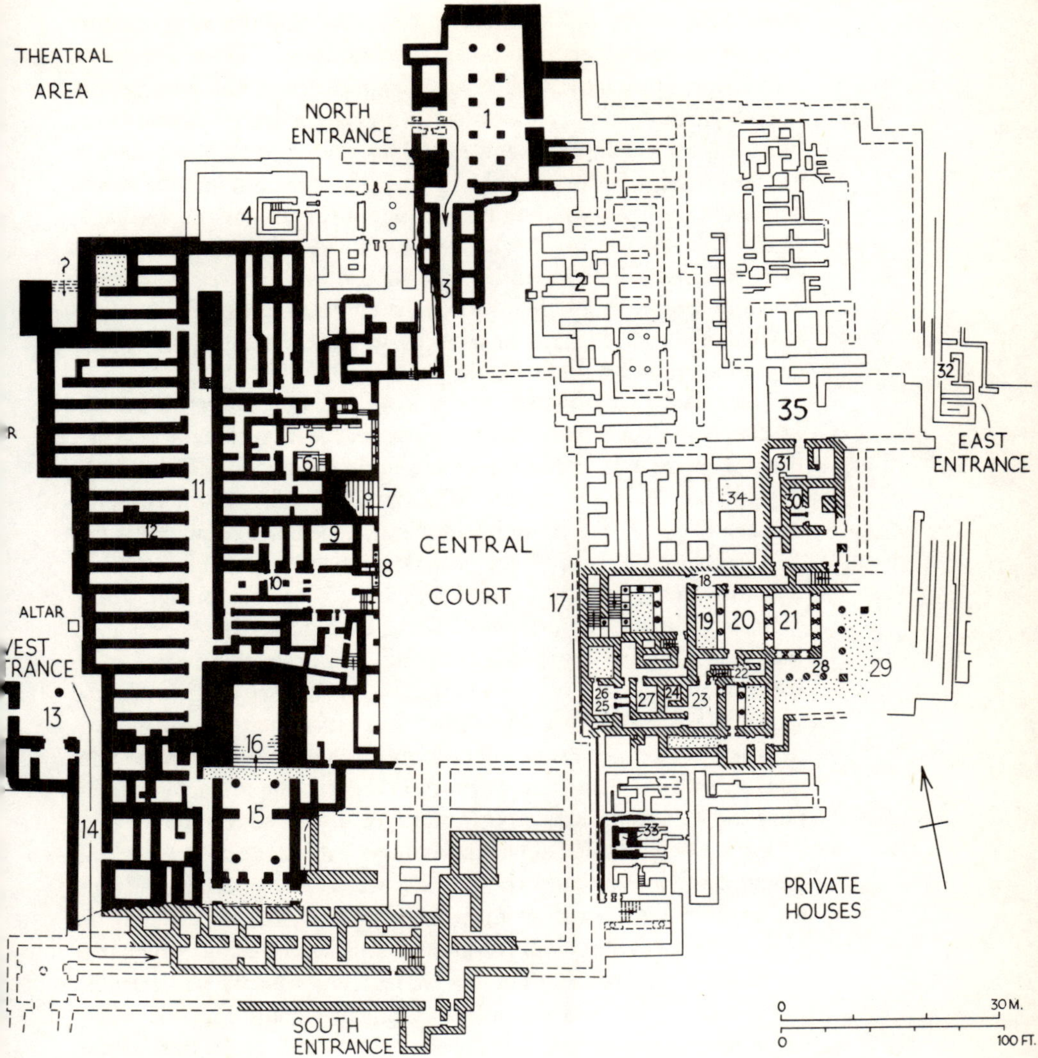

Walls in use at the time of the destruction: Ground Floor (Central Court) level

Walls in use at the time of the destruction: Lower levels

Earlier walls and foundations; some may have been in use at the time of the destruction

Conjectural walls

front of the palace and turned to reach a wide and imposing entrance (13) which opened upon an extensive paved court. This west entrance, which was apparently flanked by huge pictures of bull-leaping may have been the main ceremonial way into the palace; but there were others on the north, south and east. That on the north gave access to an open passage leading straight up the slope of the hill into the central court. On the east a winding flight of steps (32) ran down to the valley of the Kairatos stream. A channel at one side of the steps served to carry away rainwater; the rush of the water down the steep incline was carefully broken by a series of parabolic curves, while settling tanks at intervals filtered it. Perhaps the water was collected for doing the laundry on the flat ground at the foot of the palace wall.

The actual living-quarters of the king and queen were to the east of the central court as at Zakro. There was a steep slope here where the side of the hill, consisting of Neolithic occupation debris on top of which the palace was built, fell away to the valley of the Kairatos. Plate 17 As a consequence the ground floor of this Residential Quarter was two storeys below the level of the central court. This part of the palace was therefore at least three, and may have been four or five storeys high, including the ground floor. The apartments on the ground floor, built into a cutting in the side of the hill, were something like a cave, sheltered from the cold in winter but cool in summer. A monumental staircase (17) led down to them from the central court. This had stone steps and a columned balustrade opening on a well which admitted light and air. When Evans came to excavate the staircase in 1901 he found steps and balustrade miraculously preserved in their correct relationship, owing to the mud brick of which the upper parts of the walls were built having dissolved and filled all the interspace. The wooden columns and the beams which rested on them have been restored in concrete; the tapering shape of the columns and the Pompeian red colour which they are painted being copied from more or less contemporary wall-pictures.

The staircase descended to a little colonnaded court from one corner of which a door led into a narrow corridor (18). From this another door gave access to a deep columned porch (20) which formed the anteroom to what appears to have been the main living-room of the palace (21). This complex of rooms was named by Evans the Hall of the Double Axes from the double-axe signs carved on the walls of the Light

Well (19) at the west end. Against the back wall of the living-room is a low dais for a wooden throne, and traces of another wooden throne were recognized against the north wall of the porch. The other three sides of 21 had a system of multiple doorways, like the triple doorways at one end of the living-room in House A at Tylissos. These doors, which were double-leaved although the spaces for them were only about 3 feet 6 inches wide, could be kept either open or closed. They were of a primitive type in one piece with the pivot which turned in sockets in the lintel at the top and the threshold at the bottom. The floors here and in most of the rooms of this suite were paved with limestone slabs; the walls were lined to a height of some 8 feet with thin sheets of gypsum, an attractive soft veined stone something like alabaster that was quarried from the hill of Gypsades just south of the palace. Above this high dado of gypsum slabs the walls were plastered and decorated with painted designs or pictures.

What must have been a bedroom (23) was approached from the deep porch by a short corridor with a kink like a dog's leg in it. This kind of corridor prevented anyone seeing straight into the room, and helped privacy in an age of clumsy doors and embryo locks.[7] From the corner next to the door a narrow staircase (22) led to the floor above, where there may have been a similar suite of rooms. Evans thought that the ground floor suite belonged to the queen, while one on the floor above was occupied by the king, but this is highly conjectural. A nook (24) separated from 23 by a doorway and a chest-high balustrade may have been a sleeping place away from the draughts which the many doors and windows in the room would have made inevitable. Evans took it to be a bathroom, but the clay tub which he put here was actually found elsewhere in the area. A corridor led from the corner beyond this nook to a smaller room (25) with a low platform that may have been for the bed of an attendant. In a small compartment against one of the walls of this room was a lavatory (26) with a seat as in Egypt set over a drain. This was part of an elaborate system of stone-lined drains, large enough for a man to crawl through them, running below the ground floor rooms of the Residential Quarter. The drains were fed from the upper floors by means of vertical chutes.

An inside room (27) without any windows was evidently the treasure chamber or cupboard in which clothes or valuables were stored. This was unpaved and may have had a wooden floor. The main living room (21) of the Hall of the Double Axes opened on a spacious colonnade (28) to the east and south. Beyond was an open terrace (29) with a view across the deep valley of the Kairatos to the slopes of Ailias where the royal pleasure gardens may have been. The rooms adjacent to the Residential Quarter on the north appear to have been used by some of the skilled craftsmen in the service of the palace. A store of *lapis lacedaemonius*, imported from the region of Sparta, was found in a ground floor room (30) here; and the workshop of a stone vase maker had evidently been situated on the floor immediately above it. When the palace was destroyed some time in the fourteenth century BC two large unfinished stone vases were standing in this upper room. An adjacent room with benches and stone basins (31) may have been an atelier of fresco painters or a schoolroom where scribes learnt to write.

Fig. 35 *Phaistos.* The palace at Phaistos, second only in size and splendour to that of Knossos, was happier in its situation. It stood on the edge of a steep hill with a superb view over the Mesara plain to the east and the massif of Ida to the north. The main approach was from a paved court
Plate 18 on the west as at Knossos. A wide staircase (3), the equivalent of that which at Knossos was inside the building, led directly from the west court to the level of the *piano nobile.* This staircase was in the open air, and its steps were carefully sloped to shed the rain. At the top

Fig. 35 The later palace at Phaistos, destroyed in LM I B, c. 1450 BC

1 *West court*
2 *Façade of early palace*
3 *Grand Staircase*
4 *Monumental doorway*
5 *Light well*
6 *Store rooms (magazines)*
7 *Open court with garden*
8 *Staircase to garden*
9 *Main living-room of Residential Quarter*
10 *Bedroom suite (?) of Residential Quarter*
11 *Lustral Basin*
12 *Lavatory*
13 *Winter Quarters*
14 *Complex of rooms with dining-hall above*
15 *Workshops (?)*
16 *Court with smelting furnace*
17 *Part of early palace excavated since 1950*
18 *Site of later Greek temple*
19 *Line of pavement of central court, apparently dating from time of early palace*
20 *Find-place of the Phaistos Disc*

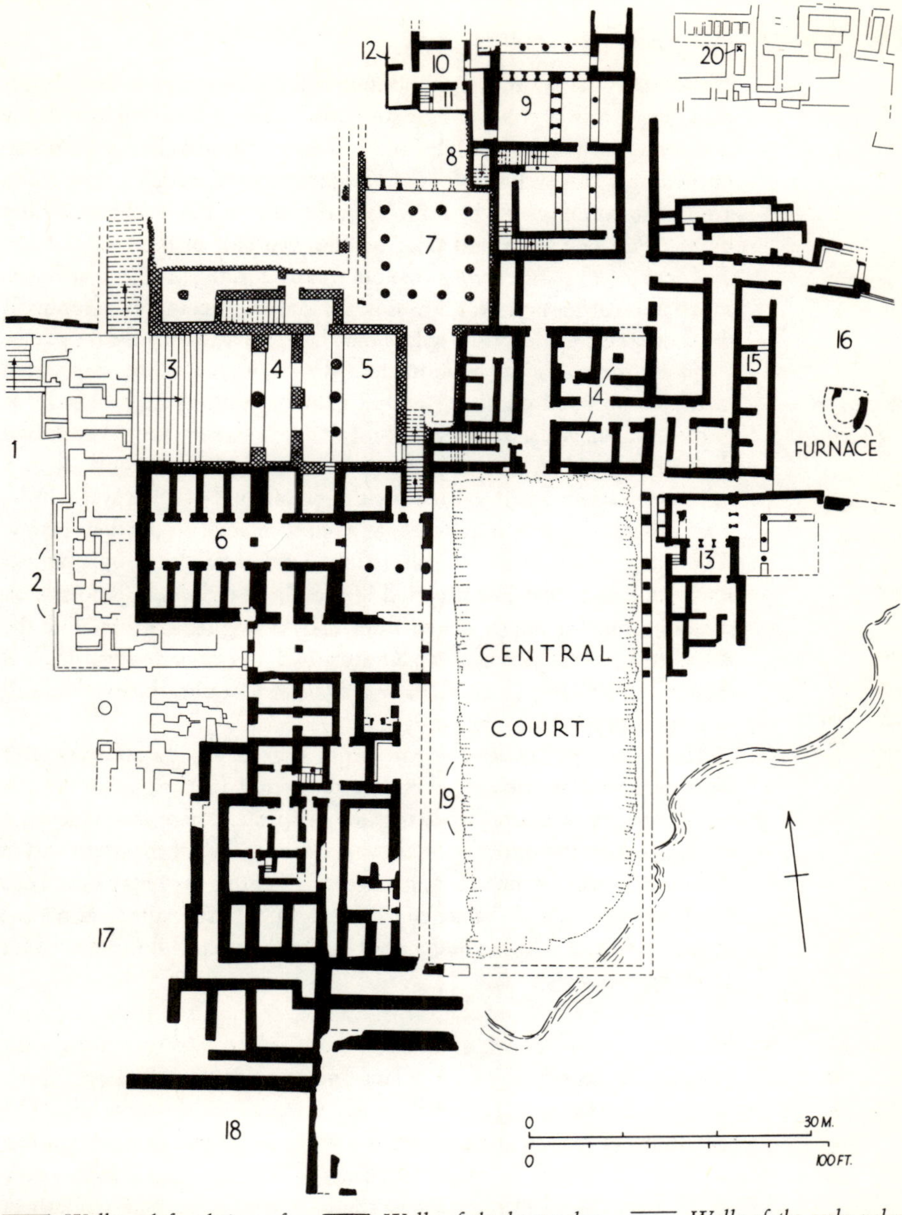

Walls and foundations of the later palace associated with floors on the level of the Central Court

Walls of the later palace associated with floors at the level of the storey above

Walls of the early palace at a lower level

of the stairs was an imposing monumental doorway (4) with a double entrance. An oval column base supported a single huge column in the front porch, while the porch behind had three columns. This back porch opened on a large light well (5) from one corner of which a door led to a stairway running down to the central court on the level of the floor below. Part of the ground floor on the west side of the central court was occupied by store rooms (6); but rooms devoted to cult were not so much in evidence here as at Knossos and Zakro. A complex of rooms in the south-west corner of the palace may have been apartments for guests.

To the north of the monumental doorway and at the same high level was an open court (7) with a colonnade along all four sides as in medieval cloisters. This was approachable both from the monumental doorway and from the north-west corner of the central court. It may have been an enclosed garden for the private use of the royal family, who could reach it by a staircase (8) from their suite on the floor below. The main living room of this (9) had multiple doors opening on spacious colonnades like the Hall of the Double Axes at Knossos. A smaller room (10) approached from it by a dog-leg corridor like the so-called Queen's Bedroom at Knossos had an elaborate sunk Lustral Basin (11) attached to it. There was a lavatory against the outside wall of a room beyond it to the north (12).

This residential quarter on the north edge of the palace may have been occupied in summer; a less spacious set of apartments on the east side of the central court (13) being for winter use. There was evidently a dining-hall on the upper floor above the rooms (14) at the north end of the central court. A line of rooms to the east of this (15) may have been workshops of skilled craftsmen. These opened on a paved court (16) in the middle of which stood a great horseshoe-shaped furnace used for smelting copper.[8]

Considerable parts of the earlier palace, destroyed *c.* 1700 BC, have
Plate 19 been exposed at Phaistos; notably the south-west corner which lay beyond the edge of the later palace and at a very much deeper level.
Plate 18 The paved west court (1) visible today is that of the earlier palace. The west court of the later palace was at a higher level and ran over the top of what was left of the earlier façade (2). This was based upon a row of large blocks of even height (orthostats) resting on a low plinth of massive flat slabs like the west façades of the later palaces at Phaistos,

Knossos and Mallia. Many of the ground-floor rooms of the early palace at Phaistos were paved, and they had cupboards in the walls and stone-built benches of the kind found in the later palaces. The destruction of the early palace at Phaistos was exceedingly thorough, and virtually nothing of it was left to incorporate in the new palace apart from the paving of the central court. The new palace appears to have been designed according to a single over-all plan, and from its measurements it has been possible to deduce the unit of length which the Bronze Age Cretans employed; a foot of 30.36 centimetres, which is only a fraction less than the standard English foot.[9] Plate 19

CONSTRUCTION AND MATERIALS[10]

An idea of how the palaces and great houses looked can be derived from little faience plaques, inlays of a wooden chest of some kind, assigned by Evans to Middle Minoan II B, *c.* 1700 BC. The small upper storey of some of these house façades may have been a sleeping place for use during the hot nights of summer on the analogy of similar roof chambers in Egyptian houses. There are windows, but only on the second floor, and no doors; because, if Evans is right, these plaques are part of a picture showing an attack upon a city, the houses being incorporated in the defence wall in a way that was foreshadowed in the early settlement of Fournou Korifi. But an ivory plaque of a somewhat later date from Knossos shows a house with a doorway flanked by narrow slit windows. Plate 22 Plate 23

The Cretans of the Bronze Age did not normally bother with foundations. Many of their buildings were erected upon exposed surfaces of rock as at Mallia. But sometimes when it seemed desirable very massive foundations were laid. At Phaistos, for instance, where the south-west corner of the later palace was built on top of the deep ruin debris of that destroyed *c.* 1700 BC, its foundations were sunk to a depth of 10 feet or more.

Walls were usually constructed of rubble packed with clay; but dressed stone might be used in the palaces and great houses for sections of wall exposed to the open air. Mud bricks, as big as a man could carry, some 18–24 inches long by 14–16 inches wide and 4 or 5 inches thick, were widely employed for the upper parts of walls. Most of the walls of a large Middle Minoan house at Mallia were built entirely of

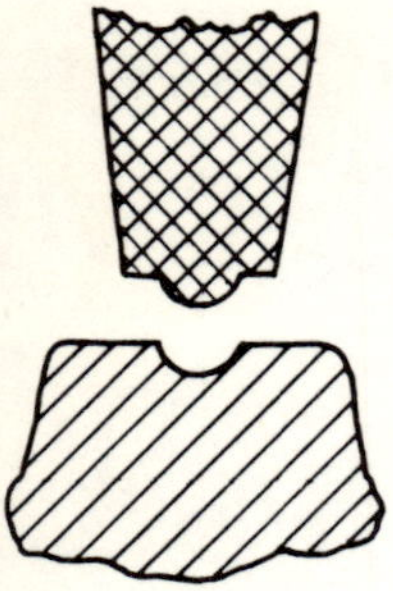

Fig. 36 Method of keying foot of wooden column into stone base

mud brick, but this appears to have been exceptional. Thin partition walls, however, were regularly made of mud bricks set on edge. Curious signs were carved on many of the stones of the palaces, and sometimes on those of houses, especially at the two great centres of Knossos and Phaistos. These were normally invisible after building had been completed, and they have been called mason's marks; but their object appears to have been religious or magical.

A standard feature in the palaces and the larger houses was the employment of a timber framework, consisting of horizontal beams let into each face of a wall, linked by cross beams and uprights at intervals. Dowel holes in the top of squared wall blocks show how the timbers were affixed to them by means of wooden pegs; and wooden pegs or dowels were no doubt employed to fasten the timbers to each other, metal nails being unknown then. This type of half-timber construction is also found in Syria, and later in Anatolia and on the mainland of Greece; but it must have been of special value in a region subject to earthquakes like Crete.

Wooden columns were lavishly employed in the palaces. These were of all sizes, the largest at Phaistos having a diameter of between 3½ and 4 feet. Columns it seems normally tapered downwards. A column of this shape is basically an inverted tree trunk with the widest end at the top to support the capital and the architrave beams laid upon it. To prevent the column slipping the top of the stone base was roughened, *Fig. 36* or had a shallow depression to fit a tenon which projected from the bottom of the column—the system by which the lintels at Stonehenge were fixed to the uprights, but in reverse. These wooden columns were usually plain, although as in Egypt they might be ribbed or fluted, sometimes with spiral flutes. Capitals of various types, some ornate and *Fig. 37* evidently inspired by Egyptian models, can be inferred from the frescoes and from the tops of stone pedestal lamps which are small versions of them. But no large stone columns or capitals of Bronze Age date have been recognised in Crete.[11] Square wooden pillars were also used as supports; larger pillars were built with dressed blocks of stone, or with rubble held together by wooden posts at the four corners. Plenty of timber was evidently available throughout the Bronze Age in Crete, the wood employed being largely pine and cypress which still grows in Plate 24 the White Mountains.[12] Beams carrying roofs and ceilings might

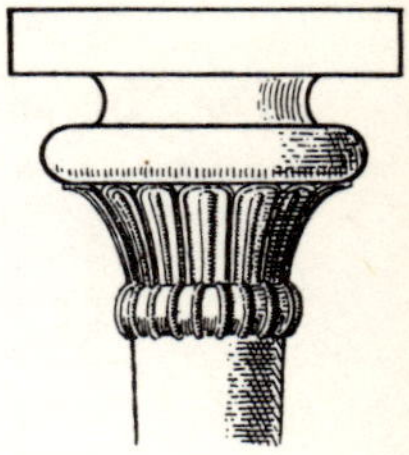

Fig. 37 Palm-capital inferred from a lamp as shown in fig. 42

have to span widths of 16 feet or more. Some of the rafters in the Temple Tomb at Knossos were 20 inches square. Roofs were apparently flat, except in the case of the domed circular tombs. These flat roofs were evidently made in the way that is still traditional in Crete: brushwood or branches being placed on the rafters, with a coat of earth several inches thick above them, and a layer of clay stamped down to make a compact watertight surface over all.

Most of the building stone was limestone, a hard grey-blue variety known as ironstone (sidheropetra) being favoured for pavements at Knossos. Slabs of soft gypsum, attractively veined, were already in use for paving and wall veneer in the early palace at Phaistos well back in Middle Minoan times. Gypsum slabs were extensively employed in the later palace at Knossos, and stone friezes, carved with rosettes or half- Plate 20
rosettes or spirals in relief, appear to have surrounded some of the monumental doorways there. But this use of carved stone was exceptional, and in Crete apparently confined to Knossos; although it was imitated in several of the palaces and royal tholos tombs of the Greek mainland.

Walls were normally coated with a fine lime plaster, except where a gypsum veneer was used. Many floors were plastered, especially in open courts and light wells, small pebbles often being mixed with the plaster to give it a better surface. Plaster was also used to fill the joints between paving slabs. But even in the palaces rooms used as offices or for storage might have simple earth floors, and wooden floors are also attested.

Cisterns and spring chambers were lined with a water-resistant plaster during the Late Minoan period if not earlier. These were often circular as at Zakro with steps leading down into them, and some may have been domed like the later spring chambers of Sardinia. Covered drains and open channels of clay and stone carried away rainwater and waste. Cunningly jointed clay pipes assigned to the earlier palace at *Fig. 38*
Knossos may have been for drainage. Evans considered that they brought water into the palace from springs outside; but if so, owing to the slope of the ground, the lines of pipes must have been carried on lofty aqueducts; unless the siphon principle was employed.

Fig. 38 Clay pipes for water or drainage

Stone was dressed with bronze axes and chisels of which the marks are often visible. Immense bronze saws, some 5 feet or more in length, were adapted for cutting timber and slicing the thin slabs of gypsum needed for wall veneer.

DECORATION

The plaster on the walls and floors of palaces and houses was often painted. Dark Pompeian red was a favourite colour for walls during the earlier part of the Middle Minoan period. Remains of red painted plaster have been found in Early Minoan contexts at Knossos and Vasiliki, and in the village settlement of Fournou Korifi. At the beginning of the Middle Minoan Period, if not earlier, walls and even floors were sometimes decorated with simple geometric designs in red and white.[13] But there is very little evidence for actual pictures before the time of the later palaces from *c.* 1700 BC onwards.

Plate 26 One of the earliest surviving wall pictures may be the Saffron Gatherer from Knossos with a background of the traditional Pompeian red. This painting could date from Middle Minoan III A (seventeenth century BC) when there was a vogue for clay vases with red bands and white spots like those here containing flowers. The flowers appear to be saffron crocuses of the kind used for making yellow dye. The head of the figure is missing, and Evans interpreted it as a boy, because of red *Fig. 39* lines on the body suggestive of dress. But it seems to be a monkey, blue being the conventional colour for monkeys in Crete as it was in Egypt. A tail, and the nose of another monkey, have been identified on fragments of the picture. The monkey is evidently a pet, and is wearing a red leather harness. So far from being usefully employed as Evans thought in collecting saffron flowers, it may be pulling the flowers out of pots in the royal gardens.[14]

There was no standard size for these wall pictures. They might occupy the whole surface of a wall above a narrow dado, or they were Plate 52 confined to small panels, like the bull-leaping scenes from Knossos with their human figures only about a foot in height. There were also Plate 28 long narrow friezes; one with hoopoes and partridges appears to have run around the top of the walls just below the ceiling in a room of the Caravanserai or hotel building south of the palace at Knossos. Figures Plate 31 vary from life-size or more than life-size, to only an inch or two in height.

Fig. 39 The 'Saffron Gatherer' restored as a monkey

Most of the remains of paintings that survive come from the palaces at Knossos and Ayia Triadha near Phaistos. But the walls of many of the houses at Knossos and elsewhere in Crete were evidently adorned with pictures during the flourishing period of the Minoan civilization between *c.* 1700–1450 BC. Even floors were sometimes decorated in this manner. The dolphins from the Residential Quarter at Knossos, which Evans conjectured came from a wall of the so-called Queen's bedroom, may in fact have adorned the floor of an upper room. The floor of a shrine by the palace at Ayia Triadha had on it a scene with similar dolphins, octopuses and other fish.[15] Plate 29

These pictures were largely in true fresco; that is to say, the colours were applied to damp plaster and sank into it. But the Cretan artists occasionally painted on a dry surface, and after the paint had dried they would add details in another colour. To guide them the painters incised lines or impressed them in the wet plaster with taut string. Life-size figures of men and animals were sometimes moulded in relief. Plate 32 These plaster relief frescoes appear to have been made at Knossos during the time before the disasters of *c.* 1450 BC, but not later.[16] Relief frescoes of the same period have been found elsewhere in Crete, notably in the east of the island. A curious technique employed in some wall paintings was like inlay. For parts of these needing more detailed Plate 25 treatment the surface was cut away and the hollow was then refilled with a finer quality of plaster. The basic colours used by the Cretan artists included red and yellow iron earths (haematite and yellow ochre), black which may have been prepared from carbonaceous shale or charred bones, and a blue that seems to be a silicate of copper and soda, that is a glass coloured by copper. But in the case of the Ayia Triadha sarcophagus the blue paint was apparently made by grinding expensive lapis lazuli from Afghanistan.[17]

Plates 59, 60

The subjects of many of these wall paintings were religious, but some of the pictures appear to have been entirely secular. These include scenes of real life, and landscapes with animals and birds of the kind which adorned the so-called House of the Frescoes at Knossos.[18] The huge reliefs of bull-leaping, however, in the west and north entrances of the palace at Knossos, and the imaginary griffins of the Throne Room there, evidently had a religious or magical significance, as did the pictures of bull-leaping and of dances watched by crowds of miniature spectators.

Plate 35
Plate 27
Plate 52

Men, women and animals were usually shown sideways-on as in contemporary Egypt and Mesopotamia. The pictures were always in one plane with no attempt at perspective; but it looks as if the figures in the same picture might vary in size according to their importance, as in Egypt. Rudimentary shading of a type found in Egypt is to be seen on griffins from the Throne Room at Knossos. Men were usually painted brown and women white, again as in Egypt. True, even there this convention was occasionally broken; but the white figures engaged in bull-leaping on a fresco from Knossos appear to be women dressed as men, as Evans assumed.

Plate 34
Plate 52

Landscape was treated in a strange way, somewhat as if seen from the air. Rocks and plants project from the sides and top of the picture as well as from the bottom after the manner of stalactites and stalagmites in a cave. This treatment, very different from Egyptian conventions, may reflect the hilly character of the Cretan countryside which affords a background to almost every view. In spite of their conventional character the landscapes painted on Cretan walls during the flourishing period of the Minoan civilization before the disasters of *c.* 1450 BC were remarkably life-like. The artists may have found inspiration in the beautiful flowers that carpet the island in the spring. But the flowers

Plates 26, 35

and plants, although they look so real, are often imaginary or highly stylized versions. Thus a rock rose is made symmetrical with six petals instead of the natural five. A favourite plant depicted in a variety of ways, sometimes hybridized with other flowers, was the papyrus native to Egypt and, if grown in Crete, exotic there. Plate 35

Figs 40, 41 Stone lamp (left) and clay lamps with protected handles

FURNITURE

Little of the furnishings of palaces and houses has survived. But stone benches along the walls of rooms are a regular feature of the palaces from the earliest times. There are also one or two stone chairs which clearly imitate wooden models. That in the Throne Room at Knossos has the seat hollowed to shape for the comfort of the occupant. The frescoes show folding stools like contemporary Egyptian ones. As in Egypt there were no doubt foot-stools, low wooden beds and tables.[20] As well as cupboards let into the walls and cists sunk in the floors, the Cretans evidently had storage chests and boxes of various kinds made of wood. These might be painted or inlaid with ivory, crystal or faience. Their lids during the Late Minoan period at least were sometimes hinged, to judge from the bronze hinges which have survived. Plate 19 Plate 27

Chests and boxes were also made in clay in imitation of wooden ones. These and clay bathtubs were often used as coffins, especially in the period after *c.* 1450 BC (see Plates 36, 21).

Lamps of clay or stone have shallow bowls for the oil and one or more troughs in the usually thick rims for a wick or wicks. Most clay lamps were portable, with a high projection from the rim to protect the handle against the heat. Stone lamps with tall pedestals were made to stand on the floor.

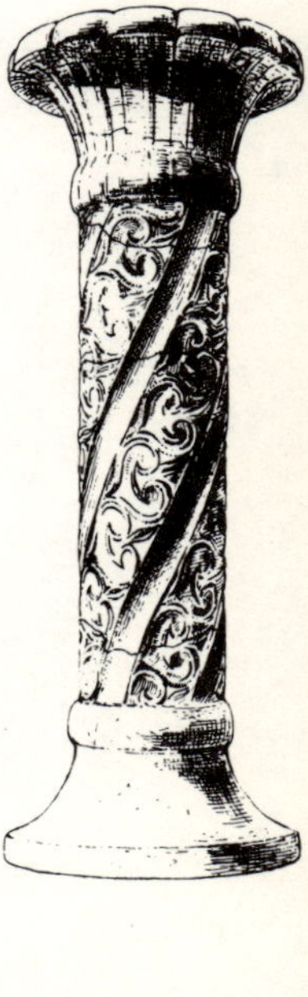

Fig. 42 Pedestal lamp from Knossos

CHAPTER VII

People, Food and Clothes

Plate 34

For the appearance of the people of Bronze Age Crete we largely depend on the lively pictures which they have left of themselves and of their gods in their own image on the walls of their palaces and houses. These all belong to the few centuries of the later palaces from *c.* 1700 BC onwards; but little figures of men and women were used as votive offerings, and some of these figures date back to the time of the earlier palaces if not before. There are also pictures on seals, and skeletons from tombs.[1]

Plates 47, 61, 62, 64

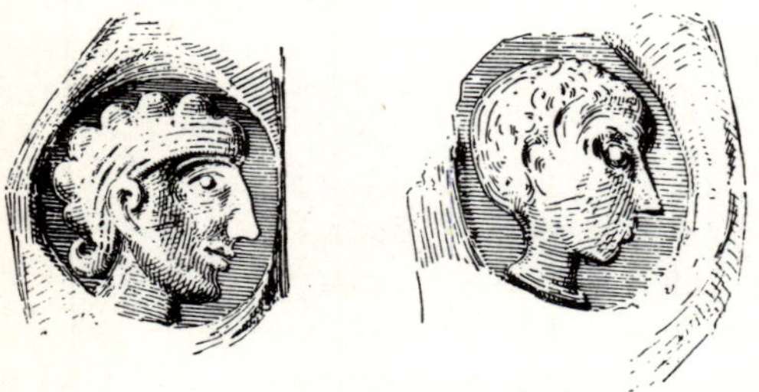

Fig. 43 'King' and 'Son': seal impressions from the Hieroglyphic Deposit (c. 1700 BC) at Knossos

From this evidence it is clear that the Bronze Age people of Crete were basically like other people of the Mediterranean area then and now; slight of build, not very tall, with dark hair and eyes and sallow complexions. The average height of skeletons of men from tombs in a cemetery of the Middle Minoan period on Ailias above Knossos was about 5 feet 6 inches, only half an inch less than the average height of men in Crete some fifty years ago before the First World War. Both men and women are usually represented with thin wasp-like waists. This may have been something of an ideal, although many of the modern Cretans are slender and thin-waisted in this manner.

Plate 62

During the most flourishing period of the Minoan Bronze Age from *c.* 1700 BC until the disasters in the middle of the fifteenth century Crete was heavily populated. Apart from the cities and towns that clustered around the palaces there were numerous smaller settlements; villages, hamlets of two or three houses, and isolated farms, many of which have disappeared without leaving a trace. Some of these farmhouses were simple one-storey bungalows as at Ayia Varvara near Mallia. But the larger villas like those at Vathipetro and Sklavokampos might have frescoed walls and all the amenities of great town houses.

These villas are often situated in places which enjoy views unusually fine and dramatic even for Crete, and this choice of picturesque situations was clearly deliberate. Such villas must have exercised control over extensive rural estates. At the same time, like the country houses of Roman Britain, they might be centres of industry. A pottery workshop appears to have been attached to the villa at Vathipetro. Several clay discs—weights from potters' wheels—were found there, along with traces of a large kiln, implying a manufacture of vases on a scale beyond that necessary for household needs. Arkhanes, site of a Bronze Age town and palace, is only half an hour's walk away down the valley to the north.

AGRICULTURE

When the Bronze Age settlements of Crete have been recorded and their character and date assessed, it may be possible to make interesting deductions about the population and economy of the island. Some work along these lines has already been done at Mallia.[2] The coastal plain there is fertile and well watered with a climate today warm enough for the growth of bananas. But this plain it seems could not have supported the population of a city the size of Bronze Age Mallia. The upland plain of Lasithi in the mountains behind Mallia may therefore have been dependent on the city, and served it as a granary as Africa later did Rome. Lasithi now is devoted to the cultivation of potatoes which like bananas were unknown to the ancients. But leaving aside exotics like these, mostly introduced in medieval and modern times, diet in Crete during the Bronze Age was basically perhaps not very different from what it is now.[3] Plate 39

Bread was made from the grain of wheat and barley, and perhaps from millet. Oil was obtained from olive trees, and wine from the grapes of the vine. Milk and meat came from cattle, sheep and goats. But hunting no doubt supplied more food than it does today when large wild animals, like deer and boar, no longer exist in Crete.

The first Neolithic immigrants were already, it seems, practising agriculture of a comparatively advanced kind when they arrived in the

Fig. 44 Plough-like sign

island. Grain, burnt (carbonized) but preserved by the action of fire, in the earliest Neolithic level 10 at Knossos included two kinds of wheat (emmer and a naked hexaploid variety) as well as barley.

To prepare the ground for sowing the people of Crete may have used wooden ploughs. Hesiod, about the eighth century BC, described a very primitive plough consisting of a piece of a tree with a fork in it; a type retained by the Romans for marking the boundaries of a new colony, and still used in parts of Syria in the late eighteenth century AD.

Fig. 44 But the signs in the earliest Cretan script which Evans interpreted as ploughs would have been of a more complex kind with the handle made of two separate pieces of wood.[4] The composite plough which Hesiod regarded as standard in his time could have derived from ones like these.

Fig. 45 The general all-purpose tool of the Bronze Age Cretans was an axe-adze with a shaft hole for mounting on a wooden handle.[5] The same tool, but made of iron, is still used throughout Crete today; the axe blade for cutting trees and clearing undergrowth, the adze for hoeing and weeding. Another standard tool in Bronze Age Crete was the double-bladed axe. Single-bladed axes and double adzes were also employed. At first the shaft holes for these tools were circular, but later they were made oval.[6] The oval shaft hole was an improvement, because the wooden handle could not twist round in it.

Until recently in Crete the ripe grain was plucked by hand in upland fields where the growth was sparse. But as early as Neolithic times curved pieces of wood or bone may have been armed with chips of flint or obsidian and used as sickles. Later, bronze sickles were made. The grain is threshed today with the help of a wooden sled with chips of flint inserted in the bottom. This is dragged by oxen round and round a circular threshing floor which is normally paved. Similar sleds armed with flint or obsidian may have been employed by the Bronze Age Cretans, but no threshing floors of theirs have yet been identified. After it was threshed the grain may have been winnowed from the chaff by flinging it into the air with long wooden forks, as is done today still. The light chaff flies away with the wind, while the heavier grain falls to

Plate 38 the ground. A stone libation vase from Ayia Triadha shows men with what appear to be sickles and winnowing forks on their shoulders, dancing in a harvest festival of some kind; but the festival may be one of sowing, and the fork-like objects carried by the men willow branches.[7]

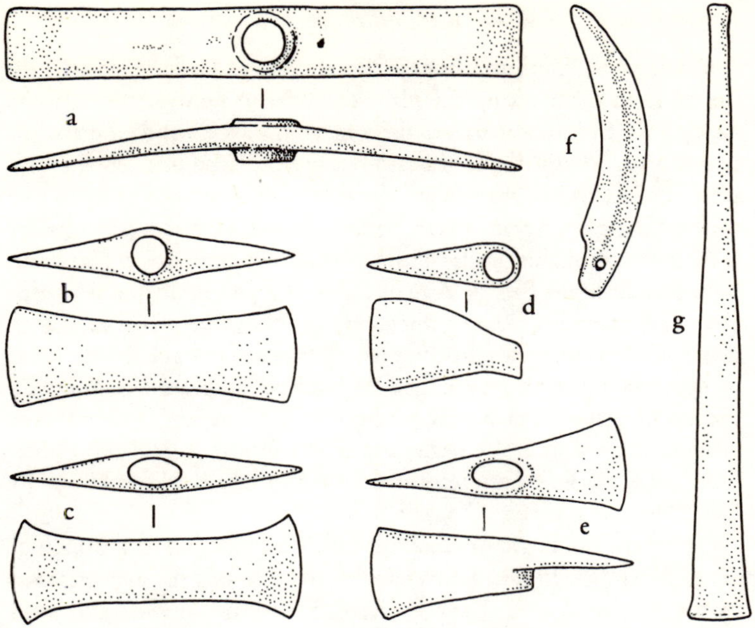

Fig. 45 Cretan bronze tools: a, *double adze;* b *and* c, *double axes;* d, *single-bladed axe;* e, *axe-adze;* f, *sickle;* g, *chisel. Approx. 1 : 4*

A group of circular rooms in the south-west corner of the palace at Mallia were perhaps beehive-shaped granaries like contemporary Egyptian ones.[8] At Knossos round pits (*koulouras*) in the West Court may have replaced the rectangular 'dungeons' (as Evans called them) of the earliest palace for the storage of grain. The curious early 'hypogaea' on the south edge of the palace may also have been silos, if they were not wells.[9] Plate 39

Fig. 46 Oil-separating jar

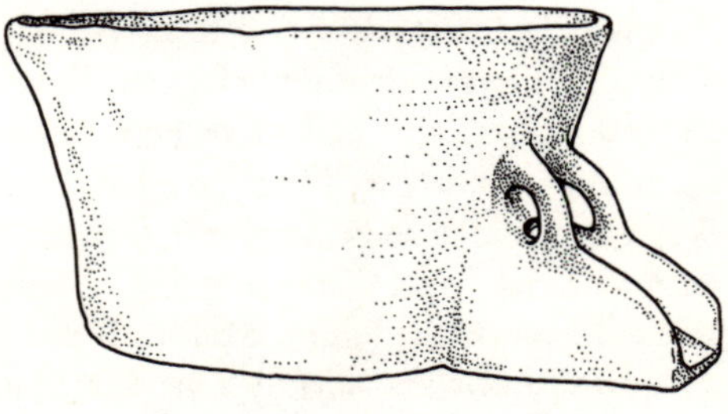

Fig. 47 Palm trees on Middle Minoan II seal

Olives are of basic importance in the economy of Mediterranean lands, the oil from them taking the place of butter in northern diet. In the autumn the fruit is beaten from the trees with sticks; it is then drenched in hot water, crushed, and the resulting pulp placed in a settling tank where the oil rises to the surface, the water being drained away in due course through a spout at the bottom. Large clay jars with spouts at the bottom suitable for use in this separating process are known from most periods of the Bronze Age in Crete. But an installation at Vathi-petro, incorporating a jar of this kind, has been interpreted as a wine press; while similar jars in the early settlement at Fournou Korifi it is suggested might have been used for crushing purple dye from murex shells. Olive trees may have been indigenous to Crete, and were probably being cultivated from the beginning of the Bronze Age if not earlier. Stones of olives have been recovered from Fournou Korifi and from the Early Minoan I well at Knossos.

Fig. 46

Plate 40

Fig trees no doubt grew in Crete and were exploited for their fruit from the earliest times. Figs and olives appear to be among the trees regarded by the Bronze Age Cretans as sacred. Pears and quinces also seem to have been native to Crete. Kydonia, the ancient Greek city which occupied the site of modern Khania, means quince and may preserve the Minoan name for it, since the Kydonians mentioned by Homer are thought to have been a remnant of the pre-Greek population retaining their independence in the far west of the island until the coming of the Dorians *c.* 1000 BC. The well-watered plain behind Khania is still an important fruit-growing district, although now dominated by the orange brought from the East during the Middle Ages. Almonds with their early blossom are a striking feature of the spring landscape all round the Mediterranean. They were presumably exploited for their nuts in Crete as elsewhere.

Date palms, often low and bush-like, grow wild in Crete today in sheltered valleys with plenty of water. But palms were almost certainly not indigenous, and may have been introduced from Egypt or elsewhere in the Levant well back in the Bronze Age or in Neolithic times. What Evans took to be a palm branch appears as a sign in the earliest script of Crete, and there are many representations of palms on vases and seal stones of the Middle Minoan II period from *c.* 1900 BC onwards. The date palm was evidently a sacred tree in Bronze Age Crete. Later

Plate 5

Fig. 47

Fig. 48 Barley ears (?) on clay jug from Knossos

it was associated with Apollo, a god who was himself probably of pre-Greek origin.

The vine, like the olive, may have been a native of Crete. Grape pips have been found at Fournou Korifi, and in storage jars of the Middle Minoan period at Phaistos and at Monastiraki, site of a Bronze Age town and palace west of Mount Ida.[10] These pips may be the remains, not of wine, but of raisins, that is, of grapes dried in the autumn sun to store and eat through the winter months. Evans thought that during the earlier part of the Bronze Age the people of Crete drank beer, and only began to crush wine from grapes during the Late Minoan period after *c.* 1600 BC. But there was wine in Egypt as early as the time of the Old Kingdom soon after *c.* 3000 BC, and the Cretans may have been making wine at the beginning of their Bronze Age if not earlier. Like the ancient Egyptians they probably grew both dark and light grapes to produce red and white wine. The red wine of Crete was much commended by travellers in the old days, and the province of Malemvizi just west of Knossos appears to have given its name to the Malmsey which was exported to England in the Middle Ages.

Beer may have been brewed from the earliest times in Crete as it was in Egypt, where traces of it have been found in clay pots dating from the Predynastic period back in the fourth millennium. Clay jugs from Knossos assigned by Evans to the seventeenth century BC have what he interpreted as barley ears in relief on them, and may have held beer for use in some religious cult. *Fig. 48*

Vegetables that grow wild in Crete include lettuce, celery, asparagus and carrots. The people of Crete today also eat the leaves of various spinach-like plants, together with the bulbs of wild hyacinths, and cultivated peas, beans and vetches. An Egyptian medical text of the beginning of Dynasty XVIII (early sixteenth century BC) mentions a 'bean of the country of Keftiou', the Egyptian name for Crete, as widely used in medicine.[11]

The wilderness in Crete today is filled with scented herbs such as thyme, sage, marjoram and mint. These may have added a flavour to ancient, as they do to modern cooking in the island. The names by which these plants are now called in Greece are probably derived from those which they had in the Bronze Age. For the ancient Greek names, which are the same as the modern ones, appear to be of pre-Greek origin.

ANIMALS, BIRDS AND FISH[12]

The only large wild animal left in Crete now is the agrimi or wild goat. This Cretan ibex (*Catra hircus cretensis*) resembles the bezoar which is found distributed from Greece eastwards through Asia Minor to Persia and north-west India. Wild goats of bezoar stock appear to be closely related to the ancestors of modern domestic goats, and the agrimi of Crete may be feral, that is to say, descended from domestic goats which were turned loose or escaped in the mountains of Crete and became wild there during the Bronze Age or before it. The Minoan artists often depicted goats that are indistinguishable from modern agrimia, with long curving horns knobbed at intervals. Sometimes these goats appear in domesticated circumstances, sitting on the roof of a shrine or drawing chariots. The occupants of these chariots may be divine; but there is no reason why goats should not have been trained as draught animals. Similar goats, however, are often portrayed bounding over a rocky wilderness or pursued by huntsmen and their hounds.[13]

Plates 114, 48

Plate 45

Pigs seem to have been domesticated in Crete as early as Neolithic times. But there were also wild boar, hunted as dangerous pests and for their meat. Their formidable tusks occur, together with other kitchen refuse in Bronze Age levels, both at Knossos and elsewhere in Crete.

Plate 41

Lions may once have lurked in the forests and mountains of Crete. They were still to be found in the fifth century BC in Macedonia in the extreme north of Greece, where there are wild boar even now. Lions were a favourite subject with Cretan seal engravers from Early Minoan times onwards. On Late Minoan seals they are often shown attacking other animals, wild deer or cattle. Lions would have been a dangerous menace, destroyers of cattle, game and men. Their pursuit and elimination with the simple weapons of early times required war-like discipline and courage. The most famous of the inlaid dagger blades found in the royal shaft graves at Mycenae on the Greek mainland shows men armed with shields, spears and bows, hunting a pride of lions. Although the dagger was found on the mainland, it may be the work of a Cretan artist, or even depict a scene in Crete. Lions also appear as sacred animals in attendance upon Cretan deities. The lion which accompanies an armed goddess on one of the clay seal impressions from the

Plates 42, 56

Plate 43

Plate 55

Fig. 49 God with lioness and opposite, goddess with lion, on seal impressions. Knossos

Figs 50, 51 Collared bitch on seal impression and men with giant dog on seal. Knossos

Temple Repositories at Knossos is balanced by a lioness walking beside a military god.

There were deer in Crete during the Bronze Age, and they survived in the mountains of the west into Roman times. Bones of cattle were recovered along with those of sheep and goat from the earliest Neolithic levels at Knossos. The original settlers may have brought their cattle with them. For there is no evidence that wild cattle ever existed in Crete. Cretan cattle seem to be descended from the giant *Bos primigenius* with long horns.[14] Cattle may have been kept for their milk rather than for their meat; but they also no doubt served as draught animals and beasts of burden, while their hides were required for the great shields used in hunting and in war.

A spectacular use of cattle was in the bull-leaping sports, which Plates 52, 85, 88 evidently had a religious or magical side to them.[15] The bulls may have been sacrificed after the leaping, but this is uncertain. While bull-leaping appears to have been practised from the remotest times in Crete, most of the evidence for the sacrifice of cattle dates from the Late Minoan Plate 59 III period in the fourteenth century BC, and then it is always in connection with funeral rites. Small altars for burnt sacrifice, however, certainly existed in the palaces by Late Minoan I, *c.* 1500 BC, if not earlier. The bulls used for the leaping ceremonies were of domestic breed to judge from their dappled, piebald or skewbald, hides. But they were evidently savage enough, as cattle allowed to live in a semi-wild state can become, and scenes like that on one of the Vafio cups vividly Plate 51 illustrate the difficulties and perils that might attend their capture.

The dog was probably the first animal domesticated by man, and dogs are attested from the earliest times in Crete. A Neolithic clay head from Knossos may be meant for one. The handles on some Early Plate 76 Minoan stone lids are shaped like dogs. The chief use of the dog was in hunting. Bitches wearing collars by which they could be held on Plate 45 leashes appear on clay seal impressions from the palace at Knossos destroyed in the fourteenth century BC. On a fine seal assigned by Evans to Middle Minoan III, a collared dog is barking at a goat at bay on a rock above. What seems to be an immense dog wearing an embossed collar is engraved on a chalcedony seal with gold end-mounts found in a Late Minoan tomb at Knossos. Evans suggested that this might be a sacred dog, recalling those described by a Roman writer at the temple

Fig. 52 Seal with cat attacking water birds

of Diktynna, a goddess of pre-Greek name and origin, whose sanctuary stood on the rugged promontory of Spatha west of Khania.

Plate 86
What seem to be cats appear on Middle Minoan seals. One of exceptional quality from Knossos has a cat-like animal engraved on it along with signs in the hieroglyphic script. Evans suggested that this might have been a royal seal, the cat being the personal badge of a Cretan prince. Wild cats were probably indigenous to Crete and still exist there. But domestic cats may have been introduced from Egypt, where they were trained to help in hunting wild fowl in the marshes.

Plate 58
An inlaid dagger from one of the Mycenae shaft graves, which like the lion-hunt dagger may be the work of a Cretan artist, has golden cats loose among water birds against the background of a stream with silver fish and clumps of papyrus reminiscent of Egypt. Several Late Minoan

Fig. 52
Plate 57
seals show cats chasing water birds, and in contemporary wall paintings they also appear stalking birds on land.

The monkey is another animal which may have found its way from Egypt to Crete. Painted blue according to Egyptian convention, monkeys feature on several wall paintings of about the sixteenth century BC both at Knossos and on Thera, where the fossilized head of one has been reported from below the debris of the Bronze Age eruption.[16]

Plate 73
But monkeys were incorporated in jewellery of the Middle Minoan period, and appear still earlier on seals. Some early seals have monkeys carved in the round as handles.

Fig. 53
Plate 49
Plate 50
Plate 28
Many of the oldest Cretan seals are in the shape of animals or birds. Birds of various kinds were engraved on Middle Minoan seals, and those of the Late Minoan period often show water birds, usually among papyrus clumps as in Egyptian pictures of them. Birds caught for food may have included partridge and hoopoe; these appear together in the frieze painted round the tops of the walls in what Evans took to be the dining-room in the Caravanserai or hotel building at Knossos.[17] Hoopoes are still common summer migrants in Crete, and Evans says that they were regarded as a special delicacy there and elsewhere in the Levant in his time. But under the name of lapwing the hoopoe is branded by Jewish law as unclean; not unjustly in view of its disgraceful nesting habits.

Did the Bronze Age Cretans have chickens? Fowl were first domesticated in India where their wild ancestors lived. The people of the

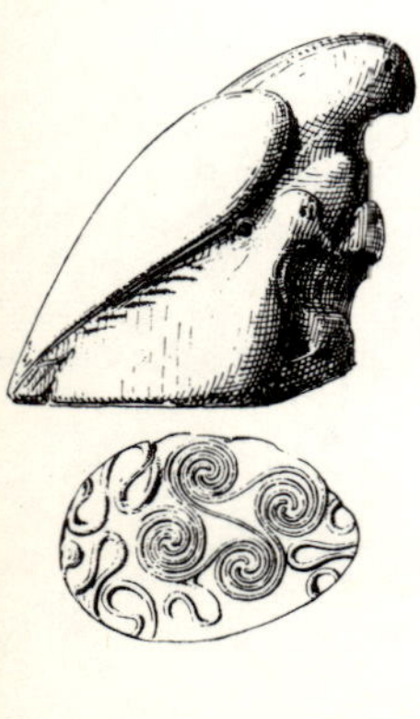

Fig. 53 Ivory bird-seal from Koumasa in the Mesara

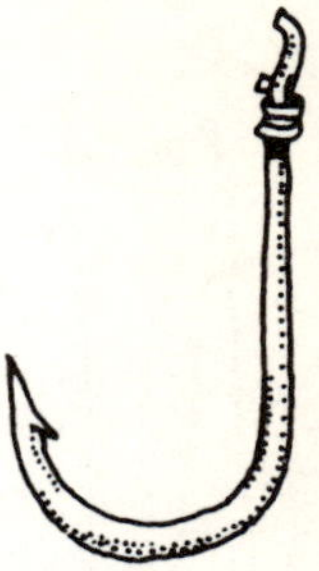

Figs 54, 55 Gold bead in shape of scarus fish, from Knossos, and fish-hook from Gournia

Indus Valley civilization were keeping fowl by 2000 BC or earlier. But there is no mention of them in Egypt until the time of Thotmes III in the early fifteenth century BC. The 'bird that gives birth every day' recorded in his annals can only refer to a chicken, but implies that it was something strange and new. There is no reason why the Cretans should not have introduced fowl from Egypt or from elsewhere in the Levant. A clay vase from Ayia Triadha looks remarkably like a chicken; but chicken bones in the early burial cave at Trapeza in Lasithi could have strayed there from the neighbouring village of Tzermiadhes in recent times.[18] Chickens were known to the later Greeks as Persian or Median birds, and are only attested from the eighth century BC onwards. If, therefore, fowl existed in Greece in the Bronze Age, they may have become extinct for a time at the end of it.

Fish must have formed an important element of diet in the numerous Bronze Age settlements round the coasts of Crete. Their bones have rarely survived; but Evans noted fish vertebrae in a cooking pot from the palace at Knossos destroyed in the fourteenth century BC. A gold ornament from the Residential Quarter of the palace seems to represent *Fig. 54*
the scarus or parrot wrasse, which was highly favoured by the Romans. Plate 44
It is still esteemed in Crete but is not common now. Flying-fish are depicted on a number of seal stones.

Ancient writers describe a wide and sophisticated variety of fishing methods; with hook and line, with nets of various kinds, both casting nets and dragnets or seines; with baskets or weels; and with spears or tridents. Some at least of these methods were already used by Cretan fishermen in the Bronze Age. Neatly barbed metal fish-hooks were *Fig. 55*
found in the town of Gournia together with a lead sinker to slip on a line and stones for weighting nets. A curious bronze double blade *Fig. 56*

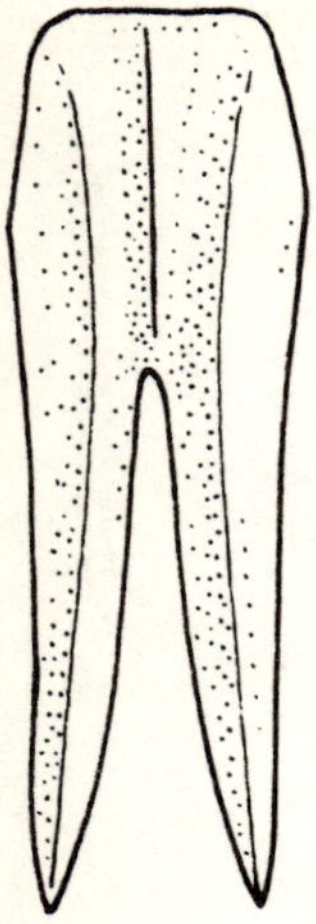

Fig. 56 Fish-spear (?) from Ayios Onouphrios

from Ayios Onouphrios near Phaistos is regarded as a fish-spear; but no other like it is known.

The octopus was no doubt a staple of diet in Crete during the Bronze Age and may have been speared by the light of torches at night, as now. It became a favourite motif in Late Minoan times (see Plate 15) when vases of clay and metal appear wrapped in its tentacles. Shell-fish were presumably eaten as well as being crushed to make dye. Edible land snails found in a vase in one of the settlements on Thera overwhelmed in the eruption *c.* 1500 BC may have been imported from Crete.[19]

A hundred years ago the eastern part of Crete was a great centre for sponge-fishing. Sponges were put to various uses by the later Greeks, as cushions inside bronze helmets and in boots. Some of the decoration on the plastered walls of the early palace at Knossos Evans thought was made with a sponge dipped in paint. A class of design on some Middle Minoan clay vases may imitate these sponge patterns in miniature.[20]

A creature of basic importance in early economies was the bee, for honey was the chief source of sugar. In Egypt bees were kept in horizontal clay cylinders, open at one end through which smoke was blown to clear the hive when the honey was to be extracted, the bees escaping through a flight hole at the other. But no clay bee-hives have yet been recognized from Bronze Age Crete, and the honey of wild bees may have been collected from hollow trees or clefts in the rocks. A remarkable gold pendant from Mallia seems to represent a pair of bees. They look more like wasps or hornets, but the Egyptians represented bees in this manner.

Plate 70

Honey may also have been used for embalming. Herodotus says that the Babylonians buried their dead in honey; and the body of Alexander the Great was embalmed in this way before being brought from Babylon to Alexandria. A curious legend describes how Glaukos, a son of Minos, was drowned by falling into a jar of honey (see p. 138). This might be a reminiscence of a time when honey was used to embalm the dead in Crete. The jars employed for burials during the Middle Minoan period could have contained honey. Occasionally these jars were lined with plaster as if to render them less porous. But there is as yet no positive evidence that honey was ever placed in them.

Plate 113

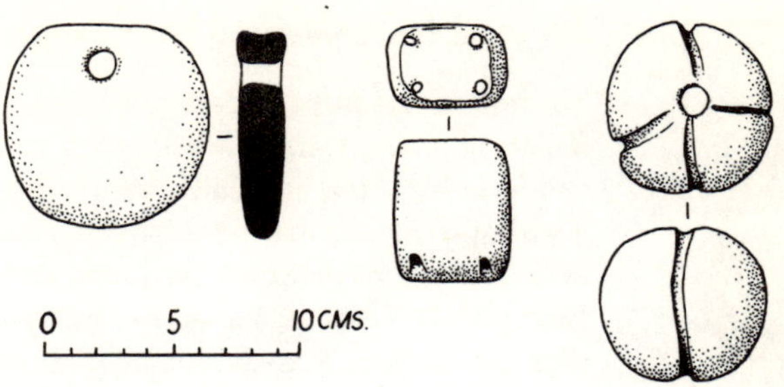

Fig. 57 Clay loom weights

Spinning and weaving of cloth were already practised in Crete before the end of the Neolithic period. These were no doubt household industries, as still today in many parts of Greece. Clay spindle whorls and loom weights are common on Bronze Age sites throughout Crete. The earlier loom weights were shaped like flat discs; but in the time of the later palaces solid globes with three or four grooves down the sides for the thread of the warp came into use. A rectangular variety of loom weight with thread holes at the four corners, occurring in the Knossian Neolithic, is still found in Late Minoan I times at Palaikastro and in the Cretan colony at Kastri on Kythera, although not at Knossos.[21] *Fig. 57*

The looms which needed these weights were of the upright type which was to remain standard throughout the Classical period (fifth–fourth centuries BC) and later in Greece. As they were made of wood the looms have not survived. But a stone in the women's quarters of the house at Ayia Varvara has two rectangular cuttings which may have held the upright posts of a loom. A pair of large hollows between these it is suggested were for oil applied to the vertical threads of the warp to keep them supple.

Wool was no doubt the staple material used for making cloth. A large proportion of the inscribed clay tablets from the palace at Knossos destroyed in the fourteenth century BC appear to refer to sheep, and may record flocks kept for their wool.[22] Perhaps woollen cloth was among the chief exports of Bronze Age Crete, and it has been suggested that the woven designs on woollens spread Cretan schemes of decoration based upon the spiral to Egypt and elsewhere in the Levant during the time of the Middle Kingdom, *c.* 2000 BC onwards.

Figs 58, 59 Seal impressions of men in kilts from Zakro and Ayia Triadha (below)

Linen seems to have been used in Crete as well as woollen cloth. Traces of it were claimed by Seager from an Early Minoan I deposit in a tomb at Mochlos. This linen was perhaps imported from Egypt, where it is already attested in the Predynastic period (fourth or fifth millennium BC), or it may have been woven from flax grown in Crete. Possibly the Bronze Age Cretans had some variety of the Coan silk, famous in later Greek and Roman times. This was a true silk, very fine and transparent, made in the island of Cos just north-east of Crete apparently from cocoons spun by a local moth, *Pachypasa otus*.[23]

An industry which probably flourished in Crete was that of making purple dye for woollens by crushing the murex shell-fish. It has been suggested that the early settlement at Fournou Korifi was a centre of this industry, but the evidence is not conclusive. Heaps of crushed murex shells at other coastal sites in eastern Crete like Palaikastro may reflect the manufacture of purple dye there in Middle and Late Minoan times if not earlier.

In cold climates at least men from the earliest times clothed themselves in the furs or skins of the animals which they hunted. But the only people wearing skins on the monuments of Bronze Age Crete are involved in ritual scenes where these may be the skins of sacrificed animals.

Plates 59, 60

There was much variety in the secular as well as in the ritual dress worn by Cretan men and women. Court dress was clearly more elaborate then ordinary wear, and local styles of dress may have existed. Some changes of fashion evidently took place over the centuries.[24]

For men, however, the basic garment throughout the Bronze Age was a loin-cloth tucked round the waist or held in place by a girdle or belt of some kind. Various shapes of loin cloth appear to have been fashionable at different times, and some of these may have been special to certain areas. Above the waist men normally went bare as in Egypt. The loin-cloth might be worn as a kilt, or folded under the groin, making it like a pair of shorts. It was a natural step from this to sew the loin-cloth into a pair of shorts, as worn by the men on the lion-hunt dagger from Mycenae, and by winged and goat-headed demons on clay seal impressions of about the same period from Zakro (see *Fig. 113*).

Plate 55

A feature of men's dress throughout most of the Bronze Age in Crete is the cod-piece. Early representations show it as straight and narrow,

sometimes, it seems, being worn with a belt alone and no loin cloth. Plate 47
But during the time of the second palaces a wide and very prominent cod-piece is often depicted in association with what appears to be a stiff kilt, cut at the sides to expose the thighs and often distinctly upturned at the back. Plates 52, 62, 96, 97 On a seal impression from Zakro this stiff kilt is shown above a flowing apron of a kind worn by a number of bronze figures of votaries assignable to roughly the same period (Late Minoan I, *c.* 1500 BC). *Fig. 58* The upturned front of the kilt on this sealing may not be meant for a cod-piece, since the latter was evidently not an invariable part of male dress in Crete by this time. *Fig. 59* A number of other Late Minoan I seal impressions show gods or men without it. There are also many representations of men in long kilts without any sign of a cod-piece.

These long kilts sloped down from back to front, where the ends may have met, the gross cod-piece being replaced by a large, often elaborately beaded tassel. The kilts were held in place by a girdle with loose ends, or, in later representations at least, by a wide belt.

This kind of kilt may have come into fashion later than the short stiff kilt and cod-piece, but both types of dress overlapped in use. Possibly the long kilt originated in the north of Crete, since most early representations of it seem to emanate from Knossos and Mallia. Plate 68 Kilts of this kind are conspicuous in the Procession fresco at Knossos dating from early in Late Minoan times. A simple form of this kilt without a tassel is worn by the Captain of the Blacks somewhat later. Plate 33

Foreigners, who appear to be meant for Cretans or other Aegean peoples, to judge from their dress and the objects which they are carrying as gifts or tribute to Pharaoh, are depicted in five tombs of high officials at Thebes, the capital of Egypt throughout the earlier part of Dynasty XVIII.[25] In one of these tombs, made for Rekhmire, Vizier for many years under Thotmes III (1504–1450 BC), these Aegean people are described as 'Princes of the land Keftiou'—that is, of Crete—'and of the isles which are in the midst of the sea', which may include the Cyclades and the coasts of mainland Greece. *Fig. 60* Some of the islands were occupied by Cretan colonies at this time, and parts of the Greek mainland may have been tributary to Crete. These people from the Aegean are wearing decorated kilts reminiscent of those in the Procession fresco at Knossos. But when the paintings in the tomb were being cleaned some twenty years ago it was found that the figures of people from the

Fig. 60 Envoys from the Aegean in the tomb of Rekhmire

Fig. 61

Aegean, and only these, had been altered. As originally painted the Aegean people had been wearing cod-pieces of the type associated in Crete with the short, stiff kilt, upturned at the back.

This alteration of dress may reflect visits of two separate embassies from the Aegean to Egypt; the second of these embassies being late in the reign of Rekhmire's master, Thotmes III, shortly before or after the disasters of *c.* 1450 BC. Perhaps the people of the second embassy were from the Greek mainland, whether sent by a king of Mycenae, or by rulers of mainland origin then in control of Knossos. But the long kilt was already being worn in Crete before this time, and it looks as if it was a fashion which developed there in the first instance, although adopted by the people of the mainland along with so many other aspects of the Cretan way of life. Similarly, the short stiff kilt with exaggerated cod-piece is still worn by a man painted on the walls of the palace at Pylos on the mainland in the fourteenth or thirteenth century BC.[26]

Seal stones, and clay figurines placed as votive offerings in sanctuaries, assignable to Middle Minoan I-II times, show women in long skirts with girdles wound double round the waist and knotted, their ends hanging down in front. Bodices, which may have been separate although depicted as if in one piece with the skirts, characteristically leave the breasts exposed but have collars rising in a high peak at the back of the neck (see Plate 47 and *Fig. 62*).

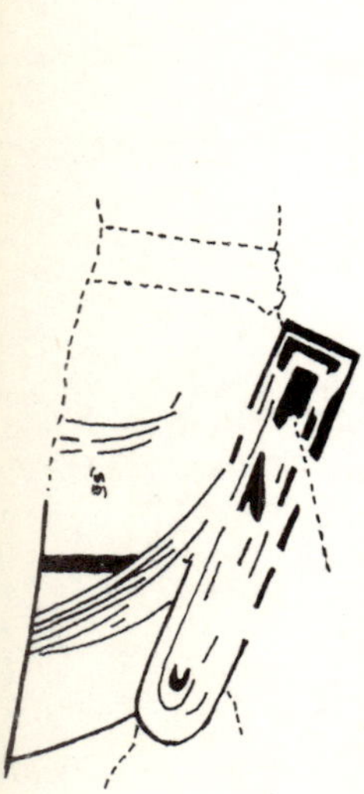

Fig. 61 Cod-piece of Aegean envoys as originally painted in Rekhmire's tomb

Fig. 62 Jasper seal with early script signs and woman in long robe

Fig. 63 Faience figurine of bare-breasted woman in long flounced V-skirt from the palace at Knossos

Many of the later representations of women appear to show priestesses or goddesses, like the snake-wielding faience statuette from Knossos. She wears a short-sleeved bodice which leaves the breasts exposed. Round her waist is a wide belt; while a double apron descending back and front conceals the top of a long flounced skirt. Women's skirts are often depicted with flounces, either squares of different coloured materials making an attractive chequer-board pattern as here, or simple bands. Flounced skirts of this kind were ultimately of Mesopotamian origin and inspiration. This statuette may represent a goddess, but her clothes are just an elaborate version of what was being worn by women of the palace at the time. Plate 63

These dresses, like the kilts worn by men about the court during the period of the later palaces, are often shown with elaborate decoration. Where the patterns were geometrical or repetitive they were no doubt woven into the cloth; but complicated designs, including pictures of animals and mythical creatures, may have been embroidered.[27]

During Late Minoan times, from *c.* 1550 BC onwards, the long skirts worn by women often have a marked V in front. Some of the skirts of this period appear to have been divided, equivalents perhaps of the shorts, or divided loin cloths, worn by men. Plate 61

Elaborate court dress of this kind was clearly not suitable for all occasions. The girl on an early ivory seal from Knossos, under the gravest suspicion as a fake but with an unusually good pedigree, wears a simple, relatively short frock, although the rectangles imply that it has flounces sewn on to it.[28] On some later seal impressions short skirts are worn by goddesses engaged in warfare or the chase (see *Fig. 49*).

Fig. 64 Girl on ivory seal alleged to come from Knossos

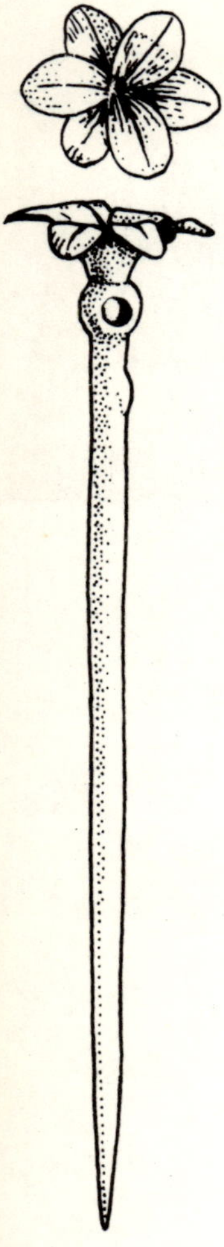

Fig. 65 Gold dress-pin from Chrysolakkos at Mallia

Capes or cloaks evidently gave protection against the rain and winter cold. Curious scaled cloaks or cuirasses are among a variety of religious garments. In Late Minoan times long single-piece robes of a distinctive type appear to be worn by certain gods and their priests, who are often represented in chariots (see Plates 38, 64).

Short pins of bone or metal were evidently used to fasten dress throughout most of the Bronze Age in Crete.[29] A gold pin with the head in the shape of a flower from Mallia has a swelling with a thread-hole like contemporary Syrian 'toggle pins'.[30] Conical stone whorls, common during the Late Minoan period, were used to weight spindles, but may have sometimes served as buttons.[31]

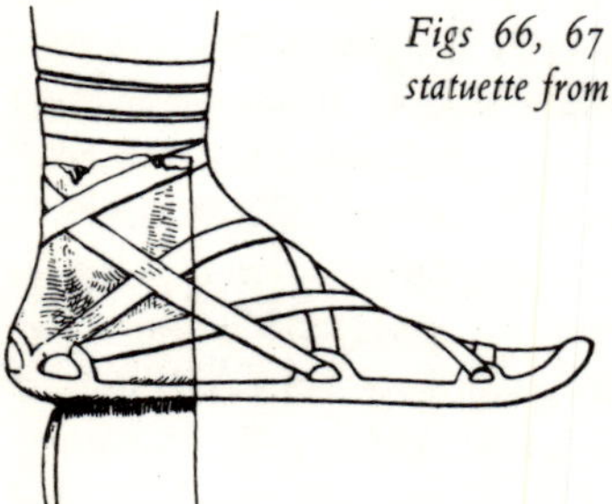

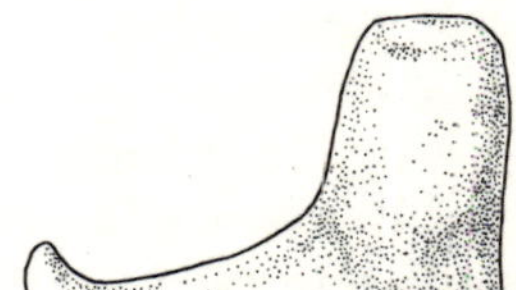

Figs 66, 67 Sandalled foot (with toes restored) of ivory statuette from Knossos and clay model boot from Mallia

In their houses and when engaged in religious ceremonies the people of Crete went barefoot. Otherwise boots may have been the standard footwear for men, as they still are in Crete. A clay figurine, assignable to the beginning of the Middle Minoan period, appears to be wearing
Plate 47 white boots with uppers of leather or woven material. The 'officer'
Plate 97 on a relief cup from Ayia Triadha is booted (see Plate 97). The larger figure has what appear to be strips of material wound round his legs like puttees. Sandals, too, were worn by men and perhaps women. The
Figs. 66, 67 Greek word *sandalon* is of pre-Greek origin and may be Minoan. Boots and sandals often had upturned toes.

Wide flat caps, or ones with short thick rolled brims, were evidently worn by men as a protection against sun or rain. Clay figurines of

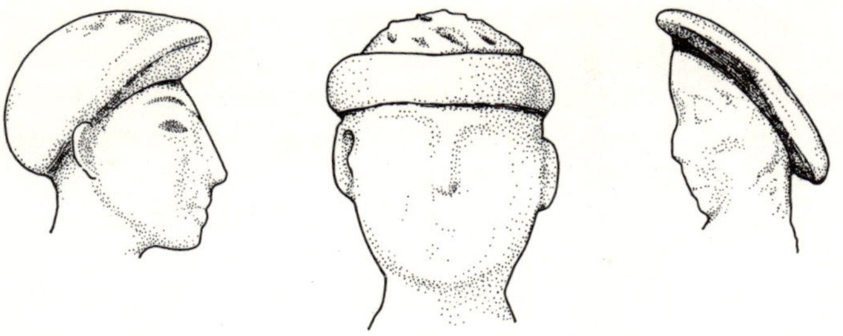

Fig. 68 Men's head-gear taken from bronze and clay figurines

women assignable to the period of the early palaces show high pointed hats like Phrygian caps that may have been adapted to the elaborate coiffures of the time. Later representations suggest a fantastic variety of headgear, much of it religious or ceremonial in character, and some of it perhaps confined to gods and goddesses. Plate 47

The men of Bronze Age Crete normally let their curly black hair grow long, with locks hanging down on each side of the face in front of the ears. Both men and gods, however, are quite often represented with short hair. Beards and moustaches, although rarely portrayed, do not appear to have been altogether foreign to Crete. Perhaps they were confined to some particular region of the island or to a special group of priests. Women, like men, wore their hair long, and early figurines suggest an extraordinary range and fantasy in hair styles. Plate 66 Plate 46

While men may have shaved with obsidian blades in early times, little cutter-like tools, common during the Early and Middle Minoan periods, appear to have served as razors. Later razors were leaf-shaped, and during Late Minoan III a type shaped like a chopper in the contemporary Egyptian manner became fashionable. Tweezers were also used for removing hair throughout the Bronze Age in Crete as elsewhere in the Levant. Paint for the eyes and face was evidently ground on rectangular stone palettes and later at any rate in stone bowls. Polished bronze discs which gave a reflection served for mirrors as in Egypt and later Greece. Their handles made of wood or ivory were often elaborately carved. For combs wood may have been used for the most part, but ivory combs appear in Crete by the Late Minoan period if not earlier. *Fig. 69*

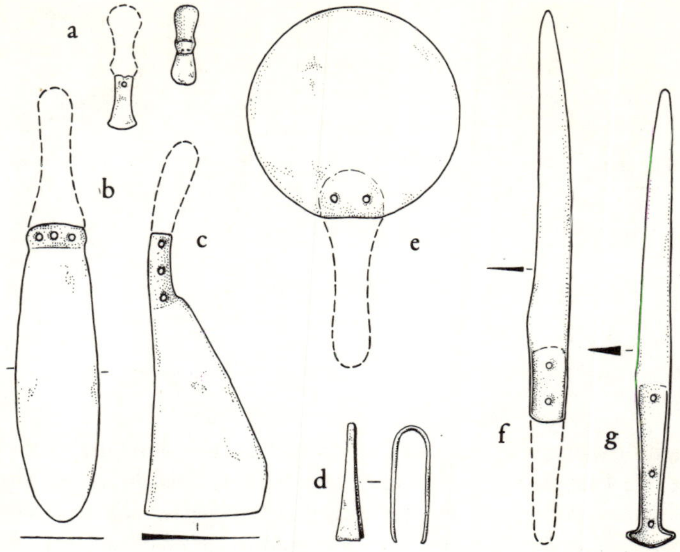

Fig. 69 a–c, *bronze razors;* d, *tweezers;* e, *mirror;* f *and* g, *knives. Approx. 1 : 4*

Jewellery, worn by men as well as women, included hair-pins and other hair ornaments, earrings which might be very large and elaborate; armlets, wristlets and anklets, of bronze or precious metal, and collars and necklaces of beads. Beads were in a wide variety of shapes, especially during the Late Minoan period, and they were made of different kinds of stone, including rock-crystal, amethyst and cornelian; also of metal—copper, silver and gold,—of paste that might be plated with gold, of

Figs 70, 71 Stone palette from Koumasa in the Mesara and gold armlet from Mochlos

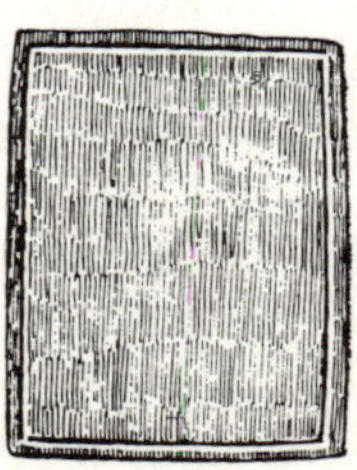

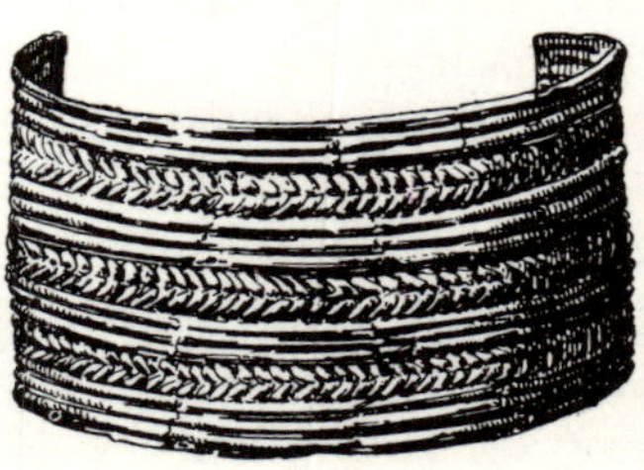

Figs 72, 73 Large triple earrings worn by a miniature frescoed head from Knossos and lapis lazuli beads from the Isopata Royal Tomb

Figs 74, 75 Gold beads in the shape of double argonauts and rosettes, and ribbed faience bead, all from the Zafer Papoura cemetery at Knossos, and a heart-shaped bead

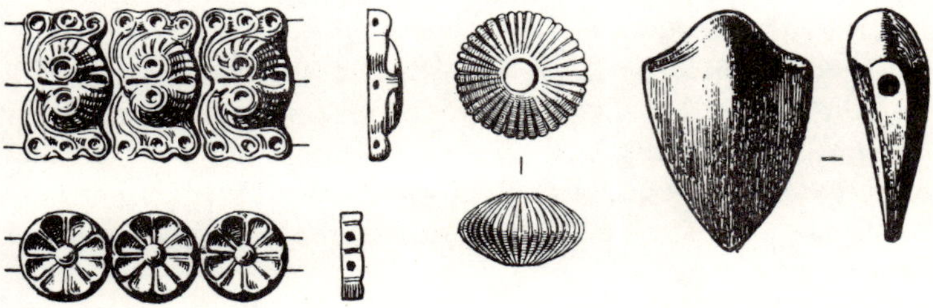

faience and eventually of glass. Bands or diadems of gold or silver, used to keep the hair in place, have been found in some of the early communal tombs. From those at Mochlos, with burials reaching back before 2000 BC, comes a varied collection of gold jewellery, including leaves and flowers set on pins which may have been hair ornaments, reminiscent of those found in the Royal Cemetery at Ur. During the Late Minoan period a simpler type of hair-pin with bent top became standard.

Plate 69

Fig. 76

A remarkable treasure of gold jewellery was acquired by the British Museum in 1892 from sponge fishers who lived on the island of Aegina within sight of Athens.[32] The treasure was said to have come from a tomb of the Late Bronze Age there, and Sir Arthur Evans who published it in 1893 therefore called it Mycenaean. But all the comparisons point to it being Cretan of the seventeenth and sixteenth centuries BC, and it may have been plundered from the great tomb at Mallia where the gold bee pendant was found by French excavators in 1930.

Besides beads of carnelian and gold, the Aegina treasure includes large and elaborate earrings, and pendants, like the bee pendant, that may have been worn in the Egyptian manner as pectorals on the chest.

Plate 70

Plate 71 The backs of these pendants are flat sheets of gold. The most striking (it may have been the head of a large pin rather than a pendant) shows a man, apparently a god, wearing a kilt with a tassel of beads hanging Plate 73 down in front. Four other jewels, each slightly different, have a pair of greyhounds wearing collars and standing muzzle to muzzle with their front paws on the heads of two monkeys; these may have been earrings, Plate 72 since they are reversible. What seems to be another earring has a lion's head at the top, with birds in flight and eggs hanging by chains. The Plate 67 chains in these ornaments are extremely fine and delicate. Similar gold chains have been recovered from tombs of this or earlier date at Knossos and Mochlos.

To judge from the finds, it looks as if gold was more plentiful than silver in Bronze Age Crete. Silver was more valuable than gold in Plate 65 Egypt at the beginning of the second millenium BC. But vases and jewellery were also made of silver, of which natural supplies may have been available in Crete itself as they were in the Cycladic islands and on the Greek mainland.

This gold and silver jewellery from Crete shows a wide range of techniques; repoussé (embossing a design on a thin sheet of metal by pressure from behind); hard soldering, and the use of it to fix wires (filigree) or minute grains of gold (granulation) to a background; and inlaying with stones or paste. By the end of the Middle Minoan period, *c.* 1600 BC, the Cretan jewellers were in effect masters of every process that was to be used in antiquity, except that of enamelling; and that may have been invented somewhere in the Aegean area if not in Crete during the course of the fifteenth century BC.[33]

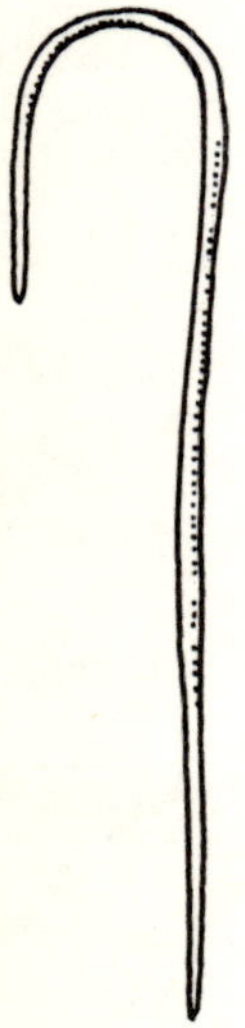

Fig. 76 Late Minoan hair-pin

CHAPTER VIII

Arts and Crafts

The Cretans of the Bronze Age were expert in the manufacture of stone vases, and in working in metal, faience and ivory. Evidence for monumental sculpture in stone is lacking, but there may have been large wooden statues. The art of writing flourished in Crete from early times, along with that of engraving seals in which Cretans excelled.

STONE VASES[1]

Stone vases were made throughout the Bronze Age in most parts of Crete, although not it seems to any great extent in the west of the island owing perhaps to lack of suitable material there. Vessels of stone began to reach Crete, apparently from Egypt, before the end of the Neolithic period, but a native manufacture is not attested until Early Minoan II, *c.* 2500 BC. Some of the earliest Cretan stone vases are incised with hatched triangles, suggestive of Syrian rather than Egyptian inspiration. (Plate 76) But numbers of Egyptian stone vases found their way to Crete throughout the Bronze Age and their shapes were sometimes copied there. (Plates 74, 75)

The earliest Cretan stone vases were made of chlorite or chlorite schist. Soon, however, the soft and easily worked serpentine, which outcrops in different parts of the island, was exploited for the ordinary run of vessels. But harder stones were in use by the time of the early palaces if not before, attractive varieties much in favour being veined orange stalactite and mottled breccia. (*Fig.* 77) Some of the finer vases during the period of the later palaces were made of rock crystal or of imported stones like obsidian. (Plate 77)

Cretan stone vases take many different forms, some of them also found in the pottery, but others peculiar to stone. They range in size from miniatures to large storage vessels, or pithoi. A distinctive early type with two or more round compartments and holes for string handles may have been used for cosmetics. Possibly vases of this type served as models for the rather similar 'block vases' that are found in the Late Neolithic of the Balkans; but these are made of clay, and usually have only one cup instead of two or more. One of the commonest bowl shapes is like a bird's nest. An attractive variety of this in fashion

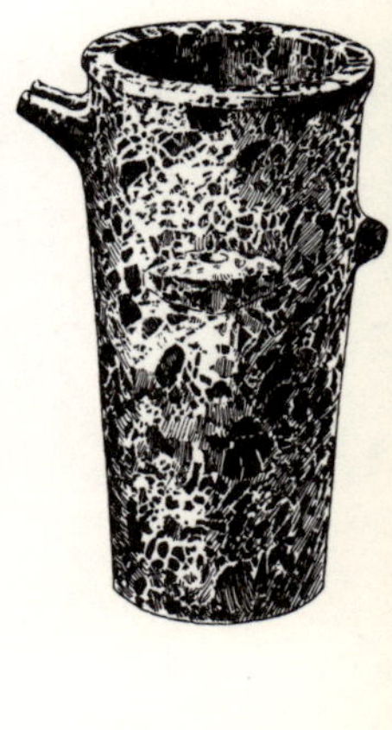

Fig. 77 Breccia jar from Mochlos

Fig. 78 Stone 'block vase' from the large tomb (A) at Platanos

Fig. 79 during Late Minoan times resembles the blossom of a flower that may have been inspired by the Egyptian waterlily (lotus).

The method used by the Cretans for making their stone vases was simple but laborious. The stone was first roughed into shape. The inside of the vase was then drilled with a hollow reed, rotated at speed by a bow, and twirling an abrasive, either sand or emery imported from the island of Naxos. The cylindrical cores thus formed were knocked away, and the vase was finished by grinding and polishing the surfaces. Vases with narrow necks were made in several pieces cunningly joined together.

Plates 38, 96, 97, 114 A remarkable series of serpentine vases with pictures in relief is assigned to the period of the later palaces before the disasters of *c.* 1450 BC. These vessels were mostly for ritual use, and some were coated with gold leaf, scraps of which have occasionally survived; an economical Plate 30 system also adopted at times for seals.

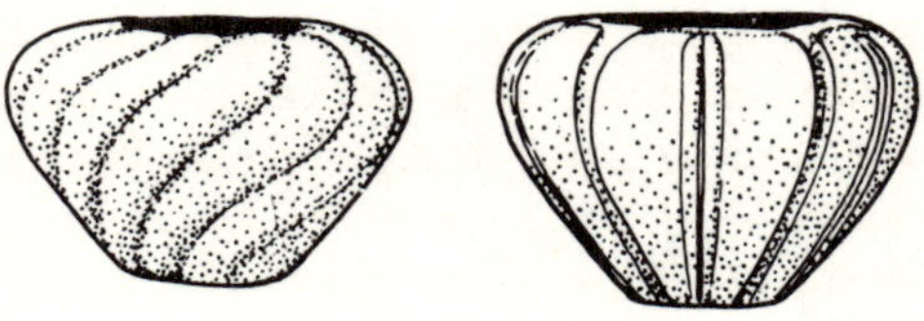

Fig. 79 'Bird's nest' and 'blossom' bowls

METALWORK[2]

From the time of the early palaces *c.* 2000 BC, if not before, the kings and great men of Crete had drinking cups of gold and silver, and *Fig. 80* vessels of copper and bronze were also in use. By the Late Minoan period, *c.* 1550 BC onwards, a large range of metal storage vases and cooking Plate 79 utensils was available. Cauldrons, large enough to boil a sheep or

Fig. 80 Bronze vessels from one of the Zafer Papoura tombs at Knossos

goat whole, were being made of several sheets of bronze held together by rivets. Sheet bronze was also used for armour.

Metal razors of various shapes are common from Early Minoan times onwards. Single-edged knives were no doubt employed for cutting meat. There was a serviceable range of bronze weapons. Tools of bronze included axes, axe-adzes, and double-bladed axes and adzes; together with sickles, chisels, saws large and small, and hammers. But stone axes of a primitive type seem to have continued in general use well into the Early Minoan period. A number of very fine perforated stone axes and mace-heads from Middle and Late Minoan contexts may have been insignia of rank or office. But stone hammers of a distinctive type with cylindrical shaft-holes and expanded ends are quite common, and appear to have been intended for some practical rather than for ritual use.

Fig. 69

Fig. 45

Plate 90

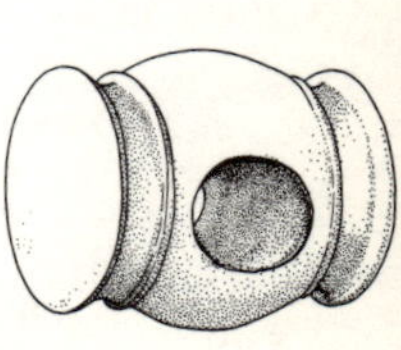

Fig. 81 Minoan stone hammer

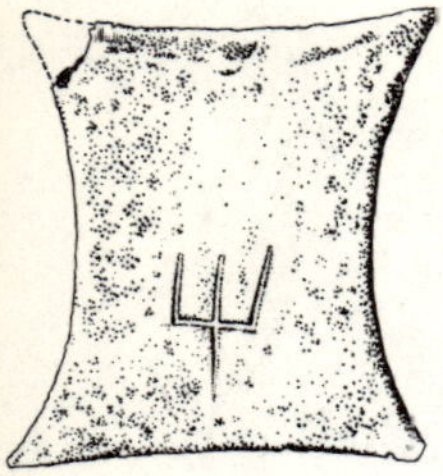

Fig. 82 Ingot with trident-like sign from Ayia Triadha

Bronze tools and weapons were cast in double moulds. The *cire perdue* process was evidently employed for the sockets of the fine decorated spear-heads of the Late Minoan period. Copper was available in some parts of Crete, notably in the Asterousi mountains which border the Mesara plain on the south, but it may have been imported from Cyprus as well. The standard type of ingot found throughout the East Mediterranean in the Late Bronze Age was about two or three feet long, with inward-curving sides and projections for a man to grasp as he carried it on his shoulder. Smaller bun-shaped ingots were also in use.[3]

FAIENCE, GLASS AND IVORY

Faience consists of a core, coated on the outside with an alkaline glaze which is in effect glass. It was being made in Egypt from early in the Predynastic period contemporary with the Neolithic of Crete. The Cretans may have learnt the art of it from Egypt at the beginning of the Middle Minoan period, *c.* 2000 BC or earlier. Faience was used for beads and pendants and eventually in the palace workshops for relief plaques, statuettes and vases. A remarkable faience vase in the shape of an argonaut was recovered from the palace at Zakro destroyed *c.* 1450 BC. Beads and other ornaments of solid glass including seals were being made in Crete before the end of Late Minoan I B *c.* 1450 BC. But the few glass vases recovered from Bronze Age contexts in Crete appear to be Egyptian imports.[4]

Plates 63, 81

Fig. 83

Plate 80

Ivory carving had a long history in Crete. The ivory itself was evidently imported, whether from Syria or Egypt. But the taste for this attractive and easily worked material may have come from Syria in the first instance. Some of the earliest Cretan seals were made of ivory and appear to have been inspired by Syrian rather than by Egyptian models. During the time of the later palaces there was a remarkable output of large ivory figurines at Knossos; but their number has been augmented by modern forgeries. The most complete of those which are certainly genuine is a slender man, apparently a bull-leaper, found in the Residential Quarter of the palace at Knossos. Though the head is much decayed that of another figure from the same deposit is very well preserved. These ivory statuettes were carved in several pieces, cunningly fastened together by an elaborate system of dowels. Ivory was also used for making inlays and for combs and spindle whorls. During the Late

Plates 82, 83

Minoan period, if not earlier, cylindrical boxes with elaborate relief decoration were being carved from sections of elephant tusk. Parts of the surfaces of figurines and other objects of ivory were sometimes coated with gold leaf. The same striking contrast of polished ivory and gold was the aim of the great chryselephantine (gold-ivory) statues of Classical Greece.

Plate 85

Plate 84

Fig. 83 Faience cups from the Temple Repositories at Knossos c. 1650 BC

SCULPTURE

During the period of the later palaces the Cretans were making exquisite statuettes in ivory, faience and solid bronze. But no large statues or reliefs carved in stone like those of contemporary Egypt are known from Crete. This is curious in the light of the magnificent plaster relief frescoes; moreover decorative friezes and large and elaborately carved stone vases show that the Cretans possessed the skill to make stone reliefs and statues. Two fragments of slabs with reliefs of bulls were found by Lord Elgin at Mycenae, where they may have once adorned the inner chamber of the Treasury of Atreus. The slabs are of gypsum, a stone found in Crete but not in the region of Mycenae on the Greek mainland, so that it is always possible that these reliefs came from Knossos.

Plate 32

Plate 20

Plates 53, 54

Stone heads from Knossos and Mirtos may have belonged to small statues with wooden bodies.[5] The existence of gigantic statues made of wood can be inferred from bronze tresses of hair found in the palace at Knossos. These appear to have come from a larger than life-size wooden figure of a goddess.[6]

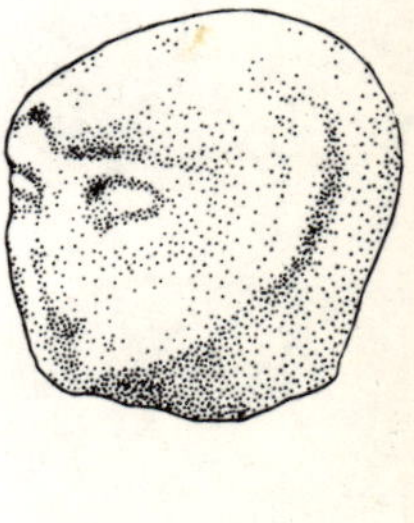

Fig. 84 Stone head from Knossos. Approx. 1 : 4

Fig. 85 Bronze tresses and suggested position on the head of a gigantic wooden statue

SEALS[7]

In an age before the invention of locks, engraved gems or seals were a way of defending property and preventing access. A lump of clay over the string which secured a door or box could not be removed and secretly replaced if stamped with a seal. The designs engraved on the seal might add the more effectual deterrent of magic to the threat of detection. Seals used as signets therefore shade into magical amulets. Considerations of magic would also affect the shapes of seals and the materials of which they were made as well as the designs on them.

Seals were apparently manufactured in Crete by Early Minoan II times, *c.* 2500 BC. Several, including half-finished ones which shows that they were being made there, were found in the early settlement at Fournou Korifi. The oldest Cretan seals are often shaped like animals or birds, or their heads. Some are cylindrical; but the designs are carved on the flat ends, and not on the curve as in the case of Mesopotamian cylinder seals and their Syrian derivatives. Oriental cylinder seals, however, were brought to Crete by Middle Minoan times, if not earlier; and during the period of the later palaces fine cylinder seals of this type were made by Cretan artists. Egyptian beetle-shaped seals (scarabs) reached Crete in considerable numbers during the time of the Middle Kingdom, from *c.* 2000 BC onwards, and were occasionally imitated there.

Plate 12
Fig. 86

A standard shape of seal in Crete during the Early Minoan period was the stamp or button, almost certainly of Syrian derivation. A signet with an elegant stalk, which may be a development of this if it was not copied from Anatolia, was among the most characteristic shapes of Middle Minoan seals. Meanwhile the Early Minoan cylinder evolved into a disc with convex ends, eventually becoming a thin lense. This

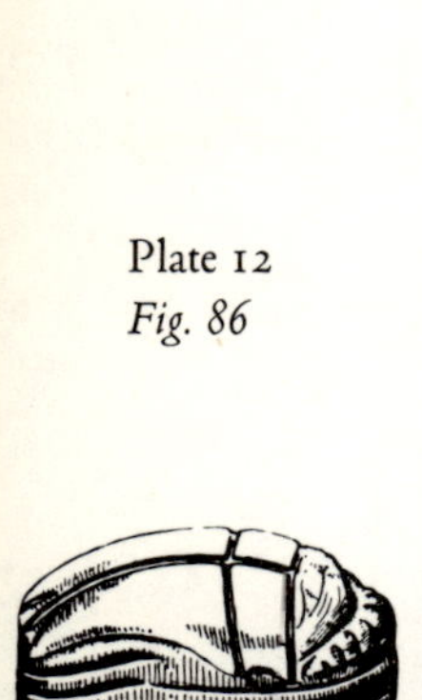

Fig. 86 Egyptian scarab of amethyst with design engraved by a Cretan artist on the base

Fig. 87 Shapes of Cretan seals: signet, disc with convex ends, and lentoid

lentoid shape was to remain the standard one for seals throughout the Late Minoan period. Another derivative of the cylinder was flattened and perforated down its length with designs on one or both of the curving faces; this was fashionable during Middle Minoan times but not later. Almond-shaped (amygdaloid) seals began to be made towards the end of the Middle Minoan period, and were in vogue until the time of the disasters of *c.* 1450 BC. A type of seal which flourished throughout the Late Minoan period was the signet ring with oval bezel. Many clay sealings from the ruins of the palace at Knossos destroyed in the fourteenth century BC have oval impressions from signet rings of this kind. The rings are usually small in diameter and may have been carried on a string round the neck. Lentoids, however, and seals of other suitable shapes, were evidently worn on the wrist like watches.

Fig. 88

Plates 44, 64

Plate 117

Signet rings were normally made of metal—gold, silver or bronze—but occasionally of stone. Other types of seal could be of metal, but were mostly of stone or, especially during the Early Minoan period, of imported ivory or a local substitute for it such as bone, antler and large animal teeth. Apart from ivory and its substitutes, soft soapstone and serpentine were usually selected for the earlier seals. But during the Middle Minoan period, when the graver was supplemented by the drill and the cutter's wheel, craftsmen embarked on harder materials, such as amethyst, rock crystal, red and green jasper, black haematite and obsidian. In Late Minoan times most of the finer seals were made of orange carnelian or banded agate, although other stones, such as imported *lapis lacedaemonius* and *lapis lazuli,* were also used. Serpentine, however, which was soft and easily carved, remained the favourite

Plate 48

Fig. 88 Flattened cylinder seal

Fig. 89 Almond-shaped seal with two-handled jar, perhaps a rain charm

material for the ordinary run of cheap seals. Seals were also sometimes made of fired clay, and during the Late Minoan period of glass.

A wide variety of motifs is found engraved on Cretan seals. Simple abstract designs are common on the earliest. A class of linear design which flourished in Middle Minoan times represents the façade of a house or shrine. From the first, pictures of animals were favoured; Plates 41, 42 usually strong, powerful beasts such as lions, bulls or wild boar, or imaginary sphinxes and griffins, but including sheep and goats, stags, dogs and cats, as well as fishes and birds. Animals are sometimes shown Plates 43, 45 attacking their prey, or being hunted. The scorpions and spiders of the *Fig. 3* early seals were no doubt chosen on account of their venomous character; the spiders being the feared rogalidhas. Human or divine figures are Plates 116, 117 found on seals of every period, and many Late Minoan signet rings were engraved with elaborate scenes of myth or ritual.

Nevertheless, the scenes on the later seals appear to be mostly secular. That is to say, the theme was no longer chosen with a view to its magical power, and this may have led to the rise of a separate class of amulets. Rather crude seals with designs incorporating spouted jars and leafy branches, made in large numbers towards the end of the Middle Minoan *Fig. 89* period, appear to have been rain charms which were never used as seals. Plates 86, 87 Seals with writing on them mostly date from Early and Middle Minoan times, and the writing is usually in the hieroglyphic or pictographic script. Many of these hieroglyphic seals are three- or four-sided. One with eight inscribed faces is virtually a cylinder.

Because they survive in large numbers seals offer a hopeful field for distinguishing any differences that may exist in content, style or spirit, between Cretan work and that emanating from the mainland of Greece. But the whole question of what is of Cretan and what of mainland manufacture or inspiration appears to be difficult and uncertain.

Cretan seal-makers no doubt had gravers of bronze or perhaps of obsidian; and by Middle Minoan II they were using the fast-twirling drill and a cutting wheel. Magnifiers may have helped them in their Plate 88 work. An exquisite miniature of a bull on the flat side of a crystal plaque less than three inches long could only have been painted with the aid of a magnifier, or so Evans thought. Crystal lenses that might have served as magnifiers were found in a Middle Minoan tomb at Knossos.[8]

WRITING[9]

Sign-like marks on clay vases suggest that writing may have been known in Crete in Early Minoan times. But the earliest certain examples of Cretan writing are on seal impressions from Middle Minoan I A deposits at Knossos. The signs on these are realistic pictures of actual things (a fish, a double axe, a human leg) after the manner of Egyptian hieroglyphs. Some of the signs of this Cretan hieroglyphic or pictographic script (as Evans named it) appear to be derived from Egypt; and a few are reminiscent of the earliest pre-cuneiform writing of Mesopotamia. But most have no obvious ancestors abroad, and the script may have evolved in Crete, unless it was derived from some as yet unknown script current in early times in the region of Syria or Cilicia. Curious similarities between the Cretan scripts and those of Cyprus and the so-called Hittite hieroglyphic script of Anatolia in much later times, are most easily explained on the hypothesis of earlier scripts in that region from which they had all borrowed.[10] *Fig. 90*

Seals were still being made with inscriptions in the Cretan hieroglyphic script at the end of the Middle Minoan period, and a few sealings impressed by such hieroglyphic seals have been found in buildings destroyed in the disasters of *c.* 1450 BC. In Egypt simplified (hieratic) versions of hieroglyphs were employed for writing with ink or paint. Similarly in Crete simplified linear versions of script are found incised on clay labels and bars, and also on clay tablets and stone ritual bowls. *Fig. 91* Clay tablets were used for writing from Predynastic times (*c.* 3000 BC or earlier) in Mesopotamia, and eventually in Syria, but never in Egypt. This again suggests that ideas about writing reached Crete from the region of Syria in the first instance. But the oldest clay tablets so far recovered in Crete are some from the ruins of the early palace at Phaistos datable to the nineteenth century BC.

Most of the surviving linear inscriptions are incised on clay tablets or carved on stone ritual vessels; although signs or short inscriptions are found on clay vases, and graffiti were painted or scratched on the walls of houses and palaces at Knossos and Ayia Triadha.[11] But inscriptions written in ink are preserved on two clay cups from Knossos, and a serpentine sphinx from Ayia Triadha with a hollow in its back Plate 89 Evans suggested might have held an inkwell on the analogy of similar animal-shaped inkstands from Mesopotamia. The bulk of what the

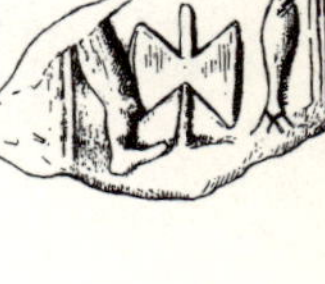

Fig. 90 Early seal impression from Knossos with pictographic signs

Cretans wrote may therefore have been in ink, either on papyrus as in Egypt, or, in the light of a later Greek tradition, on leaves of the date palm which grew then in Crete.

Plate 91

Various local scripts, or scripts for special purposes, may have been in contemporary use. A unique clay disc from a Middle Minoan III deposit in the palace at Phaistos has an inscription on each face running in a spiral. The picture-like signs, printed with wooden stamps, are at first sight so different from those of the other Cretan scripts that the disc has often been considered foreign. But other spiral inscriptions of a religious or magical character are known from Crete, and comparable signs were incised on a stone offering table from Mallia and on a bronze votive axe from a sacred cave at Arkalokhori.

In Crete with its heavy winter rains clay tablets are unlikely to survive unless they have been in a building destroyed by fire which has hardened them. Hence a number of clay tablets with linear inscriptions have been recovered from houses and palaces burnt down at the time of the disasters of *c.* 1450 BC. Most of these come from Ayia Triadha near Phaistos and from Zakro in eastern Crete. While some local differences can be detected in the signs on these tablets—it has even been suggested that the languages of the Zakro tablets and of those from Ayia Triadha are not the same—the scripts are all closely related and together with the linear scripts in use during Middle Minoan III they are classified as Linear A. The term 'Linear Class A' was devised by Evans to distinguish these earlier scripts from that ('Linear Class B') in use at Knossos at the time of the final destruction of the palace there during the fourteenth century BC. Fragments of over 3,000 clay tablets inscribed in Linear B have been recovered from the ruins of the palace and of other buildings at Knossos wrecked at that time; nearly tenfold the number of all the Linear A inscriptions known to date.[12]

Tablets with writing in the Linear B script were discovered in 1939 in the ruins of a palace at Pylos on the Greek mainland destroyed at the end of the Bronze Age *c.* 1200 BC. Since 1945 similar tablets have been found elsewhere on the mainland, at Mycenae, Tiryns and Thebes. In Crete the Linear B tablets from Knossos are the only ones so far assign-

Fig. 91 Inscribed clay label and bar, pierced with holes for tying; both from the Hieroglyphic Deposit at Knossos, c. 1700 BC

able to a period after the disasters of *c.* 1450 BC. But vases with signs or short inscriptions painted or scratched on them from Khania and elsewhere in the west and centre of the island suggest that the practice of writing was not confined to Knossos then. Vases with similar painted signs are known from several mainland sites.[13] Plate 92, *Fig. 96*

Many of the Linear B signs differ from those current in the Linear A scripts. The signs for numerals are dissimilar, and the system used for fractions has been changed from one corresponding to the Egyptian system to one that appears to be based upon the Mesopotamian.[14] Such changes may have been inspired by considerations of convenience. The Linear B script seems to have evolved from some variety of script in use at Knossos earlier. This evolution probably took place at Knossos itself during the period after the disaster of *c.* 1450 BC.[15]

DECIPHERMENT AND DOUBT

Both the Linear B script and the language written in it are clearly one and the same at Knossos and on the Greek mainland. After the Second World War a number of leading archaeologists working on the Aegean Bronze Age came to the conclusion that the Linear B language might be Greek; and it was eventually deciphered as Greek by Michael Ventris, an English student of the script, in 1952. Ventris was a young architect, distinguished in his profession, who had early taken a serious interest in the problem of the Linear B script. In the sense that he was not actually paid to do it, his work on the script was amateur, but he was probably as expert on the subject as anyone in Europe at the time. His decipherment has won a wide measure of acceptance; it is questioned, however, by some of those who have examined it, and a few who at first accepted it have since become sceptical.[16]

Sceptics argue that the kind of Greek this decipherment extracts from the tablets is not right for such early times, and is not like real Greek at all. But this is a matter of opinion. In the last resort the rejection of the decipherment is based, not so much upon the character of the Greek obtained by it, as upon the nature of the decipherment itself. The rules postulated by it are so lax that it is difficult to believe they are ancient; a system of writing based upon such rules would have been hopelessly inefficient and ambiguous. For instance, no less than eight quite different Greek words are obtainable by the rules of the decipherment from the sign group which it renders as PO-LO. And the sign group rendered as PA-TE has actually been interpreted as the Greek word *pantes* (= all) in one context, and as *pater* (= father) in another!

Convincing sense could scarcely be extracted by means of a false decipherment from long narrative texts like those of Egyptian inscriptions or Mesopotamian cuneiform documents. But the Linear B tablets consist of short lists and inventories. These often have pictures (ideograms) which represent the items enumerated, and it is therefore possible even without knowing the language to guess the subject matter of some of the tablets. Moreover, it seems likely that many of the words in these lists are names, and it is therefore reasonable to interpret as a proper name of non-Greek origin any word which cannot be forced into an appearance of Greek by the rules of the decipherment. In short, the nature of the Linear B tablets is such as to open the door to the possibility that a false decipherment can be made to work.

Fig. 96

The Linear B script, like the earlier Cretan linear scripts, is basically syllabic. This is clear from the number of the signs (at least seventy in common use as opposed to twenty or thirty needed for an alphabet), and from the length of the sign groups, divided by vertical strokes from each other and evidently standing for words. The rules of the decipherment assume that each sign, except for those set apart as ideograms, stands for a syllable consisting of a vowel (A, E, etc.) or of a consonant followed by a vowel (NA, NE, etc.). During the four years between his first announcement of the decipherment and his lamented premature death in a motor accident in 1956, Ventris only published summary accounts of the methods he had used. Those who are convinced of the correctness of the decipherment by the results it gives when applied to the texts tend to accept these accounts as adequate. But those who remain unconvinced have looked more closely at the other evidence about the nature and validity of the methods of decipherment. Most of this evidence is contained in a series of 'Worknotes' which Ventris circulated to colleagues during the months of 1951–52 before the decipherment was announced.

The Worknotes do not give every step in his reasoning. But it seems clear that Ventris began with the idea that the language of the Linear B tablets was of non-Greek origin, and perhaps related to Etruscan brought to Italy early in the first millennium BC by immigrants from western Anatolia, which on one hypothesis was the home of the language originally spoken by the Bronze Age Cretans.[17] Many leading archaeologists, however, already thought that the language of the Linear B tablets might be Greek, and one of them suggested this to Ventris in the autumn of 1951.[18] But Ventris always claimed that he did not try Greek as a possible solution until about six weeks before he announced his decipherment in a wireless broadcast on 1st July, 1952.[19] Since his death the truth of this claim has been challenged by some sceptics of the decipherment, who have urged that Ventris was in fact attributing values to signs on the assumption that the language of the script was Greek already some months earlier. But the latest findings by critics of the decipherment have confirmed the truth of what Ventris said, and have emphasised the way in which he made a number of important changes in the values for the signs about six weeks before he made his announcement. These changes appear to reflect a shift from seeking a non-Greek to experimenting with a Greek solution for the script.[20]

For many people the truth of the decipherment was proved by the subsequent publication of a tablet found at Pylos on the Greek mainland. This tablet, like most of the others, is a list, but it has comparatively long sentences. The sentences end with ideograms representing vases of various shapes including tripod cooking pots. The rules of the decipherment when applied to this tablet obtain reasonably sensible Greek from it, and in particular the words TI-RI-PO and TI-RI-PO-DE (interpreted as *tripous* in the singular and *tripode* in the dual) appear in sentences ending with ideograms of these tripod bowls with numbers for one or two against them. Those who accept the decipherment argue that coincidence is excluded; while those who reject it point to various difficulties and imperfections in the translation of the rest of the tablet.[21]

The controversy about the decipherment may be incapable of resolution without long consecutive texts or bilinguals like the Rosetta stone. But even if this particular decipherment is false, it does not necessarily follow that the language of the Linear B tablets is not Greek; moreover, even if the language proves to be non-Greek, it is always possible that rulers of Greek speech controlled Knossos at the time, retaining an alien written language for administrative purposes.

CHAPTER IX

Society, War and Trade

The many palaces suggest that Crete before the disasters of *c.* 1450 BC was divided among a number of independent states. But Knossos may always have enjoyed some kind of primacy, essentially perhaps religious in nature (like that of Babylon among the ancient Sumerians), but amounting at times to an actual hegemony, whether shadowy or substantial, over other parts of the island.

GOVERNMENT

The palaces imply kings and queens. Large country houses like that at Vathipetro were evidently the centres of landed estates, and there may have been a class of nobles and territorial magnates. The cities and towns with their variety of houses, some large and splendid, others mere hovels, suggest free citizens of varying economic status. These no doubt included craftsmen and professional men such as priests and scribes.

The extensive storerooms in the palaces may have housed the produce collected as taxes in an age before the use of coinage, and it has been argued that one important function of the palaces was to serve as public markets or centres of barter-exchange.[1] But shops have been identified in the towns at Mallia and Palaikastro; and a row of what may have been shops at Ayia Triadha, the harbour town of Phaistos, has a spacious colonnade in front like the shop-stoas of later Greece. There must have been a class of merchants, even if the bulk of overseas trade was directly controlled by the government, and the Cretans doubtless had slaves like other contemporary peoples of the Near East. However there is no hint of great slave enterprises like the Lavrion silver mines of Classical Athens, or the latifundia—the slave estates—of southern Italy in Roman times.

It has been suggested that alongside the kings in Crete there may have been senates or councils of elders if not popular assemblies. The wide paved squares that flank the palaces would have been ideal meeting places for large masses of people, and a series of interconnecting basements by the square west of the palace at Mallia has been interpreted

Plate 18

as a council chamber since nothing was found there apart from some storage jars. Customs and traditions were apt to survive in Crete after they had disappeared in other parts of the civilized world of the Near East, and according to one view the rulers of ancient Sumer were in early times controlled by councils of elders or even by popular assemblies of some kind. But the evidence for this appears to be ambiguous.[2] The kings of Bronze Age Crete were probably as absolute as their contemporaries in Egypt or Syria at the time.

WOMEN

What was the position of women in Bronze Age Crete? The dominance of goddesses in religion meant that women took an important part in religious rites and ceremonies, as they continued to do in the cults of female deities descended from those of the Bronze Age in Athens and other states of Classical Greece. Women even seem to have joined in the bull-leaping games which were religious or magical in their origin. Plate 52 The queens as high priestesses, if not themselves divine, clearly had important ritual functions. Indeed, there is some reason to suppose that the stone seat in the Throne Room at Knossos was not a throne of Plate 27 Minos but of Ariadne, used in ritual by the queen as representative of the goddess.[3] But this would not imply that Crete was ruled by queens. Tradition and analogy suggest that power was in the hands of kings, although it is always possible that succession to the throne was through the female line by marriage to the king's daughter.

It seems likely enough that customs of the kind described as Matriarchy (Mother Rule) persisted in Crete.[4] These arise in primitive societies where people do not comprehend when a baby is born who its father can be. The children are therefore named after their mothers, and all inheritance is through the female line. Primeval traditions of this kind survived in western Anatolia into Classical times. Thus, among the Carians on the west coast of Anatolia succession was still through the mother in the fourth century BC; and in Lycia to the south-east of Caria children were named after their mothers. Both Carians and Lycians were peoples with an Aegean Bronze Age background, having close contacts with—if not actually related to—the people of Bronze Age Crete. Indeed Herodotus says that the customs of the Lycians were partly of Cretan origin.

Wall paintings from Knossos show richly dressed women in the place of honour, while others mingle in the crowd with men, watching ritual of some kind. These have helped to suggest that women in Bronze Age Crete enjoyed more respect and freedom than they did in later Greece. But this does not necessarily follow from the undeniable importance of women in ritual and cult.

WARFARE

A field which men appear to have reserved for themselves is that of warfare. It is often assumed that the Bronze Age Cretans were of a peaceful and unwarlike disposition. Their chief towns are rarely situated with an eye to defence, while many are in flat ground by the sea or near it. But the city at Mallia appears to have been protected by a wall at the beginning of the Middle Minoan period, and there are hints of fortifications elsewhere, although none have been dated. The wall at Mallia was evidently built of mud or mud brick on a stone foundation which is all that has survived.[5]

That assaults on fortified cities were among aspects of life familiar to Bronze Age Cretans is suggested by the little faience plaques of the Siege Mosaic from Knossos. These inlays from a chest or box of some kind were evidently part of a scene showing a town under attack. Evans compared with them the picture on the so-called Siege Rhyton, a silver relief vase which may be of Cretan origin, although found in one of the shaft graves at Mycenae.[6]

Plate 22

There has been much discussion as to whether the scene of an attack upon a walled town here represents some historical event. But even if the vase is Cretan and the scene historical, the town may lie outside Crete. The colonies established by Cretans overseas, if tradition is any guide, were not always the result of peaceful infiltration. That at Ayia Irini on the island of Kea was certainly fortified.

The weapons used by Cretans during the earlier part of the Bronze Age included short daggers and swords of types evolved in Syria in the first instance. Curious wide flat blades peculiar to Crete may have been hafted as spear-heads. But in Middle Minoan times socketed spear-heads were made, together with long swords or rapiers. Some of these rapiers were nearly three feet in length. Their hilts were riveted to short tangs which projected from the shoulders of the blade. Large

Fig. 92

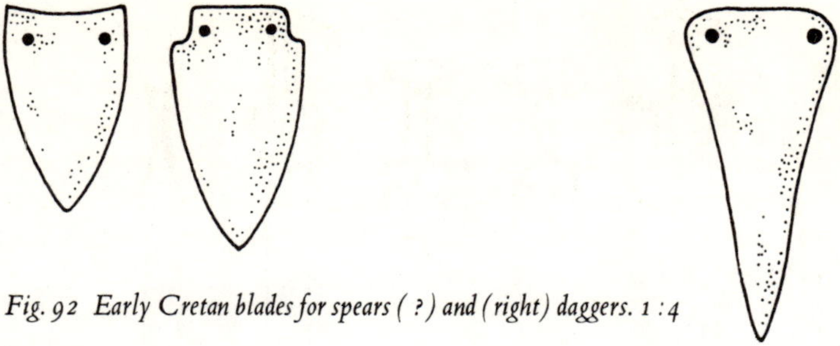

Fig. 92 Early Cretan blades for spears (?) and (right) daggers. 1 : 4

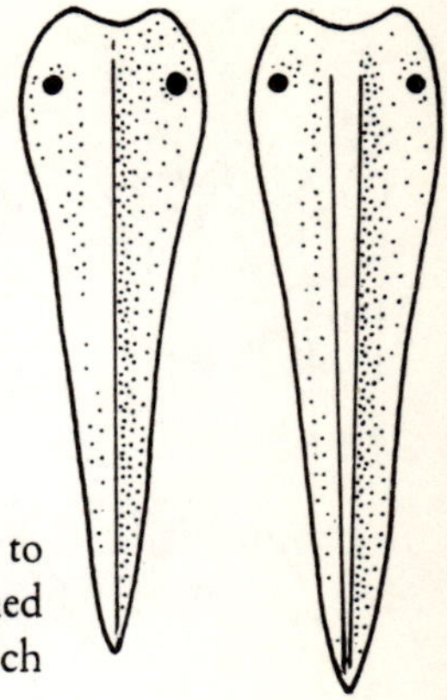

pommels of stone or ivory, or of wood plated with gold, helped to balance the weight of the long blades. These weapons were designed for thrusting and they had rounded shoulders like the daggers from which they had evolved.

The shoulders of rapiers and daggers at the beginning of the Late Minoan period were often given horn-like projections. Many of these horned rapiers were found in the shaft graves at Mycenae. Eventually horns were replaced by short lateral projections making the shoulders cross-shaped (cruciform). This fashion it has been suggested may have developed on the Greek mainland, but Crete has an equally good claim to be the home of it. Unlike the earlier rapiers, both horned and cruciform swords have long flanged tangs for the hilt plates.[7] *Fig. 93*

During the course of the Late Minoan period the blades of swords were reduced in length, and short swords or daggers adapted for slashing as well as thrusting were evolved. These slashing weapons tend to have leaf-shaped blades of a kind which appear as ideograms on the so-called Sword Tablets of the fourteenth century BC from Knossos. At the very end of the Bronze Age a comparatively long, heavy slashing sword is found in use throughout Greece. It is widely believed that this type of sword (known as Naue II) was introduced by invaders from European lands to the north, where swords of this kind are extremely common. But there are some reasons for thinking that the type may have been first invented in the Aegean.[8] Earlier in the Bronze Age double axes could have served as slashing weapons as well as tools. Depictions of embattled Amazons wielding double axes are frequent in later Greek art, and this may be a reminiscence of a time when men used them in war.[9] Plate 95 *Fig. 94*

Projectile weapons included throwing-spears or javelins. Pebbles seem to have been used as sling-stones. Arrows may have been tipped

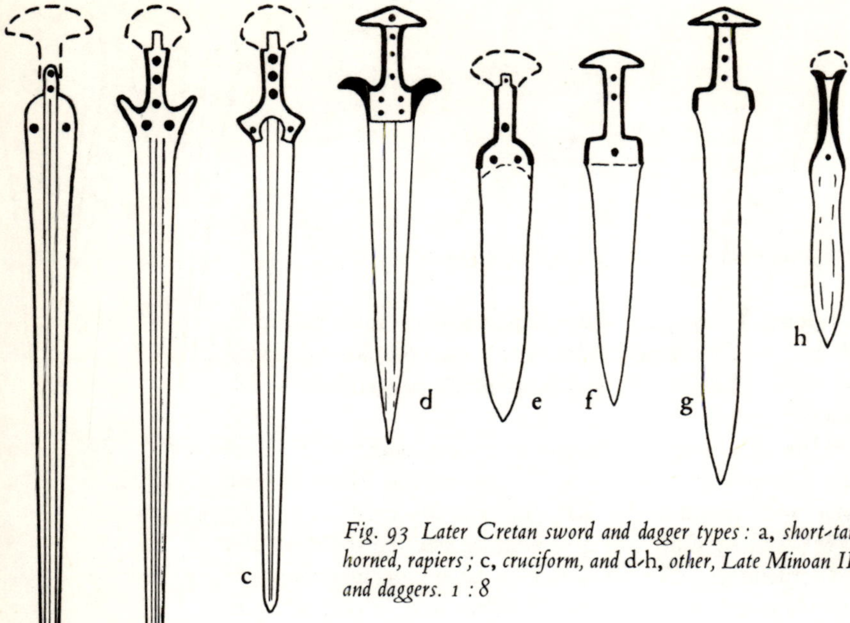

Fig. 93 Later Cretan sword and dagger types: a, *short-tanged, and* b, *horned, rapiers;* c, *cruciform, and* d-h, *other, Late Minoan II-III swords and daggers. 1 : 8*

with hard wood, or with bone as in Neolithic times. The few metal arrow-heads assignable to the Early and Middle Minoan periods have sockets. An Oriental variety of tanged arrow-head occurs from Late Minoan I times onwards; but flat arrow-plates, hollow-based or tanged, appear to have been introduced from the Greek mainland after *c.* 1450 BC. Arrow-heads of stone or obsidian, common on the mainland, are very scarce in Crete and do not seem to have been made there. Large numbers of metal arrow-heads, and one of flint, were found together with a clay tablet listing 8,630 arrows in the Armoury building at Knossos destroyed along with the palace in the fourteenth century BC. Other tablets from the Armoury show horns of wild goats from which bows of the composite type could be made. But one-piece wooden bows may also have been used in Crete.

Some of these Armoury tablets have pictures (ideograms) of chariots, and appear to record the issue of military equipment to the warriors who manned them. An object drawn alongside the chariot on several tablets was interpreted by Evans as a corslet made of metal strips. An actual suit of bronze armour of this kind has since been found in the

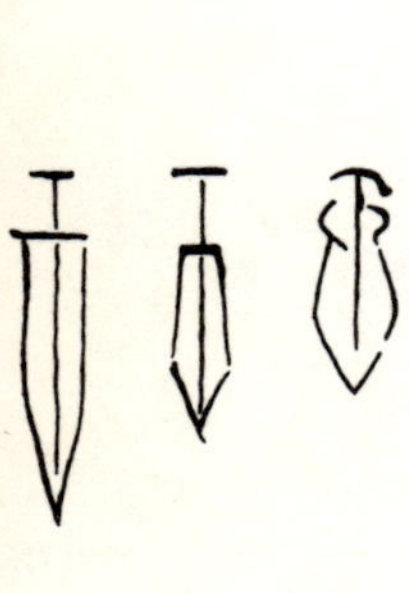

Fig. 94 Swords on Linear B tablets from Knossos

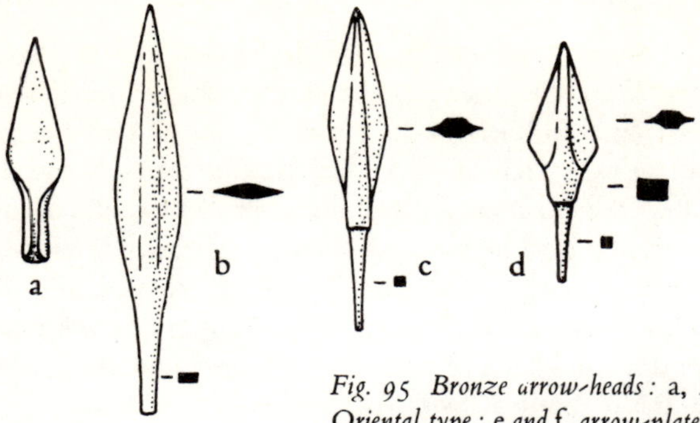

Fig. 95 Bronze arrow-heads: a, *Middle Minoan;* b-d, *Late Minoan of Oriental type;* e *and* f, *arrow-plates of mainland derivation. Half-size*

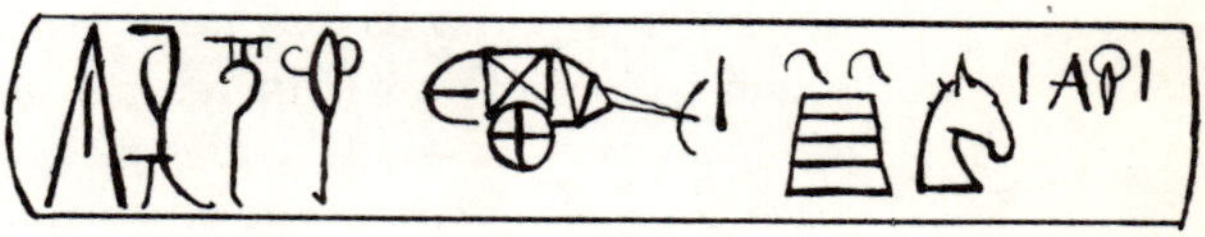

Fig. 96 Linear B tablet from the Armoury at Knossos

tomb of a warrior buried *c.* 1400 BC at Dendra near Mycenae on the mainland.[10] But scraps of bronze armour were recovered many years ago from more or less contemporary tombs at Phaistos, and a small stone vase from Knossos is in the shape of a corslet with shoulder pieces *Fig. 97*
like the Dendra one.[11] Metal armour may have been developed in Crete in connection with chariot warfare in the fifteenth century BC or earlier. Corslets of leather also appear to have been in use during Late Minoan times. Bronze greaves have been found in Late Bronze Age tombs on the mainland and in Cyprus, but are not yet attested as early as this in Crete.

The traditional weapon of defence in Crete appears to have been a Plate 55
huge shield, rectangular or like a figure-of-eight in shape, made of bull's hide on a wooden frame or centrepiece and covering a man from head to foot. Shields like this may have been in use from early in the Bronze Age, although no certain representations of them are datable before Middle Minoan III B, *c.* 1600 BC, when smaller rectangular shields are also shown (see *Fig. 49*). Light-armed troops evidently dispensed even with shields (see Plate 33).

Fig. 97 Stone vase from Knossos in the shape of a corslet

Fig. 98 Helmetted head on faience plaque found with the house façades, see plate 22

Helmets in Crete were traditionally conical. Figures in the Siege Mosaic of *c.* 1700 BC from Knossos wear helmets of this shape which may be meant for metal ones. Soldiers in the Royal Tombs of Ur, dating from well before 2000 BC, had copper helmets. But the only metal helmet of the Bronze Age that has yet been found in Crete comes from the grave of a warrior buried at Knossos about the same time as the Plate 94 warrior of the Dendra armour *c.* 1400 BC. This is bell-shaped, and is surmounted by a knob with a hole through it for a plume of some kind. The metal is quite thin, and had been attached by holes round the edges to a lining of leather or quilted material. Helmets of this shape with waving plumes are depicted on Late Minoan seals and vases. Some of these helmets were evidently made of padded leather, while others were Plate 93 covered with metal discs or with slivers of boars' tusks. The helmet found with the Dendra armour had been adorned with boars' tusks, although its cheek-pieces were of metal like those of the bronze helmet from Knossos. What seem to be metal helmets but of a different shape, Plate 96 something like the Corinthian helmets of later Greece, are worn by men boxing with knuckle-dusters on one of the stone relief vases from Ayia Triadha.

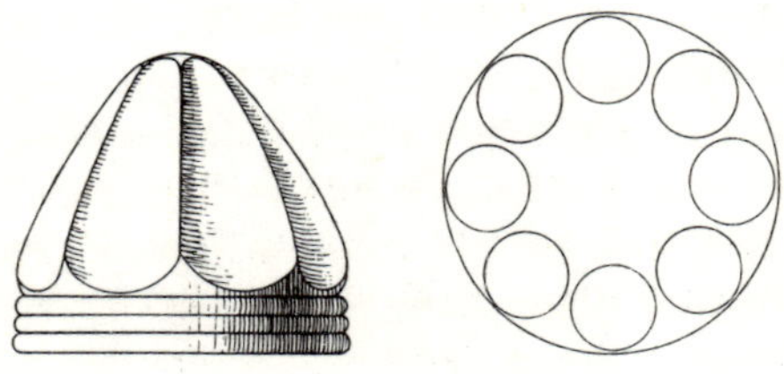

Fig. 99 Ivory gaming-piece from Knossos

SPORTS AND GAMES

Other men on this vase from Ayia Triadha are wrestling or leaping bulls. The sports depicted here may have had religious or magical connotations. Purely secular sports no doubt included hunting, jumping Plate 98 and running, as in later Greece. The acrobatics so necessary for the bull-leaping rites do not appear to have been confined to them.

Plate 100 Stones with cups round the edge and a larger central hollow occur on Bronze Age sites in Crete from the Early Minoan period onwards and were evidently used for some kind of game, although it may have been Plate 99 one with a religious or magical side to it.[12] A draught-board from

Fig. 100 Ivory gaming-pieces from Phaistos

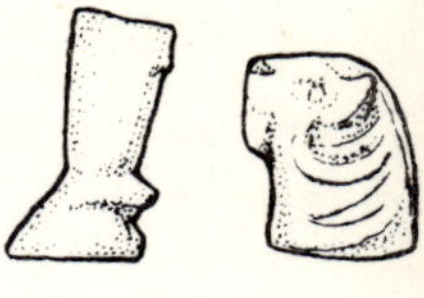

Fig. 100

Knossos was nearly three feet long, made of ivory plated with gold and inlaid with rock crystal and faience. Large ivory cones from the same area of the palace may have served as men for it.[13] From the early palace at Phaistos destroyed *c.* 1700 BC come small ivory gaming-pieces, one taking the form of a bull's leg, the other that of a lion's head with a gold mane. They were found together with a circular dice in a clay goblet which appears to have been the dice box.[14] Another dice consisting of a knuckle-bone marked with numbers from 1 to 4 was recovered with two sets of two men each from a Late Minoan tomb at Katsamba by the harbour town of Knossos.[15]

TRADE[16]

There is abundant evidence for trade between Crete and countries overseas, especially the neighbouring islands of the Aegean and Egypt. While much of this foreign trade may have been controlled by the palaces, a class of private merchants no doubt existed as in Egypt and elsewhere in the Levant at the time. The bulk of what was exchanged probably consisted of raw materials such as wood, together with foodstuffs and perishable goods like textiles, which have rarely survived.

For the basic needs of their way of life the Cretans of the Bronze Age were self-supporting. They did not have to bring food or materials for building ships or houses from abroad; in this they had the advantage over the people of Mesopotamia with their lack of stone, or the Egyptians who must import wood. When it came to metal, some copper may have been imported, although it was available in Crete. The tin for mixing with copper to make bronze was almost certainly brought from outside, whether from Central Europe where tin abounds in the Erzgebirge mountains of northern Bohemia, or from Etruria on the west coast of Italy. The earliest Italian metal daggers reflect Cretan types, and some of these Italian daggers it has been suggested may even have found their way back to Crete.[17]

Most other raw materials imported to Crete were in the nature of luxuries. Gold and silver doubtless came from the Aegean islands, or from western Anatolia; emery, useful as an abrasive in the manufacture of stone bowls, from Naxos. Fine stones brought for making bowls and seals included *lapis lacedaemonius* and *rosso antico* from the southern Peloponnese; black obsidian from Anatolia and the spotted variety of it

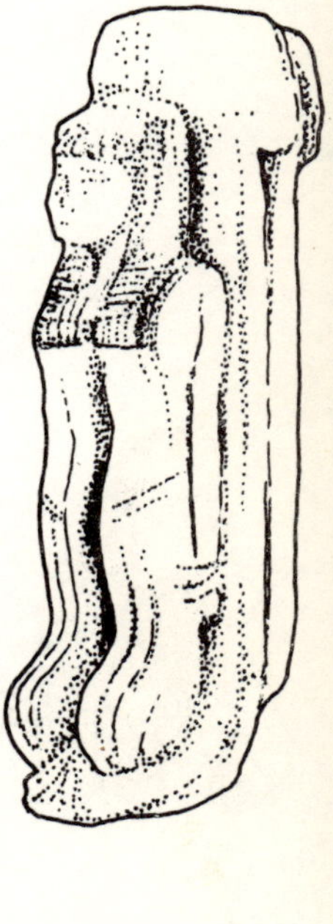

Fig. 101 Egyptian ivory sphinx from Mallia

from Yiali near Cos, together with veined white alabaster from Egypt.[18] Among rarer stones made into seals, beads and pendants, were amethyst perhaps from Egypt, and lapis lazuli from distant Afghanistan.

Plate 85

Another luxury material that was reaching Crete from early in the Bronze Age was ivory, used at first for seals and amulets, later for inlays and statuettes, and for circular boxes cut from sections of tusk. Most of this ivory may have come from Syria where elephants lived until they were hunted to extinction about the ninth century BC. Ostrich eggs and apparently plumes as well were imported from North Africa or Egypt. The eggs were transformed into libation vases, of which an example, almost certainly of Cretan origin, was found in one of the royal shaft graves at Mycenae. In Crete this egg-shape was copied for libation vases of stone and clay.

Plate 38

Plate 12

Fig. 101

Fig. 102

Foreign manufactures reaching Crete included beads and pendants, mostly perhaps from Egypt, together with Egyptian scarabs. An ivory sphinx, inlay from a piece of furniture, which was found in a house at Mallia, is Egyptian work assignable to the time of Dynasty XIII, *c.* 1700 BC.[19] Two ivory figurines of boys from Palaikastro may also be Egyptian imports of this period, unless they are exceptionally good local imitations. Faience vases and many stone vessels found their way from Egypt to Crete. Some Egyptian stone vases recovered from contexts of the fifteenth or fourteenth centuries BC in Crete are of much earlier date, assignable to the Old Kingdom back in the third millennium. These might have been handed down in Crete as heirlooms, but some could have been brought there along with contemporary Egyptian imports, since antique stone vases are not uncommon in Egyptian tombs of the time. Stone vessels inscribed with royal names may have been presents from Egyptian Pharaohs or high officials whether in exchange for 'tribute' offered to them or not.

Plate 75

Plate 11

Plate 101

Seal stones and other objects reached Crete from Anatolia, Syria and Mesopotamia. A silver cylinder seal from one of the early tombs at Mochlos it is suggested was made in Mesopotamia during the time of Sargon of Akkad (*c.* 2350 BC).[20] If Oriental imports are less prominent in Crete than Egyptian ones, it may be because they are more difficult to recognise and distinguish from native products. For example, the ink-stand in the shape of a sphinx Evans thought was Anatolian, while others have argued that it came from Syria; but it may in fact be

Fig. 102 Ivory boy from Palaikastro

Cretan. It has holes in the neck and tail for inlays as commonly found on Cretan stone vases; and although the idea of a man with a woman's head is Oriental, sphinxes were being engraved on Cretan seals by Middle Minoan II, *c.* 1800 BC or earlier. A few clay vases were brought to Crete from the islands of the Aegean and from the Greek mainland, as well as from distant Cyprus, whether by way of regular trade or as curiosities.[21] Plate 89 Plate 103

The decorative painted pottery of Crete on the other hand may have been exported in response to a demand for it overseas. It was the finest pottery in the civilized world in its day, as that of the great trading cities like Corinth and Athens was to be later. From early in the Middle Minoan period, *c.* 2000 BC, onwards Cretan painted ware was reaching Cyprus, Syria and Egypt. About the same time vases of precious metal that may have been made in Crete appear in Syria and Egypt, and Cretan bronze daggers in Cyprus. Stone vases and lamps of Cretan types have been found at Atchana in Syria and at Troy as well as in the Aegean islands and on the Greek mainland. Many of the treasures from the Mycenae shaft graves and from later tombs on the mainland are Cretan in style; but it is hard to distinguish what was made in Crete and what locally by Cretan craftsmen or by native craftsmen under Cretan influence. Plates 55, 56, 58, 51

The bulk of Cretan exports probably consisted of raw materials and perishable goods such as foodstuffs and cloth. Woollen cloth for instance may have been sent to Egypt in exchange for linen and papyrus. Timber was perhaps exported to Egypt from Crete as it was from Syria. Olive oil is a staple product of modern Crete and may have been exported in the Bronze Age. The storerooms of the palace at Knossos were apparently filled with oil at the time of the final destruction in the fourteenth century BC; some of it may have been awaiting export. That oil was exported earlier in the Bronze Age is suggested by a clay seal impression of *c.* 1700 BC from Knossos. If Evans is right, the branch signs above the ship here are sprays of olive. Other exports from Crete to Egypt included beans and medicines. What might be called an invisible export was Cretan magic, which the Egyptians seem to have valued. Plate 37 *Fig. 103*

In an age before the invention of coinage trade was by exchange of goods or by payment with an agreed weight of gold or silver. Scales

Fig. 103 Seal impression from Knossos with ship and olive sprays

therefore played an important part in business life, and bronze scale pans and lead weights are found even in tombs.

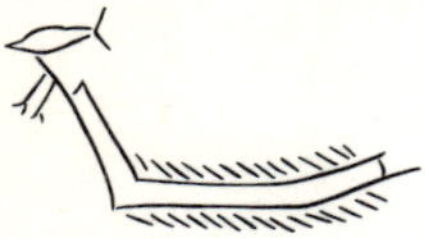

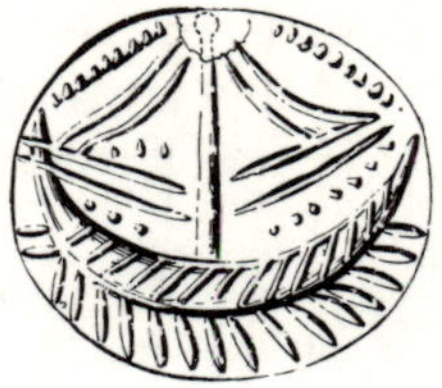

Figs 104, 105 Boat on clay vase from Syros and many-oared ship on Cretan seal

SHIPS AND THE SEA[22]

This overseas trade was carried in ships. Many representations of Cretan and other Aegean ships of the Bronze Age survive, but most of them are on a small scale, engraved on seal stones or appearing as signs in
Plate 106 the various scripts. The standard sea-going ship had a single mast for a square sail and paddles or fixed oars. In the earlier ships the prow was high while the keel projected some way from the stern like a rudder. The high prow would have been an advantage in breasting the waves of the open sea, while the projecting keel may have helped to steady the vessel.

Plate 108 There are also clay models of mastless boats of this type. Similar
Fig. 104 mastless boats with many paddles or oars were scratched on clay ritual vases by the people living on the Cycladic island of Syros during the period corresponding to Early Minoan II in Crete. The high end which appears to be the prow on these Cycladic boats carries a fish ensign. Later it seems the projecting keel went out of use both in Crete and in
Plate 107 the islands. A lead model of a boat from the island of Naxos has a high prow with a holder for an ensign of some kind, but the stern is also raised. Models of similar mastless boats made of stone or ivory were being placed in tombs in Crete during the Late Minoan III period in the

Fig. 106 Warship with ram on vase from Tragana

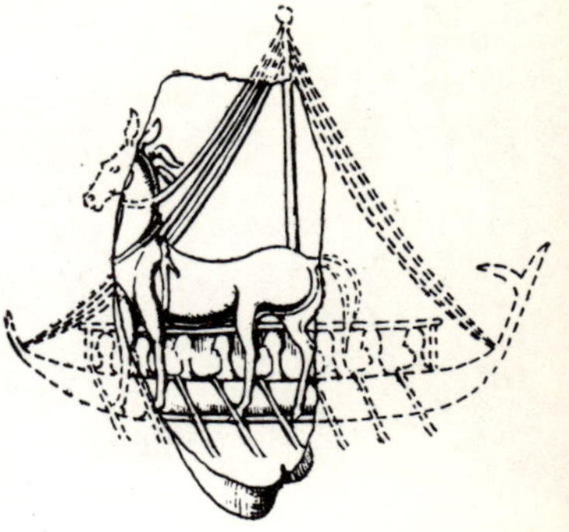

Fig. 107 Ships with raised central decks, one with a horse superimposed, on seal impressions from Knossos

fourteenth century BC. All these have comparatively high prows; but some Aegean boats were canoe-shaped, high at prow and stern, while others may have had high sterns and low prows like many river craft in Egypt. As in Egypt, ships were steered with a large oar or paddle, or a pair of them, at the stern. *Fig. 105*

Most of these early Aegean boats and ships were probably quite small, and could be drawn up on the beach or tied to the shore in shallow water; a simple matter in the tideless Mediterranean. But some of the ships built in Crete during the Bronze Age may have attained a length of a hundred feet or more. One ship on a seal stone which formerly belonged to Evans is depicted with a row of some fifteen oars. It could be meant for what the later Greeks called a pentekonter, a fifty-oar ship with twenty-five oars a side, this being the standard size for a warship until Classical times. *Fig. 105*

Greek warships had rams, and were long, low and narrow, as opposed to merchant ships with their wide beams. A warship of this type was painted on a vase assignable to the very end of the Bronze Age (twelfth or eleventh century BC) found at Tragana near Pylos on the mainland. This, like later Greek warships, has a raised deck or gangway along the centre and high platforms at stem and stern. Above the ram is a large fish, reminiscent of the ensigns on the prows of Cycladic boats at a much earlier date. Warships like this are unlikely to represent a new development at the very end of the Bronze Age; both the central deck or gangway and the platforms at stem and stern are already visible in pictures of ships on Cretan seals or their impressions assignable to the fourteenth century BC and earlier. It looks as if warships with rams *Fig. 106* *Fig. 107*

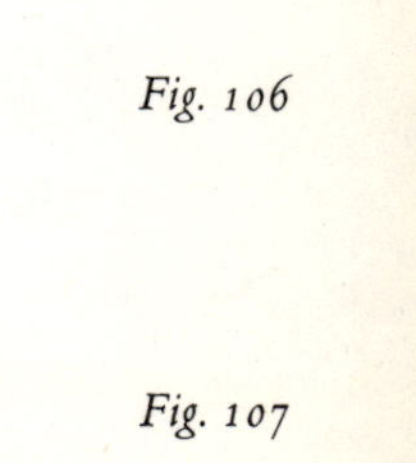

Fig. 108 Ship sign on Phaistos disc, see plate 91

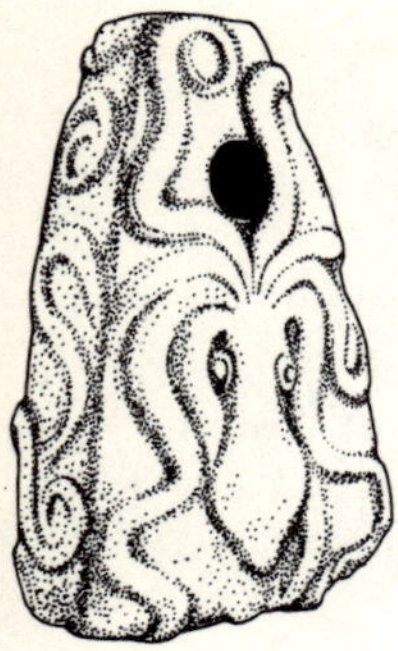

Fig. 109 Stone anchor from Knossos

were being built in Crete if not elsewhere in the Aegean before the end of the Middle Minoan period, *c.* 1600 BC. There is a sketch of one on a fragment of a Middle Helladic vase from Volo in Thessaly, and what appears to be a ship of the same kind is among the signs on the Phaistos disc (see *Fig. 108*). A graffito in the Temple Tomb at Knossos Evans thought was intended to depict the prow of a warship with its ram.

At Cape Gelidonya on the southern coast of Turkey a Bronze Age shipwreck has been excavated. But little of the ship itself survived apart from the stone ballast and what appears to have been an anchor at the stern. Large stones with holes for ropes were commonly used as anchors. What may have been a royal anchor of purple stone with
Fig. 109 octopuses in high relief was found in the palace at Knossos; but Evans interpreted it as a talent weight.[23]

TRANSPORT BY LAND

Much of the trade between different parts of Crete may have been carried by sea along the coast as it was before the building of the present network of car roads about fifty years ago. Until then inland traffic was by pack animals, and roads for wheeled vehicles only existed in some of the less mountainous areas. Assyrian merchants in the early part of the second millennium BC were using donkeys for long-distance
Plate 105 transport. A clay model from Phaistos assigned to the end of the Bronze Age, *c.* 1200 BC or later, represents a horse or donkey loaded with jars. Oxen may also have been used as beasts of burden. One way of carrying heavy loads is by slinging them on long poles with groups of bearers at each end. This principle was certainly applied to passenger trans-
Plate 109 port in Bronze Age Crete; a clay model of a sedan chair was found with other relics of a toy-sized shrine at Knossos assigned by Evans to Middle Minoan II B, *c.* 1700 BC. Mobile chairs of this kind were no doubt used in everyday life as well, and litters in which the passenger could lie at ease may also have been employed as they were in Egypt and later in Rome.

A number of terrace walls which supported roads are assignable to the Bronze Age. Similar road terraces and even bridges have been recognized in the region of Mycenae and elsewhere on the mainland.[24] The ancient Greek word for a bridge, *gephyra,* appears to be of pre-Greek origin and may therefore be Minoan. One of the most convincing of

Cretan road terraces climbs the north side of Mount Juktas leading from Knossos to the Bronze Age sanctuary on the highest summit. This road was narrow and steep, and clearly not intended for the use of wheeled vehicles. But a massive terrace wall running across a disused cemetery of the Middle Minoan period on the slopes of Ailias east of Knossos may have supported a road suitable for wheeled traffic. Roads in the large towns were often paved or cobbled, and might have a narrow raised strip of smooth pavement in the centre for the comfort of pedestrians. But in the countryside most of the routes were probably narrow unpaved tracks of the kind which still exist all over the island. Plate 111

HORSES AND CHARIOTS

Wheeled vehicles were in use in Crete at a comparatively early date to judge from a clay model found at Palaikastro assignable to the beginning of the Middle Minoan period *c.* 2000 BC. The wagon which inspired this model evidently had solid wooden wheels and was surely drawn by oxen rather than horses. But animals on some early Cretan seal stones look remarkably like horses; although they may be meant for donkeys or asses.[25] Apart from these seals there is no evidence for the existence of horses in Crete before the fifteenth century BC. Their bones have been identified in Late Minoan I deposits at Tylissos west of Knossos, and there are many contemporary representations of them. Horses appear to have been introduced to the mainland of Greece by invaders from the north about the beginning of the second millennium. But horses of a more refined breed may have reached Crete before then from Syria or Egypt. Horses doubtless served as mounts in Aegean lands during the Bronze Age as they did elsewhere in the Near East at the time. But riding had its limitations before the invention of saddles

Plate 110

Plate 106

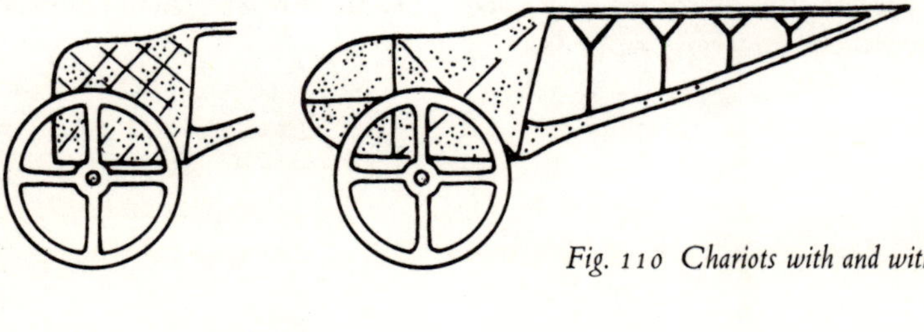

Fig. 110 Chariots with and without semicircular wings

and stirrups; and the advantages which the mounted warrior enjoyed were literally precarious. The chief use of the horse in the civilized world of the Near East during the Bronze Age was therefore as a draught animal with the light spoke-wheeled chariot.[26]

This appears to have been in the first instance a military invention, produced somewhere in the Levant—in Syria perhaps or northern Mesopotamia—early in the second millennium. The basic technological break-through was the development of light spoked wheels to replace the heavy solid wheels of the slow-moving ass-drawn battle carts used by soldiers in Mesopotamia in earlier times. The speed potential of the horse could then be exploited, and the warrior had a swift mobile platform from which to shoot his arrows or thrust his spear. No army could afford to be without this revolutionary invention which seems to have spread with rapidity throughout the civilized world.

That chariots formed an important part of the army of Knossos during the period after *c.* 1450 BC is clear from the inscribed clay tablets found in the ruins of the palace and its dependencies destroyed a century or so later. One group of these lists chariot parts, while another appears
Fig. 96 to record the issue of chariots and horses and other military equipment to individual warriors. More than four hundred chariots it is estimated are listed on the Knossian tablets. These chariots were drawn by a pair of horses, as the yoke shows. The main pole leading from the floor of the car was reinforced by a second one projecting from the top of the car rail, the two poles being laced together by a system of thongs. The sides of the car were normally covered with hide, and they were lengthened at
Plate 48 the back by means of semicircular wings which may have been intended to give additional protection against weapons fired or thrust from the
Fig. 110 flanks. Some representations, most but not all of them early ones, show chariots without these semicircular wings. Chariots were used in hunting as well as in warfare, and probably for travel where the character of the country and the roads allowed. They are also depicted in religious processions and carrying gods.

CHAPTER X

Religion and Burial Customs

Our knowledge of the Bronze Age religion of Crete has been compared to a book of pictures without a text. This is perhaps unnecessarily pessimistic. We have the remains of shrines and of a bewildering variety of cult furniture and votive offerings, like the mysterious clay 'sheep-bells' common at Knossos at the beginning of the Middle Minoan period.[1] There are also pictures of religious stories or cult scenes, which can be interpreted on the analogy of what is known of contemporary religions in the Near East and of later survivals in Greece. For it is clear that a great deal in the religion of Classical Greece, including cults and names of gods, was of Bronze Age origin; although how much beliefs and practices had become modified in the course of the centuries after the Dorian invasion, and how much of what survived from the Bronze Age was ultimately of Cretan as opposed to mainland derivation, is uncertain. *Fig. 111*

GODS AND GODDESSES

The chief deity worshipped by the Bronze Age Cretans was evidently a goddess; either a single goddess under different aspects, or a group of goddesses with different names but basically similar in character. The Cretan goddesses were versions of the Goddess of Fertility worshipped throughout the Near East in the earliest times. She appears as Ishtar in Mesopotamia, and by a corresponding name, Astarte, in Syria; as Isis in Egypt. With her are associated a male god or gods in the roles of son and husband. The death and resurrection of a god of vegetation were evidently central to her cult. In Crete the tradition of a dying god survived into later Greek times, for the tomb of the king of gods and men, Zeus, was still being shown to people in Crete then. It was this tradition of a Zeus who died (an idea repugnant to normal Greek sentiment, for how could Zeus, the Immortal die?) that earned the Cretans the reputation of 'liars', quoted by St Paul, apparently from the poet Epimenides, who was himself, however, a Cretan.[2]

The name Zeus is Greek, and has replaced the original Bronze Age name of the god. It may have been Velkhanos, still worshipped at

Fig. 111 Clay 'sheep-bell'

Fig. 112 Seal from Mochlos with horned imp

Gortyna during the Classical period. His name is pre-Greek, and virtually the same as Vulcan, the Etruscan god adopted by the Romans and equated by them with the Greek Hephaistos. In the west of Crete there were still sanctuaries of the Bronze Age goddess Diktynna in Greek and Roman times. Other titles or epithets of Bronze Age goddesses which survived in later Greek tradition were Britomartis, said to mean Sweet Virgin, and Ariadne, meaning Very Holy, like Panagia, the title by which Mary the mother of Jesus is known throughout Greece today.

It is often difficult to distinguish representations of gods from those of their priests and worshippers. According to one theory, while gods might be represented in pictures, no cult statues of them were made in Crete before *c.* 1450 BC, when anthropomorphic cult images were
Plate 63 introduced from the Greek mainland. But the snake-entwined figurine from Knossos has the aspect of a goddess rather than of a priestess, and looks as if intended for cult.[3] Apart from deities in human shape,
Plate 119 animal-headed figures reminiscent of the gods of contemporary Egypt
Plate 102 also appear in religious contexts. Minotaurs, with a bull's head and a man's body, are found on a number of Late Minoan seals. A horned
Fig. 112 imp with a phallus on its head on a Middle Minoan seal from Mochlos may be an earlier version of the same idea. A creature with scaly back,
Plate 104 demon or kindly genius, commonly represented on seals and ornaments, appears to have been inspired by the Egyptian crocodile goddess Ta-Urt. Dragons, difficult to distinguish on seals and their impressions from horses, are of Babylonian origin.[4] But winged and goat-headed figures
Fig. 113 wearing shorts have no counterparts in Egypt or elsewhere. A seal
Fig. 114 impression from Knossos seems to depict a monster of the deep, prototype perhaps of Homer's Skylla.

Figs 113, 114 Seal impressions: goat-headed monster from Zakro and boat and sea-monster from Knossos

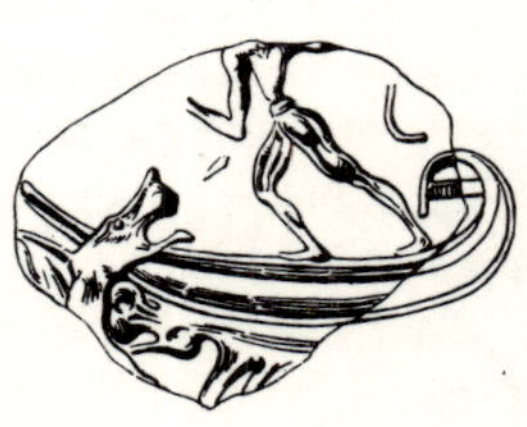

SHRINES AND SANCTUARIES

The simplest type of shrine was a single room with a bench for cult objects and votive offerings. Shrines like this with a shallow porch in front resemble some early Greek temples, which may be descended from them. But the classic Greek temple, long and narrow and surrounded by columns, appears to stem from a different tradition without Minoan antecedents. Some Cretan single-room shrines are assignable to Late Minoan III times and none are certainly earlier. It can therefore be argued that shrines of this type were introduced to Crete towards the end of the Bronze Age, but this is disputable. *Fig. 115*

A shrine consisting of a single room without a porch stood in the centre of the town at Gournia. In it was found a large clay idol of a snake-entwined goddess with hands upraised in the traditional way, together with fragments of several other clay statues of goddesses or priestesses or worshippers. These had evidently been placed on a bench round the walls of the room. On the floor was a low circular tripod altar, and upon this stood the base of a tall splayed tube, one of five recovered. These tubes may have been supports for vessels with offerings, like similar Egyptian vase stands. One of those at Gournia has snakes in relief and a handle surmounted by what Evans termed horns of consecration. These seem to be stylized versions of bulls' horns used to denote the sanctity of a place or object somewhat like the cross or the crescent in later times.[5] *Fig. 30* *Fig. 116*

The shrine at Gournia may go back to the beginning of the Late Minoan period or earlier. But there is room for argument as to whether the cult objects found in it date from before *c.* 1450 BC when the town was destroyed, or from the subsequent reoccupation of part of the town site in Late Minoan III. The little Shrine of the Double Axes at Knossos is Plate 112

Fig. 115 Late Minoan shrine building on site of palace at Mallia

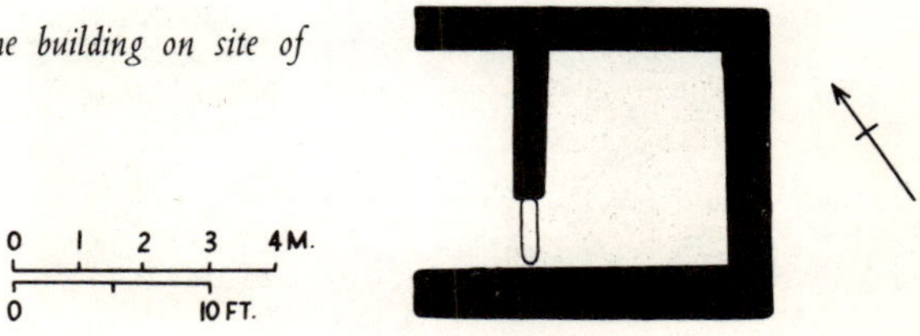

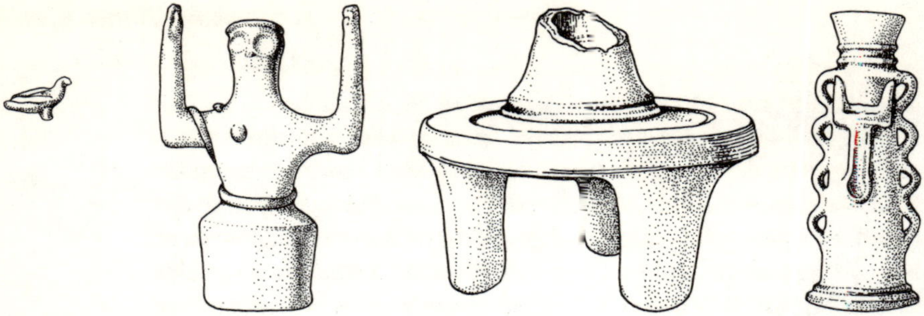

Fig. 116 Cult furniture from the shrine at Gournia: clay dove, goddess, tripod altar with base of tubular stand on it, and complete tubular stand with handle surmounted by horns of consecration

certainly of Late Minoan III date, although it is disputable whether it formed an integral part of the palace destroyed in the fourteenth century BC, or was set up afterwards in its ruins. It consists of a small *Fig. 117* room with a bench at the back on which stood little clay images of a goddess and a god and their attendants or worshippers, together with two pairs of horns of consecration with holes in the top for inserting cult objects: either bronze double axes, as Evans thought, or leafy twigs or branches. Clay vases on the floor in front of the bench may have

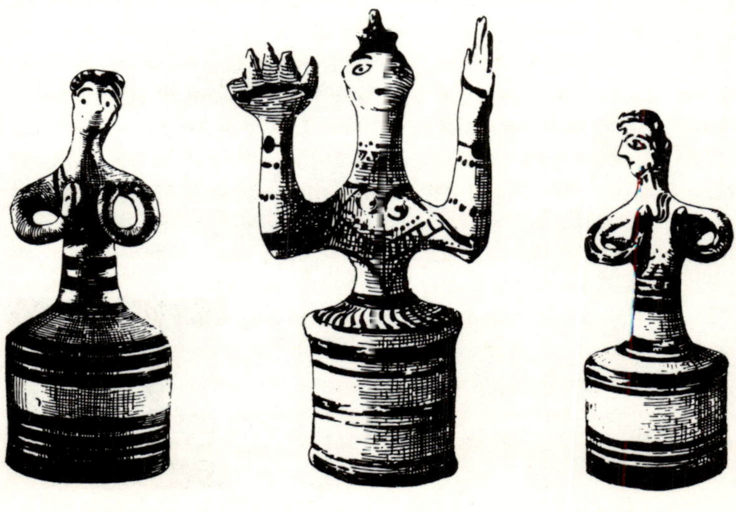

Fig. 117 Goddess with attendants from the Shrine of the Double Axes at Knossos

held offerings of food and drink. Set into the floor was a circular tripod altar like the one in the shrine at Gournia. *Fig. 116*

The goddess from the Shrine of the Double Axes has arms raised in the customary manner, and is wearing a long skirt and many necklaces and bracelets. On each wrist she carries a seal stone. Marks on her hands may be meant for fishes. On her head is a dove. Doves with their traditional capacity for love were appropriate birds for a goddess of fertility, and remained special to Aphrodite, who in many of her aspects was of Bronze Age descent. Animals associated with Cretan goddesses apart from snakes and doves included goats, lions, and imaginary sphinxes and griffins which were merely lions, usually with wings, and with the heads of women or of birds. *Fig. 117* *Fig. 118*

Besides simple one-roomed shrines there were more complex sacred buildings with several rooms. One of these has been excavated in the city at Mallia; another which was destroyed by fire, apparently at the time of the disasters of *c.* 1450 BC, stood by a stream in open countryside at Rousses near Khondros in the south of Crete.[6] As in later Greece, there were also open-air sanctuaries or consecrated areas. What seem to be walled enclosures, with sacred trees inside them, are represented on a number of signet rings and impressions made by them assignable to the early part of the Late Minoan period. Plate 117

Shrines were often set on the tops of hills and mountains. Many of these peak sanctuaries, as they are called, were perhaps in origin, if not always, open 'high places' without buildings. The peak sanctuaries appear to have been places of pilgrimage to which worshippers clambered to pray for blessings or relief from pain and sickness, or to give thanks for what they had received. Large numbers of votive offerings have been recovered from these sanctuaries; vases that held food or drink, together with model animals which may have been cheap substitutes for sacrifices, and figurines of men and women left by the pilgrims to represent themselves in constant attendance at the shrines.[7] Plate 47

These votive gifts are for the most part assignable to the Middle Minoan period, and especially to the earliest phase of it, Middle Minoan I. But some of the sanctuaries continued in use into Late Minoan III times; among them one of the largest and most impressive on the highest peak of Mount Juktas. Here a massive 'Cyclopean' wall enclosed a

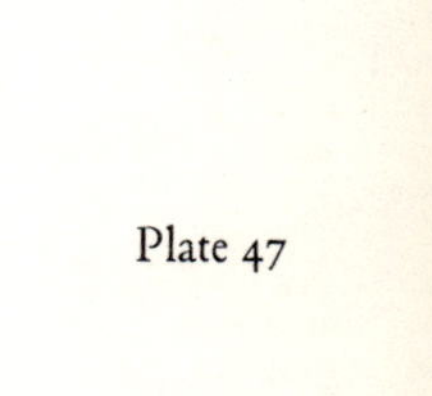

Fig. 118 Seal impression from Knossos showing a goddess on a mountain flanked by lions, with a worshipper in front and a shrine behind

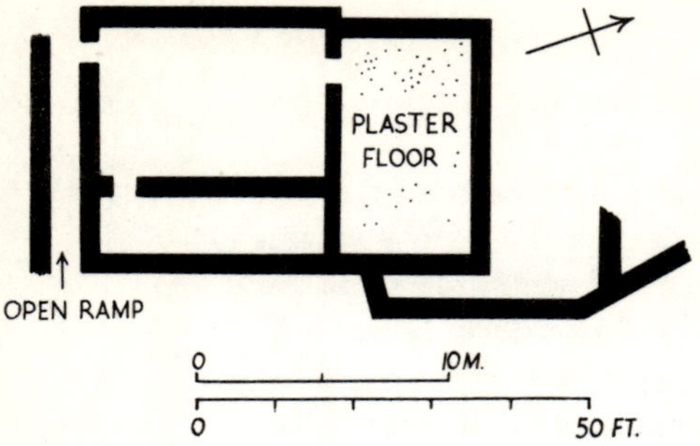

Fig. 119 Shrine building on the summit of Mount Juktas

Fig. 119 wide area round the summit, on which stood the shrine building explored by Evans in 1909. The shrine had three rooms approached by a ramp on the south. Fires had evidently been lit in the open air round it, either as part of ritual or for warmth during night-long vigils.

Plate 114 A relief vase from Zakro shows what may be a peak sanctuary, to judge from the rocky background and the goats sitting on top of the shrine. This consists of a high central part flanked by lower wings, which are surmounted by horns of consecration and have poles like the flag-staffs in Egyptian sanctuaries on either side.[8] Just below the spiral-decorated central part of the shrine is a small altar with a narrow waist; a standard shape in Crete for small stone altars suitable for offerings of incense, vegetables or fruits. But rectangular bases in the west court of the palace at Knossos may have belonged to larger altars used for animal sacrifices. A sunk altar of burnt sacrifice stood in the middle of the central court at Mallia.

The shrine on the Zakro vase may be just a façade. Elaborate shrine façades appear to have been erected by the open courts which flanked the great houses at Vathipetro and Nirou Khani, and by the central court of the palace at Knossos. This Knossian shrine façade seems to be represented in wall-paintings from the palace which show a tripartite structure as on the Zakro vase with columns and horns of consecration.

Trees and wooden columns, as well as square stone pillars, were evidently objects of cult.[9] Besides these, the Bronze Age Cretans venerated natural concretions of stone, and stalagmites and stalactites in caves. Several of the caves in which Crete abounds were used as sanctuaries in the Bronze Age, and in a few instances, like the Idaian cave, the cult appears to have continued without a break into Greek and Roman times.

Fig. 120 Woman blowing conch-shell trumpet on seal from the Idaian Cave

Fig. 121 Clay model of woman on swing between dove-topped posts, from Ayia Triadha near Phaistos. Height: 15 cm.

RITES AND CEREMONIES

The religious rites and ceremonies in use in Bronze Age Crete were no doubt varied and elaborate. The bull-leapings so prominent in Minoan art may have been connected with fertility rites. Boxing and wrestling perhaps formed part of initiation ceremonies of some kind. This boxing was clearly savage in character; the men engaged in it wearing bronze helmets and knuckle-dusters. Minoan religion like that of many early peoples may have had a dark side to it. Human sacrifice and suttee, the killing of a wife when her husband dies, were perhaps not unknown in Bronze Age Crete.

Plate 52

Plate 96

Processions and dances are among more attractive aspects of Minoan religion. Some of the religious dances appear to have survived into later Greek times, and may even be ancestral to the dances for which Crete is still renowned.[10] On the stone vase from Ayia Triadha men are singing and dancing in some festival of sowing or harvest time. But women also danced, and on a gold signet ring from Knossos they appear to be doing so to invoke the goddess and bring her down to them. The woman blowing a conch-shell trumpet on a crystal seal from the Idaian Cave may have the same idea in mind. Behind her is a sacred tree, and she faces a waisted altar, which is surmounted by horns of

Plate 38

Plate 116

Fig. 120

consecration and leafy branches, and flanked by a curious object like a stylized idol and a star. Among other ceremonial activities women partook in was swinging, which is found in many parts of the world as a fertility rite.[11] The Cretans of the Bronze Age may have used opium to encourage a state of ecstasy in their religious ceremonies; a large clay goddess from Gazi west of Knossos is wearing poppies in her crown.

Fig. 121

Plate 115

A number of metal signet rings assignable to the sixteenth and fifteenth centuries BC are engraved with scenes of ritual or with myths about the gods. The distinction, however, may be somewhat artificial, because a large part of ritual probably consisted of stories about the gods enacted by priests as was customary throughout the Near East at the time. The interpretation of the scenes on these signet rings is difficult, and the difficulties are increased by the large number of modern forgeries of gold signets which fill museums and collections. But the death and resurrection of the god, consort of the goddess, must have been among the chief features in the myth and enacted ritual of Bronze Age Crete as it was elsewhere in the Levant. A number of metal signet rings may show scenes connected with this theme.

Plate 117

On a bronze signet from Knossos the goddess is standing outside a shrine or enclosure built of squared masonry with a sacred tree in or behind it. A little female attendant appears to have climbed the wall of the enclosure and is vigorously pulling down a bough of the tree. The goddess stoops as if in sorrow, while behind her on the right is a curious object, in shape like a storage jar, or pithos, of the kind used for burials in many parts of Crete during the Middle Minoan period from *c.* 2000 BC onwards. A gold signet ring with a similar theme was recently found in a tomb at Arkhanes south of Knossos. In the middle is the goddess wearing an elaborately flounced dress. On the right a man attacks a tree set in or behind a shrine with a high central part flanked by lower wings as on the Zakro vase. On the left another man clasps what might be a large storage jar upside down in the way that burial jars were often placed in tombs. Do these scenes and others like them represent some rite of mourning for the dead god, while search is made for a magic bough or fruit to restore life to him? Some ritual of this kind may lie at the back of the curious legend about Glaukos, the son of Minos, drowned in a jar of honey, but restored to life with a herb which a snake revealed.

Plate 113

Fig. 122 Gold signet ring from Mochlos showing goddess in boat

On a fine gold signet ring from Mochlos the goddess is sitting in a curious boat with the head of an animal at one end and something like a plant at the other. In or behind the boat is a shrine with a tree, while on land to the right stands another substantially built shrine or enclosure. Boats were a regular part of funerary apparatus in Egypt, and models of them are sometimes found in Bronze Age tombs in Crete. It is just possible that the scene on this signet represented some journey of the goddess across the water in search of her dead consort.

BURIAL CUSTOMS

The idea of an Elysion, or Isles of the Blessed, a tolerably pleasant heaven as opposed to the murky underground Hades of the Homeric poems, is thought to be a legacy from Bronze Age Crete. The way in which the Cretans tended their dead suggests that like the Egyptians they believed in an after-life of some kind. A clay model assigned to the end of the Middle Minoan period, *c.* 1600 BC, from the large circular tomb at Kamilari near Phaistos shows two couples with altars or tables in front of them upon which offerings of food and drink are being placed. The couples who receive the offerings may be the deceased, unless they are meant for gods. Plate 118

There is less room for doubt in the case of a similar scene painted on the remarkable stone sarcophagus of the fourteenth century BC from Ayia Triadha in the same area. The dead man here stands in front of his tomb, while two women pour libations into a large vase set between a pair of pillars surmounted by elaborate double axes with birds on top of them. Three men dressed in skins bring the dead man a pair of bulls or models of them, along with a boat which he may need for his voyage to the Isles of the Blessed. Another man in a long robe has a lyre with seven strings like the standard Greek lyre until the fifth century BC, when the number of strings was increased to eight or nine. But a lyre with eight strings already appears on an early seal impression from Knossos, along with a simpler four-stringed instrument. A man on the other side of the Ayia Triadha sarcophagus is playing double pipes resembling the later Greek *aulos*. The music of the Greeks, like so much of their religion, may have been derived from Bronze Age Crete. Plate 60 *Fig. 123* Plate 59

During the earlier part of the Bronze Age the people of Crete normally buried their dead in collective tombs. These were used by a single

Fig. 123 Seal impression with lyres from the hieroglyphic deposit at Knossos, c. 1700 BC

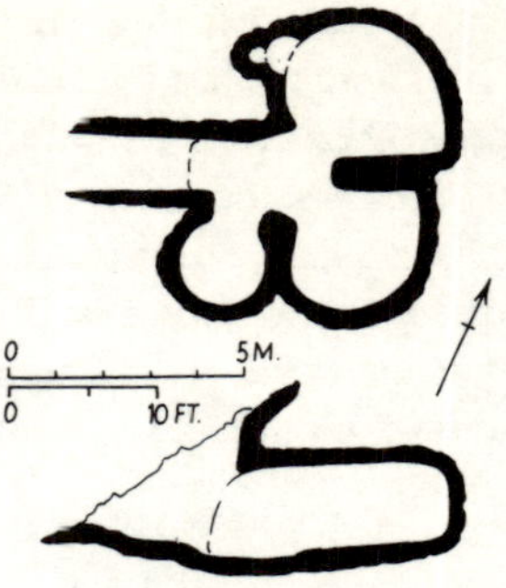

Fig. 124 Rock-cut tomb in the Mavrospilio cemetery adjacent to Ailias at Knossos

clan or extended family over many generations, and often contained hundreds of burials. Small settlements may have only one such tomb, as if all the inhabitants belonged to a single clan. But two or three tombs are regularly found outside the larger settlements. A city like Knossos was ringed with tombs.

The usual rite of burial was inhumation. Cremation hardly occurs in Crete before the end of the Bronze Age. Isolated cremation burials in tombs of the Ailias cemetery at Knossos dating from the end of the Middle Minoan period, *c.* 1600 BC, may be those of foreigners who had married into local clans. In some parts of Anatolia, for instance, cremation appears to have been general by this time.

During the Middle Minoan period and earlier the body was normally trussed tight, knees to chin. The idea may have been to make it like the foetus in the mother's womb. The trussed body was then laid on the floor of the tomb, or squeezed into a large jar of the kind used for storing food in the houses. Some oblong clay coffins from Pirgos and elsewhere are assigned to the Early Minoan period; but at Knossos clay coffins only began to replace storage jars for burials towards the end of Middle Minoan times. The reason for this change was no doubt convenience, it being easier to fit a body into a coffin than into a storage jar.[12]

Plate 113

At Knossos the early collective tombs were carved out of the soft white marly limestone (*kouskouras*) of the region, and were usually irregular in shape, often with several interconnecting chambers. Collective tombs of this kind were still being used in the Knossos area at the beginning of the Late Minoan period. One with a large pillared

Fig. 124

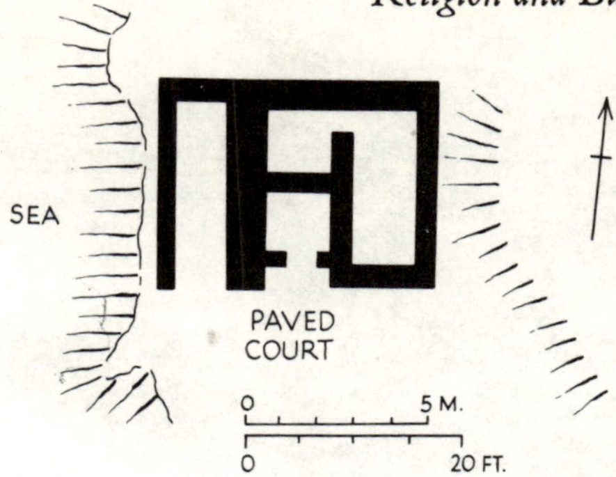

Fig. 125 Built tomb at Mochlos

chamber and very rich finds assignable to Middle Minoan III and Late Minoan I times has recently been excavated at Poros, the harbour town of Knossos.[13]

In some parts of Crete, where the rock was hard and difficult to excavate, caves were used for burial as in Neolithic times, or tombs were built above ground like houses. Many of these built tombs had rectangular rooms or compartments. Some tombs of this kind at Mochlos, excavated by Seager in 1908, belonged to leading families of the region to judge from the wealth of gold ornaments found in them. They stood on a wide ledge in a cliff overlooking the sea on the west side of the peninsula where the town was. The peninsula is now an island owing to the rise of sea level here since ancient times. *Fig. 125*

Round the Mesara plain of southern Crete the standard type of collective tomb was a circular domed structure. A small circular tomb built at Knossos towards the end of Middle Minoan II, *c.* 1700 BC, may have belonged to a clan of southern Cretans who had settled in the

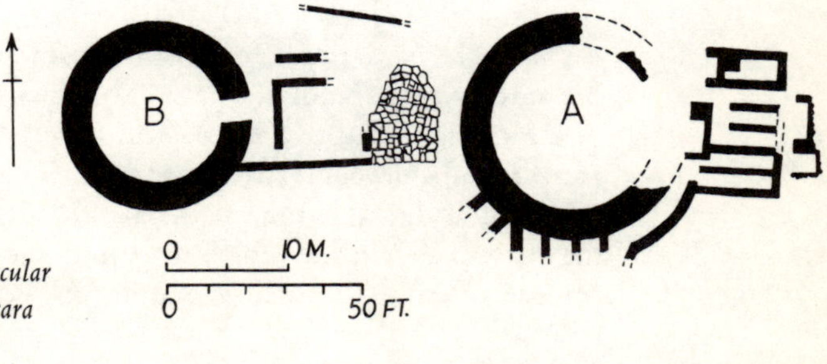

Fig. 126 Pair of large circular tombs at Platanos in the Mesara

Fig. 127 Restored view and plan of the tomb at Apesokari, overlooking the Mesara plain

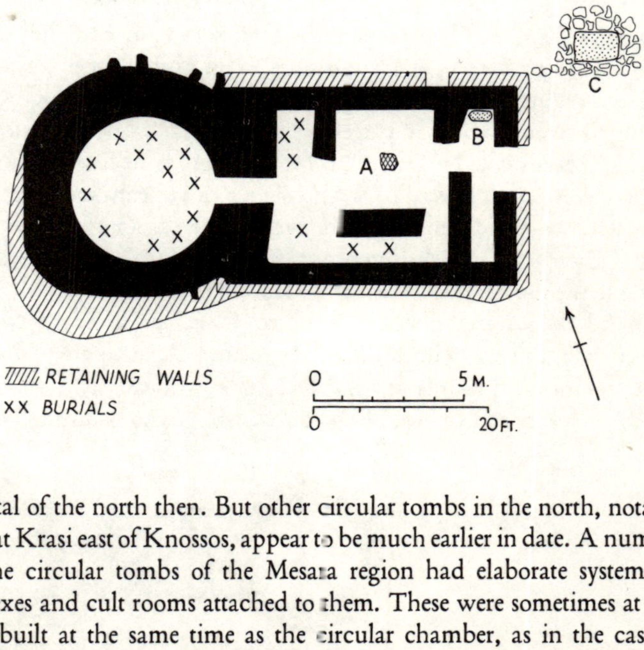

capital of the north then. But other circular tombs in the north, notably one at Krasi east of Knossos, appear to be much earlier in date. A number
Fig. 126 of the circular tombs of the Mesara region had elaborate systems of annexes and cult rooms attached to them. These were sometimes at any rate built at the same time as the circular chamber, as in the case of
Fig. 127 the tomb at Apesokari, which dates from the early part of the Middle Minoan period in the centuries round 2000 BC.[14]

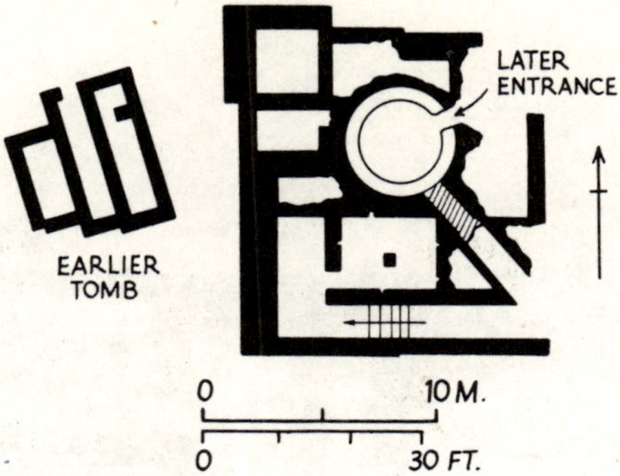

Fig. 128 Earlier and later tomb complexes at Arkhanes

The circular chamber here, and some of the outer ones, had served for burials, while a large room with the stone base for a wooden pillar (A) was apparently used for cult. Cult rooms of this kind with pillars of wood or stone are regularly found in the more elaborate Bronze Age tombs of Crete as well as in palaces and houses. A niche (B) just inside the entrance on the right at Apesokari held a small bench or altar on which a natural concretion of stone had evidently been placed to serve as a cult image. Another larger altar (C) suitable for sacrifices stood outside in the open on the edge of a paved area with the remains of many clay vases which had contained offerings of food and drink.

A more elaborate burial complex which appears to be later in date was discovered in 1966 at Arkhanes south of Knossos. It had replaced an earlier collective tomb with rectangular compartments like the tombs at Mochlos. This earlier tomb was used for a considerable length of time, some two hundred skulls being recovered from it. Its entrance eventually became choked with burials, and the roof had to be removed to insert the latest ones. The new tomb with its circular chamber was built some time after 2000 BC, and it may have remained in use over five hundred years into the fourteenth century BC or later. The circular burial chamber with a bench round the inside was an integral part of the complex which included a pillar room as at Apesokari. A staircase led to an upper storey which also appears to have housed burials. At some point the floor of the circular chamber was raised; the original passage leading into it was blocked, and a new and shorter entrance was made on the east side. This would have brought the tomb into line with the circular tombs of southern Crete where the doorways invariably face east.[15] *Fig. 128*

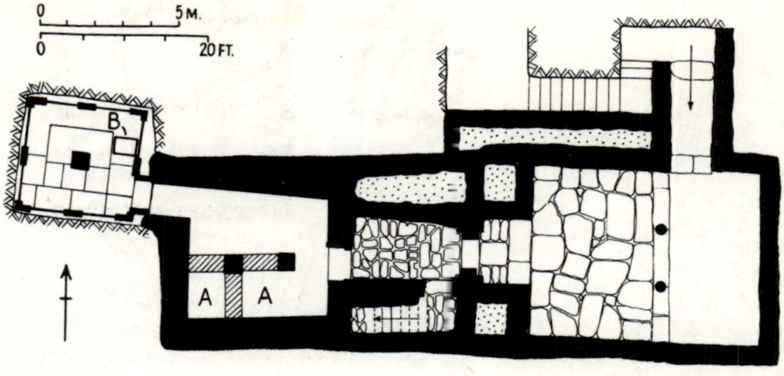

Fig. 129 The Temple at Knossos

Fig. 129

A remarkable burial complex known as the Temple Tomb was discovered by Evans in 1931 on the southern edge of the Bronze Age city at Knossos. This had an upper storey and a pillar crypt like the tomb at Arkhanes, but it appears to have been constructed some centuries later, towards the end of Middle Minoan times. It may have been a royal sepulchre, but if so, it was plundered and re-used during the period after the disasters of *c.* 1450 BC. The tomb was entered from an enclosed open courtyard on the east. A dark crypt with a pair of massive square stone pillars was built up against the face of a low cliff of soft white *kouskouras* in which the burial chamber was cut. The south side of the pillar crypt had been used as an ossuary, and in walled compartments here (A) were found the bones of some twenty individuals—earlier burials, or sacrifices to the royal dead; or, as Evans thought, stressing the dual character of the complex as tomb and shrine, worshippers who had gathered here but fell victims to one of the great earthquakes about the time of the eruption of Thera. The rock-cut burial chamber was paved with slabs of gypsum, and gypsum slabs lined its walls, while a pillar of the same stone helped to support the roof which appears to have been painted blue. A little pit in the floor (B) contained objects which may have belonged with the latest burials in the tomb, an elderly man and a child it seems, laid to rest in the early fourteenth century BC. Decorated clay vases assignable to the same period or a bit later, on the floor of the pillar crypt and in the open outside the entrance to the tomb, show that a cult of the dead continued here at least until the final destruction of the palace at Knossos.[16]

Apart from the Temple Tomb no certain example of a royal or princely tomb of the period before *c.* 1450 BC has been recognized in Crete. In earlier times it seems even kings and their families were buried like everyone else in the tombs which belonged to their clan, although the tombs of royal clans were larger and more elaborate. There is a tomb which may have belonged to a royal clan on the north-eastern edge of the city at Mallia near caves used for collective burials in Early and Middle Minoan times. This takes the form of a large rectangular building with a colonnade along the east side and a maze of rooms or compartments within. It had been wrecked and thoroughly plundered before the French came to excavate it in the 1920's.[17] Most of the plundering seems to have been done in the last century, and the name of the place, Chrysolakkos or Gold Hole, suggests what the robbers may have found. In spite of the plundering a certain amount of jewellery, including a gold pin and the remarkable bee pendant, was recovered during the French excavations; and there is reason to suppose that the 'Aegina treasure' acquired by the British Museum in 1892 really came from here. *Fig. 130* Plate 70

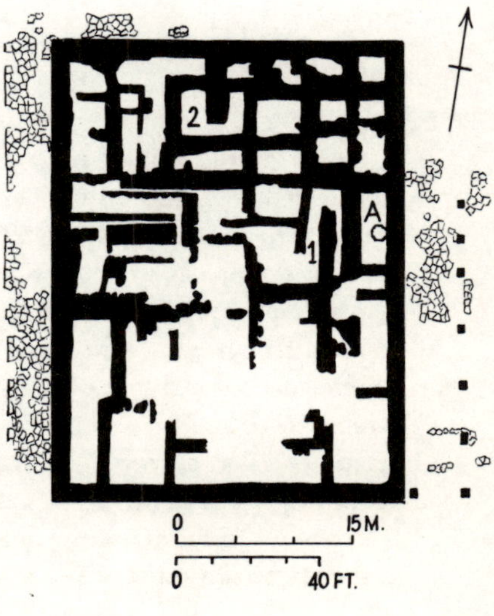

Fig. 130 Great tomb at Chrysolakkos, Mallia, with altar (A) and find-spots of (1) gold pin (fig. 65) and (2) bee pendant (plate 70)

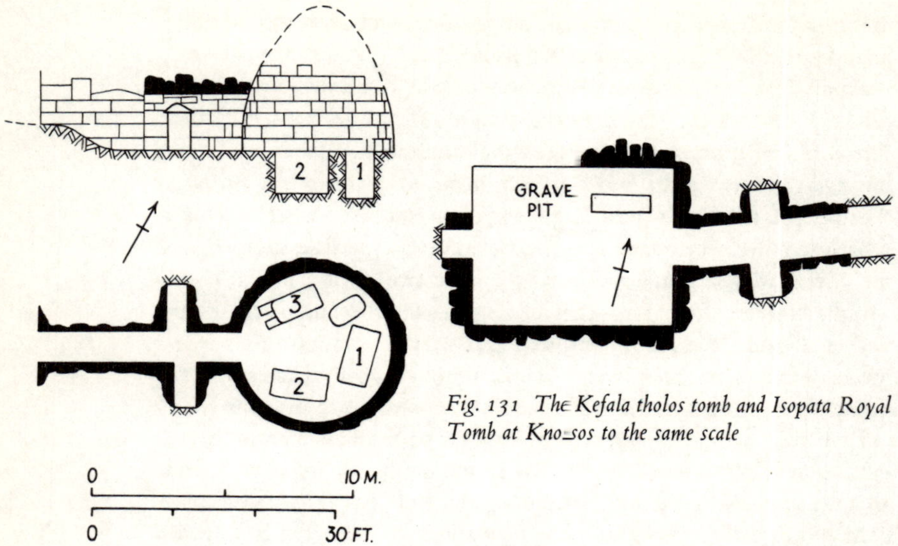

Fig. 131 The Kefala tholos tomb and Isopata Royal Tomb at Knossos to the same scale

This tomb may therefore be the burial place for the royal family of Mallia during the Middle Minoan period, and perhaps beyond that until the time when the palace there was destroyed in the disasters of *c.* 1450 BC.

Some built tombs at Knossos may be those of kings or princes who were ruling there during the period immediately after *c.* 1450 BC; *Fig. 131* notably a tholos tomb with circular chamber sunk deep in the ground at Kefala on the Isopata ridge north of the Bronze Age city, and the Isopata Royal Tomb on the north end of the same ridge overlooking the sea. In the latter a large rectangular chamber with a high stone vault was approached down a long passage from the east.[18] There are scattered examples of similar stone-built princely tombs of the Late Minoan III period in other parts of Crete. Most of these were long ago emptied of their treasures by marauders, but at Arkhanes the burial of a princess with a great wealth of jewellery has been found in the unplundered rock-cut chamber attached to an underground tholos tomb about fifty yards north of the complex already described. This burial is assignable to the eve of the final destruction of the palace at Knossos in the fourteenth century BC.

The practice of collective burial survived in some parts of Crete until the end of the fifteenth century BC or later, and a few of the old communal tombs continued in use, notably that at Kamilari near Phaistos. Plate 120 But after the middle of the fifteenth century BC burial was for the most part in small tombs holding a group of three or four immediate relatives, or a couple, or even a single individual. This revolution in burial custom was no doubt accelerated by the events of *c.* 1450 BC, but it appears to have been under way before then. It may have been stimulated in the first instance by the increasing wealth and complexity of Cretan society with a consequent loosening of clan ties. The gap between rich and poor had no doubt become wider during the flourishing period of the later palaces from 1700 BC onwards, while the force of custom grew weaker. The rich probably began to want to furnish their burials in a more expensive and lavish manner.

Many if not most of the burials in the old collective tombs were unaccompanied by grave goods, and any personal valuables left with the dead, such as their jewellery or seal stones, were an easy prey to unscrupulous members of other burial parties. One of the last burials in a collective tomb in the Ailias cemetery at Knossos throws a vivid light on this: under the clay coffin the relatives had pushed a fine chalcedony seal stone and a finger ring of solid gold. Dislocation caused by the eruption of Thera *c.* 1500 BC, with the wrecking of many of the old collective tombs by earthquakes about that time, may have fanned the winds of change; while the corrupting example of Egypt with its fantastic wealth and luxurious sepulchres stuffed with grave furniture perhaps helped to stimulate the break with tradition.

The new-style exclusive chamber tombs which began to be dug at Knossos and on the mainland of Greece during the Late Minoan period may indeed owe something to Egyptian models. *Fig. 29* Burials are either placed on the floor of the chamber, or in graves dug into the floor as in the Isopata Royal Tomb. Plate 21 The bodies are sometimes contained in clay bathtubs, or in rectangular clay coffins with low feet. Plate 36 These coffins, often elaborately decorated, have gabled lids and panelled sides suggesting that they are copies of the wooden chests used for storing clothes and textiles in houses at the time. Occasionally painted wooden storage chests were used for burials, but this extravagance appears to have been confined to the very rich.

CHAPTER XI

Epilogue

After the final destruction of the palace at Knossos in the fourteenth century BC Crete may have become the province of an empire ruled from Mycenae on the Greek mainland. No later palace has been identified at Knossos or elsewhere on the island.

Eventually at the end of the thirteenth century BC immigrants from the mainland appear to have settled in Crete in large numbers. Their presence is reflected in the pottery assignable to the beginning of the Late Minoan III C period, which has acquired many mainland characteristics. Perhaps these settlers were refugees from the Peloponnese, ravaged by invaders from the north shortly before 1200 BC.[1]

Some fifty years later, a second wave of people from the Greek mainland reached Crete; and to judge from the distribution of their pottery, they occupied the fertile centre and south of the island, the region of Knossos and Phaistos, where the Homeric Catalogue of Ships places the cities controlled by Idomeneus, Greek king of Knossos and leader of the Cretan contingent in the Trojan War. These newcomers may have been Achaians or East Greeks who first invaded Crete and conquered the central parts of it at this time. But this view depends upon the assumption that the language of the Linear B tablets of the fourteenth century BC is not Greek.

Now, if not earlier, many of the previous inhabitants of the island began to take refuge in the hills where their settlements are found on high, inaccessible peaks like Karfi (the Nail) on the northern edge of the Lasithi plain. Others may have escaped overseas; the Philistines, who settled on the coast of Palestine in the twelfth century BC, according to tradition came from Crete.

These movements of people into Crete at the end of the thirteenth century and again *c.* 1150 BC were followed by a final mass invasion. The Dorians, last of the peoples of Greek speech to enter the Peloponnese, overran the central parts of Crete which were already occupied by Achaians or East Greeks. They also settled in the mountainous and thinly occupied west of the island, which is studded with their little cities. Eventually the whole of Crete came under Dorian control.

But in the far east of the island pockets of the original pre-Greek population, known to the Greeks as Eteocretans or true Cretans, appear to have maintained their independence for a time, and their language is preserved in a few official inscriptions of the Greek cities of Dreros and Praisos assigned to the sixth and fifth centuries BC.

APPENDIX

Date of the final destruction of the palace at Knossos (see Bibliography)
Great masses of Linear B clay tablets and seal impressions were found by Evans during his excavations in the palace at Knossos from 1900–5. These tablets and sealings had evidently been involved in the final destruction of the palace by a fire which had hardened and preserved them. Evans dated the destruction *c.* 1400 BC.

In 1960 L. R. Palmer, Professor of Comparative Philology at Oxford, suggested that the final destruction of the palace actually took place at the very end of the Bronze Age *c.* 1150 BC. This choice of date was inspired in the first instance by philological considerations; the assumption being that the Greek obtained by the decipherment from the Linear B tablets of Knossos showed later forms than that of those from Pylos on the Greek mainland which was destroyed *c.* 1200 BC. But this assumption has been disputed by other philologists who agree with Palmer in accepting the decipherment of the Linear B tablets as Greek.

It should be possible to date the final destruction of the palace at Knossos by means of the pottery found by Evans during excavations in the burnt ruins with the tablets. But there has been much controversy as to what pottery Evans found with the tablets and there is disagreement about the date of some of it.

Three main groups of pottery are involved (see S. Hood, *Studi Micenei* 2, 1967, pp. 63–70). (1) A small group of fine decorated vases from the southern edge of the palace area, assignable to Late Minoan III B (*c.* 1300–1200 BC). (2) A quantity of fine decorated ware, which has been studied by M. Popham and shown by him to be assignable to Late Minoan III A 2, and perhaps to an early phase of it *c.* 1375 BC or not much later. (3) A mass of plain ware, and a number of vases (notably large storage stirrup-jars) with comparatively simple decoration.

The pottery of this last group (3) is the crux. It was assigned by Evans to a period of reoccupation of the palace site after the final destruction of the palace as such. But Palmer, on re-examining the evidence of the excavation reports with the help of the original note-books kept by Evans and his assistant D. Mackenzie, argued that this pottery of group (3) was actually found with the clay tablets and seal impressions in the burnt ruins of the final destruction of the palace.

According to the usually accepted view, the pottery of this group (3) dates from Late Minoan III B, and is therefore considerably later in date than the pottery of group (2) which is assignable to Late Minoan III A 2. Palmer has accepted this dating for the pottery of group (3), and assigned it (along with the few vases of group (1), which are by general agreement of Late Minoan III B date) to the final destruction of the palace. On this view the fine decorated ware of group (2), dating from Late Minoan III A 2, must reflect some earlier horizon of destruction in the history of the palace.

I believe myself that Palmer is right in his conclusion that the pottery of group (3) was found by Evans in the burnt ruins of the final destruction of the palace. But I have argued that the usually accepted date (Late Minoan III B) for this pottery of group (3) is wrong, and that it is in fact earlier and contemporary with the fine decorated ware of group (2) which is assignable to Late Minoan III A 2. On this view the vases of group (3) are merely the plain and coarse wares which were in use alongside the fine decorated table wares of group (2) in the palace at Knossos at the time of its final destruction in Late Minoan III A 2 *c.* 1375 BC or not much later.

There is some evidence from Mallia which suggests that this may be the right view. For large stirrup-jars, identical with one of those from the palace at Knossos belonging to group (3), were apparently found in the fire-destroyed ruins of a house there along with fine decorated ware assignable to an early phase of Late Minoan III A 2 (O. Pelon, La Maison E de Malia reconsidérée, *BCH* 91, 1967, pp. 494–512).

In agreement with J. Boardman I would assign the vases of group (1), which are admittedly Late Minoan III B in date, to some kind of reoccupation in a limited area on the southern edge of the palace site after the final destruction of the palace itself. This reoccupation might reflect a religious cult, which continued into Classical Greek times, when the palace site appears to have been a sanctuary with a small temple, and perhaps a grove of cypress trees, dedicated to Rhea (Evans, *PM* II, pp. 5 ff.).

Notes on the Text

For key to abbreviations, see Bibliography, page 164.

PREFACE

1 For the life of Evans see Joan Evans, *Time and Chance. The Story of Arthur Evans and his Forebears,* London, etc. 1943.

2 Seager, *Mochlos,* 1912, p. 1.

3 For the view that Greeks were in Crete from the earliest times, e.g. C. Renfrew, Crete and the Cyclades before Rhadamanthus, *Kr Kh* 1964, pp. 107–41.

INTRODUCTION

1 Work at Knossos before Evans began excavations there is described by G. Perrot and C. Chipiez, *Art in Primitive Greece,* London 1894, Vol. I pp. 439–43.

CHAPTER I

1 Descriptions of Crete in Pendlebury, *The Archaeology of Crete,* 1939, Ch. I, and Hutchinson, *Prehistoric Crete,* 1962, Ch. I. For the economy of the island in recent times, L. G. Allbaugh, *Crete. A Case Study of an Underdeveloped Area,* Princeton 1953.

2 The rise of the sea level in eastern Crete is discussed by J. Leatham and S. Hood, *BSA* 53–54, 1958–59, pp. 263 ff. At Chersonesos between Herakleion and Mallia the sea is now level with the top of the Roman quay, while Roman fish-tanks cut in the rock of the foreshore there and at Mochlos further east are totally submerged. But the slipway for a warship near Siteia in the far east of the island appears to be at about the same height above the water as it was when in use *c.* 300 BC (*K. Davaras, *AE* 1967, pp. 84–90). For oscillations in the rise and fall of sea level at Mallia since Roman times see *Études Crétoises XIII*, 1963, pp. 29–31.

3 The rise of the land in western Crete was studied by Spratt, *Travels and Researches,* 1865, Vol. II, pp. 135 ff. Cf. pp. 227 ff. for Phalasarna, and pp. 241 ff. for the maximum rise. There is no evidence for a sudden and cataclysmic rise as suggested by Pendlebury, *The Archaeology of Crete,* 1939, p. 3.

4 Caves as places of refuge, Faure, *Fonctions des Cavernes,* 1964; Antiques Cavernes de refuge dans la Crète de l'Ouest, *AAA* II, 1969, pp. 213–16.

5 R. M. Dawkins, *BSA* 20, 1913–14, pp. 1–17. Cf. Graham, *The Palaces of Crete,* 1962, p. 4. For the Diktaian Cave see J. Boardman, *The Cretan Collection in Oxford,* Oxford 1961, pp. 1–3.

6 While the forests were certainly more extensive, the higher slopes of the Cretan mountains were probably bare of trees in the Bronze Age as they are now (*Études Crétoises* XIII, 1963, pp. 31–2).

7 S. Payne, *PPS* 34, 1968, p. 375.

8 Marinatos and Hirmer, *Crete and Mycenae,* 1960, p. 11.

CHAPTER II

1 *BSA* 38, 1937–38, p. 50 fig. 21.

2 There was a Neolithic village not far from the sea at Katsamba north of Knossos (**PAE* 1953, pp. 305–8; 1954, pp. 370–4).

3 For Neolithic Knossos see S. S. Weinberg, *CAH* rev. ed. Vol. I, Ch. X, pp. 51–61. *Old excavations:* Evans, *PM* I, pp. 32–55; II, pp. 1–21. A. Furness, *BSA* 48, 1953, pp. 94–134. *New excavations:* J. D. Evans, *BSA* 59, 1964, pp. 132–240; 63, 1968, pp. 239–76. Excavations were resumed by J. D. Evans in the summer of 1969.

4 Non-pottery Neolithic in Thessaly, *D. R. Theokharis, *I Avyi tis thessalikis Proistorias,* Volos 1967, pp. 171–2 (English summary). V. Milojčić, *Argissa-Magula* I, Bonn 1962. Cf. J. Mellaart, *Earliest Civilizations of the Near East,* London 1965.

5 Middle Neolithic house at Knossos, J. D. Evans, *BSA* 59, 1964, pp. 174–6 fig. 16. For Late Neolithic houses there, Evans, *PM* II, pp. 8–21 fig. 8A.

6 For obsidian see C. Renfrew, J. R. Cann, and J. E. Dixon, *BSA* 60, 1965, pp. 225–47, and p. 239 for a scrap of central (southern) Anatolian origin from a Late Neolithic house at Knossos.

7 Figurines are listed and discussed by P. J. Ucko, *Anthropomorphic Figurines of Predynastic Egypt and Neolithic Crete,* London 1968.

8 Carbon 14 dates for the Knossian Neolithic in *BSA* 63, 1968, pp. 271–2, reckoned with the 'conventional' half-life for the C14 atom of 5,570 years. There does not seem to have been a long gap between the occupation of level 10 and the appearance of pottery in level 9, as suggested by Weinberg, *CAH* rev. ed. Vol I, Ch. X, pp. 58–9.

9 J. D. Evans, *BSA* 63, 1968, pp. 273–4, advances strong arguments for a western Anatolian origin for the Cretan Neolithic. The sherds allegedly found by T. E. Lawrence at Byblos in Syria (C. L. Woolley, *Liverpool Annals of Art and Archaeology* 10, 1923, p. 39 pl. IX.2) appear to be in fact Knossian Neolithic (A. Furness, *BSA* 48, 1953, p. 134 note 119).

CHAPTER III

1 The Early Minoan settlement on a hill above the Cave of Hermes at Melidhoni may have replaced a Neolithic one on lower ground to the west (*BSA* 59, 1964, pp. 58–9).

2 For copper sources in Crete see P. Faure, Les minerais de la Crète antique, *Revue archéologique* 1966, pp. 45–78. K. Branigan, *Copper and Bronze Working in Early Bronze Age Crete,* Lund 1968.

3 Evans, *PM* II, p. 14, fig. 3 *f.*

4 A telescoped chronology for the Cretan Early Bronze Age was suggested by D. Levi in *La Parola del Passato* 71, 1960, pp. 116 ff; modified in *Studi in onore di Luisa Banti,* Rome, 1965, pp. 223–39.

5 For high pedestals and pattern burnish in the latest Neolithic at Knossos see *PM* II, p. 10 fig. 3m, 12 fig. 4, and *BSA* 59, 1964, p. 229.

6 Libyan elements in the Minoan civilization are discussed by Evans in *PM* II, pp. 22–59.

7 Round tombs in Crete, S. Xanthoudides, *The Vaulted Tombs of Mesara,* London 1924. Other listed by Pini, *Beiträge zur minoischen Gräberkunde,* 1968, and K. Branigan, *The Tombs of Mesara,* London 1970. For their roofing system and relationship to later

tholos tombs see S. Hood, *Antiquity* 34, 1960, pp. 166–76.

8 P. Dikaios, *Khirokitia,* Oxford 1953.

9 A circular hut assignable to the Late Neolithic or Early Minoan period has been recognized at Phaistos (D. Levi, in *Studi in onore di Luisa Banti,* Rome 1965, p. 223).

10 Circular shrines: 1, Egypt. E. J. Baumgartel, *The Cultures of Prehistoric Egypt,* Oxford 1955, p. 46. 2, Crete. *AJA* 40, 1936, pp. 371–2, at Gazi west of Herakleion.

11 Models of circular buildings found in Crete include an Early Minoan example from Lebena, *ILN* 6. 8. 60, p. 227 fig. 16. Cf. S. Korres, *CIM,* 1968, p. 81 pl. 1 fig. 1. One from Zakro is assigned by Korres to LM III but may be LM I in date. There is one datable to LM III B from Amnisos, *BCH* 91, 1967, pp. 777–8. For other late examples from Karfi and elsewhere see *BSA* 55, 1960, pp. 27–8. One of the Subminoan period from Knossos (*PM* II, pp. 128 ff., fig. 63) has a goddess inside, like the Protogeometric example published by *S. Alexiou, *Kr Kh* 1950, pp. 441–62.

12 For Narmer in Palestine, S. Yeivin, *Israel Exploration Journal* 10, 1960, pp. 193–203. Cf. *Oriens Antiquus* 2, 1963, pp. 205–213. S. Moscati, *Oriens Antiquus* 3, 1964, p. 5, admits an Egyptian invasion, but questions the evidence for a sack at Tell Gat.

13 Palestinian features in the earliest Bronze Age pottery of Crete are noted by Weinberg, in Ehrich, *Relative Chronologies,* 1954, p. 95, and *Chronologies,* 1965, p. 307.

CHAPTER IV

1 The separate existence of Early Minoan III was independently argued by *A. Zois, *Acts of the Second Cretological Congress* Vol. I, Athens 1967, pp. 141–56.

2 The embryo of a palatial system of periods was suggested before the Second World War by N. Åberg, *Bronzezeitliche und Früheisenzeitliche Chronologie* IV, Stockholm 1933; and more recently by D. Levi, Per una nuova classificazione della Civiltà minoica, *La Parola del Passato* 71, 1960, pp. 81–121. Cf. N. Platon, in Zervos, *L'Art de la Crète,* 1956, pp. 509–12.

3 D. Levi, La Varietà della primitiva Ceramica cretese, in *Studi in onore di Luisa Banti,* Rome 1965, pp. 223–39. The Phaistos 'Neolithic' may be partly or wholly contemporary with Early Minoan at Knossos, as noted by J. D. Evans, *BSA* 63, 1968, p. 276, citing Pernier.

4 F. B. de la Roque, G. Contenau, F. Chapouthier, *Le Trésor de Tôd,* Cairo 1953. For lapis lazuli, G. Hermann and J. C. Payne, *Iraq* 30, 1968, pp. 21–61.

5 There is some confusion as to what should be understood as belonging to the earlier phase A and what to the later B of MM II, but the vases from the Royal Pottery Stores at Knossos, which were defined by Evans in *PM* I as MM II A, appear to be distinctly earlier than the material from the final destruction of the early palace at Phaistos. Evans saw this, and in *PM* I classified the pottery from the early palace at Phaistos available in his time as MM II B. He was not consistent, however, and in later volumes of *PM* he referred to the same material as MM II A. A. Zois, in a careful study of all the pottery from the early palace at Phaistos, including that recovered in excavations since 1950, also calls this material MM II A (**AE* 1965, pp. 27–109). But at Phaistos

there seems to be clear evidence for two distinct periods of building in the early palace (E. Fiandra, *Kr Kh* 1961–62, I, pp. 112–26). The pottery from the level of destruction, apparently due to an earth-quake, at the end of the first of these building periods (phase I b) seems comparable with that from the Royal Pottery Stores at Knossos, and assignable therefore to Middle Minoan II A. The great deposit of seal impressions (D. Levi, *Annuario* 35–36, 1957–58, pp. 7 ff.) appears to belong to this horizon. An earlier phase of occupation of which there are traces in the palace (phase I a) is assignable to Middle Minoan I B.

6 Octopus and palm tree motifs on vases of this period are discussed by P. Pellagatti, *Kr Kh* 1961–62, Vol. I, pp. 99–111.

7 A date well after 2000 BC for the beginning of the Middle Minoan period is argued by P. Aström, *The Middle Cypriote Bronze Age,* Lund 1957, and New Evidence for Middle Minoan Chronology, *Acts of the Second Cretological Congress,* Vol. I, Athens 1967, pp. 120–7.

8 For the evidence from Tholos B at Platanos see K. Branigan, *Studi micenei* 5, 1968, pp. 12–30 and V. E. G. Kenna, *AJA* 72, 1968, pp. 321–36.

9 The date given by Evans for the deposit with the lid of Khian is challenged by Palmer, *The Penultimate Palace of Knossos,* 1969, pp. 53–8. Cf. Nestor 1. v. 1964, pp. 323–5, and 1. viii. 1964 pp. 342–3 for a defence of Evans's date by S. Hood.

CHAPTER V

1 For Crete and the Levant as being within the same zone of the most favourable Mediterranean climates see K. W. Butzer, *CAH* rev ed. Vol. I, Ch II.

2 The views of R. P. Charles, *Anthropologie archéologique de la Crète,* Paris 1965, about immigration into Crete from the north in Early Minoan times seem improbable.

3 Caskey, *CAH* rev. ed. Vol. I, Ch. XXVI (*a*), p. 38, suggests a flow of refugees there from the Peloponnese at the end of Early Helladic II.

4 For the Lerna sealings, M. Heath, *Hesperia* 27, 1958, pp. 81–121. The problem of comparisons with Cretan seals is discussed by *A. Sakellariou-Xenakis, *Kr Kh* 1961–1962, Vol. I, pp. 79–87.

5 Both at Knossos and at Phaistos there are deposits of pottery that appear to reflect destructions in MM II A and MM II B (see note 5 Chapter IV). What has been called phase 3 of the early palace at Phaistos, marked by deposits of pottery assignable to MM III A really seems to be an early phase of the later palace (*N. Platon, *AE* 1968, pp. 1–58). The later palace at Phaistos was destroyed in LM I B *c.* 1450 BC.

6 For the palace at Monastiraki see Matz, *Forschungen auf Kreta,* 1951, pp. 27 ff. But some of the rooms assigned to the palace may have belonged to houses in the town round it.

7 For Luwians in Crete see Huxley, *Crete and the Luwians,* 1961, and Palmer, *Mycenaeans and Minoans,* 1965. Criticized by G. E. Mylonas, *Hesperia* 31, 1962, pp. 284–309, and F. Schachermeyr, *Kadmos* 1, 1962, pp. 27–39.

8 The later palace at Mallia may be to a large extent a survival of the early palace there as noted by E. Chapouthier and P. Demargne, *Études Crétoises* XII, 1962.

9 J. W. Graham in E. L. Bennett, *Mycenaean Studies,* Madison 1964, pp. 195–215, offers some strong arguments against a derivation of the Cretan palaces from the Anatolian ones.

10 Cretan colonies overseas are listed by P. Warren, *PPS* 33, 1967, pp. 37–56. That at Ayia Irini on Kea was apparently founded back in MM III A.

11 Huxley, *Crete and the Luwians,* 1961, p. 16.

12 Recent work in the Bronze Age settlement near Akrotiri on Thera is described by S. Marinatos, *Excavations at Thera. First* and *Second Preliminary Reports,* Athens 1968, 1969.

13 The theory of an eruption with long intervals between the different phases, based upon observations by Fouqué (1879) and Reck (1936), was outlined by D. Ninkovich and B. C. Heezen, *Santorini Tephra,* reprinted from Vol. XVII of the *Colston Papers,* London 1965. Cf. J. V. Luce, *The End of Atlantis. New Light on an Old Legend,* London 1969, and A. G. Galanopoulos and E. Bacon, *Atlantis: the Truth behind the Legend,* London 1969, both informative and well illustrated; D. L. Page, *The Santorini Volcano and the destruction of Minoan Crete,* London 1970; L. Pomerance, *The Final Collapse of Santorini (Thera),* Göteborg 1970. But most of the volcano experts at the International Scientific Congress held on Thera in September, 1969, seemed to oppose the idea of a long gap between the different stages of the eruption, and they rejected the samples of what had been thought to be volcanic 'bombs' from the ruins of the palace at Zakro (B. C. Heezen, A Time Clock for History, *Saturday Review,* Dec. 6, 1969, pp. 87–90).

14 **PAE* 1950, p. 249 figs 10–11.

15 The LM I A votive deposit at Nirou Khani was reported by *N. Platon, *Kr Kh* 1954, pp. 449–50. Cf. I. Tzedakis, Pumice from Khania, *AAA* 1, 1968, pp. 313–4, for a possible survival of cult inspired by the eruption of Thera into LM III times.

16 For tholos tombs and their origin see S. Hood, *Antiquity* 34, 1960, pp. 166–76.

17 There has been much confusion in the past about the LM I B horizon of destruction in Crete. The most distinctive LM I B pottery was for many years classified with that of the succeeding period, LM II. Gradually, however, the characteristics of LM I B pottery came to be recognised and distinguished from those of LM II and LM I A wares. But until a few years ago the comparative scarcity of LM I B deposits at Knossos itself made it possible to equate the LM I B destruction horizon in the rest of Crete with that of the final destruction of the Knossian palace early in LM III which took place half a century or more later (see Appendix, p. 149).

18 Evidence for destruction in LM I B at Knossos: 1, some LM I B pottery from the Court of the Stone Spout suggests damage or rebuilding in that part of the palace then. 2, the South House on the edge of the palace area was apparently destroyed in LM I B and never afterwards rebuilt (M. Popham, *BSA* 62, 1967, p. 341 note 14). 3, a building on the Royal Road was destroyed by fire in LM I B (S. Hood, *AR 1961–62,* pp. 25–9).

19 For the house of mainland type at Gournia see F. Oelmann, Ein achäisches Herrenhaus auf Kreta, *Jahrbuch* 27, 1912, pp. 38–51.

20 N. Coldstream, The Thera Eruption: some thoughts on the survivors, *LIMS*, Feb. 19, 1969.

CHAPTER VI

1 P. Warren, *ILN* Feb. 17, 1968, pp. 25–7; Feb. 8, 1969, pp. 26–7.

2 K. Branigan, *Kadmos* 8, 1969, p. 3, notes the possibility that this building with a curved wall may have been a shrine.

3 The palatial building at Vasiliki may have had a central court according to Branigan, *The Foundations of Palatial Crete,* 1969, p. 44; but it seems doubtful if there was room on the small hilltop for this.

4 O. Pelon, *BCH* 90, 1966, pp. 552–85.

5 See the *Bibliography* under D. Sites for Tylissos House A.

6 For the capacity of the West Magazines at Knossos, J. W. Graham, *Gnomon* 1964, p. 622 note 1, correcting his own previous estimate.

7 Minoan locks are discussed by Graham, *The Palaces of Crete,* 1962, pp. 173–9.

8 For the copper smelting furnace at Phaistos and its date, D. Levi, *Bol. d'Arte* 1951, p. 5.

9 The length of the Minoan foot was calculated by J. W. Graham, *AJA* 64, 1960, pp. 335–41. Cf. *Acts of the Second Cretological Congress* Vol. I, Athens 1967, pp. 159–65.

10 See Graham, *The Palaces of Crete,* 1962.

11 What may be the ornamented stone abacus of a capital was recovered from the porch of the megaron of the palace at Mycenae (H. Plommer, *BSA* 60, 1965, pp. 207–11).

12 For woods used, see S. Marinatos, *AA* 1935, pp. 254–5.

13 For an early painted floor at Phaistos, D. Levi, *Bol. d'Arte* 1955, p. 148 fig. 6.

14 The 'Saffron Gatherer' was restored as a monkey by *N. Platon, *Kr Kh* 1947, pp. 505–24; 1960, p. 504. M. Cameron suggests a later dating for this fresco. Cf. G. Rodenwaldt, *Der Fries des Megarons von Mykenai,* Halle 1921, p. 9 and note 22.

15 The painted floor at Ayia Triadha is described by L. Banti, *Annuario* 3–4, 1941–43, pp. 31 ff.

16 An unpublished fragment of a relief fresco found at Knossos during the excavations by the British School of Archaeology from 1957–61 appears to be of MM II B date.

17 Paints used on the Ayia Triadha sarcophagus are listed by D. Levi, *Archaeology* 9, 1956, pp. 192–9.

18 For the House of the Frescoes at Knossos see now M. Cameron, *BSA* 63, 1968, pp. 1–31.

19 Graham, *The Palaces of Crete,* 1962, Ch. XIII.

20 For chairs and stools, *N. Platon, *Kr Kh* 1951, pp. 385–412. The ivory decoration from a foot-stool has been reported by I. Sakellarakis from Arkhanes (*CIM* pp. 245–61).

CHAPTER VII

1 R. P. Charles, *Anthropologie archéologique de la Crète,* Paris 1965, discusses the physical remains of Bronze Age Cretans and has a good summary of earlier work in this field although reaching some highly improbable conclusions. For skeletons from Ailias see J. C. Trevor in Hutchinson, *Prehistoric Crete,* 1962, pp. 58–64.

2 The economy of the Mallia region is discussed in *Études Crétoises* XIII, 1963, Ch. III.

3 For remains of fruits and plants from various sites see S. Marinatos, *AA* 1935, pp. 254–5.

4 For the 'plough sign' in the earliest Cretan script see Evans, *Scripta Minoa* I, 1909, p. 190

No. 27; but is it really a crude version of No. 28, the distaff with spindle?

5 Tools: J. Deshayes, *Les Outils de Bronze, de l'Indus au Danube (IVe–IIe millénaire)*, Paris 1960. For tools in the Late Bronze Age see G. F. Bass, *Cape Gelidonya: a Bronze Age Shipwreck,* Philadelphia 1967, pp. 87 ff., and H. W. Catling, *Cypriot Bronzework in the Mycenaean World,* Oxford 1964.

6 Oval and circular shaft holes in double axes are listed by S. Piggott, *PPS* 19, 1953, pp. 224–6.

7 The scene on the Harvester Vase from Ayia Triadha is interpreted as a sowing festival by J. Forsdyke, *Journal of the Warburg and Courtauld Institutes* 17, 1954, pp. 1–9.

8 For the Mallia granaries see Graham, *The Palaces of Crete,* 1962 pp. 134–5.

9 The hypogaea at Knossos were described by Evans, *PM* I, pp. 104–7. Compare the great storage pit at Megiddo, R. S. Lamon and G. M. Shipton, *Megiddo* I, Chicago 1939, p. 66 fig. 77, although this dates from the eighth–seventh century BC. Wide pits with stairways down to springs are also found in Syria and Palestine, e.g. R. S. Lamon, *The Megiddo Water System,* Chicago 1935.

10 Grape pips: Fournou Korifi, *ILN* Feb. 8, 1969, p. 27; Phaistos, *Bol. d'Arte* 1956, p. 254 and note 29; Monastiraki, Matz, *Forschungen auf Kreta,* 1951, p. 38.

11 Vercoutter, *Essai sur les Relations*, 1954, p. 88.

12 See in general, F. E. Zeuner, *A History of Domesticated Animals,* London 1963.

13 For sheep and goats, S. Payne, *PPS* 34, 1968, pp. 368–84.

14 Cattle: C. Keller who reported on animal bones from Tylissos (*AE* 1912, pp. 231–2) distinguished two breeds there at the beginning of the Late Minoan period *c.* 1500 BC; one descended from *Bos primigenius* with long horns, the other a short-horned variety akin to the cattle of the Swiss lake villages which he had also studied. But the existence of this second breed in Crete seems dubious.

15 For bull-leaping see Evans, *PM* III pp. 203 ff. Cf. J. D. Evans, Cretan Cattle-Cults and Sports, *Royal Anthropological Institute, Occasional Paper* No. 18, 1963, pp. 138–43. A. Ward, The Cretan Bull Sports, *Antiquity* 42, 1968, pp. 117–22, agrees with Graham that the bull-leaping took place in the central courts of the palaces. Some objections to this view are noted by S. Hood, *AJA* 58, 1964, p. 309.

16 Fossilized monkey's head (?) from Thera in Galanopoulos and Bacon, *Atlantis,* 1969, p. 153; or is it a natural stone?

17 Partridges are discussed by Evans, *PM* II, pp. 112 ff. Lithgow, *Rare Adventures,* 1906, p. 84, describes them as being kept like chickens on some of the Greek islands in the early seventeenth century AD.

18 For chickens in Egypt and the Levant see Smith, *Interconnections,* 1965, p. 29. Chicken bones from the Trapeza Cave are noted in *BSA* 36, 1935–36, p. 131. The vase from Ayia Triadha is illustrated by Zervos, *L'Art de la Crète,* 1956, No. 184. Chickens on the Greek mainland in Middle and Late Helladic times, J. L. Caskey, AJA 72, 1968, p. 316, and E. Vermeule, *Greece in the Bronze Age,* Chicago 1964, p. 204 fig. 50a.

19 For edible snails from Crete in Thera, S. Marinatos, *AAA* 1, 1968, p. 220 fig. 12; *Excavations at Thera* II, Athens 1969, p. 52 fig. 41.

20 Sponge-diving in Cretan waters was described by Spratt, *Travels and Researches,* 1865, Vol. I Ch. XX. W. Arndt, *Sitzungsberichte der Gesellschaft naturforschender Freunde,* Oct. 26, 1935, pp. 182–92, denied the use of sponges for making the patterns claimed by Evans.

21 For varieties of loom weights see *BSA* 60, 1965, pp. 304–5 fig. 19, from Palaikastro.

22 The Knossos Sheep Tablets: J. T. Killen, The Wool Industry of Crete in the Late Bronze Age, *BSA* 59, 1964, pp. 1–15. Criticisms by D. Young, *Kadmos* 4, 1965, pp. 111–22; 8, 1969, pp. 39–42. Reply by Killen, *Kadmos* 7, 1969, pp. 105–23, and 8, 1969, pp. 23–38.

23 Coan silk is discussed by F. E. Zeuner, *A History of Domesticated Animals,* London 1963, pp. 487–8.

24 Dress in general: Evans, *PM,* and S. Marinatos, Kleidung; Haar-und Barttracht, *Archaeologia Homerica* Bd I, A, B. For male dress, *E. Sakellarakis, *Minoikon Zoma,* shortly to be published.

25 Aegean embassies in Egypt: Vercoutter, *Essai sur les Relations,* 1954, and *L'Égypte et le Monde égéen,* 1956. F. Schachermeyer, Das Keftiou—Problem, *Jahreshefte des Österreichischen arch. Inst. Wien* 45, 1960, pp. 44–68.

26 The fresco from Pylos with a man wearing the short stiff kilt is among the earliest of those found there according to M. L. Lang, *The Palace of Nestor* Vol. 2: *The Frescoes,* Princeton 1969, p. 77, 36. H. 105.

27 Embroidery was known in Egypt in the time of Dynasty XVIII; but the use of it in the Aegean area is disputed, e.g., S. Marinatos, *Archaeologia Homerica* I A, p. 16, with references.

28 For the pedigree of the ivory seal with the girl in a short frock see M. A. Gill, *Kadmos* 6, 1967, pp. 114–8; but V. E. G. Kenna, *Kadmos* 7, 1968, pp. 175–6, may be right in doubting its authenticity.

29 Dress pins in the Bronze Age are discussed in *BSA* 63, 1968, p. 214.

30 For Syrian toggle pins with perforated swellings see E. Henschel-Simon, *Quarterly of the Dept. of Antiquities in Palestine* 6, 1938, pp. 169–70. One from Palaikastro in East Crete is surmounted by a dog wearing a collar (*BSA Suppl.* I, 1923, p. 121 fig. 101).

31 For uses of conical stone spindle whorls see *BSA* 53–54, 1958–59, p. 246, IV. 2.

32 The 'Aigina treasure' was recognised to be Minoan by R. A. Higgins, *BSA* 52, 1957, pp. 42–57.

33 For techniques of jewellery, Higgins, *Minoan and Mycenaean Art,* 1967. Even the art of making 'Sheffield Plate' was practised in Crete by c. 1700 BC if J. A. Charles is right (*Antiquity* 42, 1968, pp. 278–85, and K. Branigan *ibid.* 43, 1969, pp. 137–8 for the date).

CHAPTER VIII

1 See *Bibliography* and various articles by P. Warren, The First Minoan Stone Vases and Early Minoan Chronology, *Kr Kh* 1965, pp. 7–43; Minoan Stone Vases as Evidence for Minoan Foreign Connexions in the Aegean Late Bronze Age, *PPS* 1967, pp. 37–56; and A Stone Vase-Maker's Workshop in the Palace at Knossos, *BSA* 62, 1967, pp. 195–201.

2 K. Branigan, *Copper and Bronze Working in Early Bronze Age Crete,* Lund 1968. P. Faure, Les minerais de la Crète antique,

Revue archéologique 1966, pp. 45–78.

3 Ingots: G. F. Bass, *Cape Gelidonya,* Philadelphia 1967, pp. 52 ff., with references to the basic work of H.-G. Buchholz.

4 Glass vases from Bronze Age Crete: G. Weinberg, *Kr Kh* 1961–62, I, pp. 226–9.

5 Stone heads: from Knossos, Hutchinson, *Prehistoric Crete,* 1962, pp. 166–9; and Mirtos, *BSA* 59, 1964, p. 94.

6 The evidence for large wooden statues is discussed by Evans, *PM* III, pp. 522–5.

7 See *Bibliography.* For cylinder seals, V. E. G. Kenna, Ancient Crete and the Use of the Cylinder Seal, *AJA* 72, 1968, pp. 321–36. Cf. H.-G. Buchholz, in G. F. Bass, *Cape Gelidonya,* Philadelphia 1967, pp. 148–59.

8 H. C. Beck, Early Magnifying Glasses, *Antiquaries Journal* 8, 1928, pp. 327–30.

9 See *Bibliography.* For marks on EM II vases, K. Branigan, *Kadmos* 8, 1969, pp. 1–22. Similar marks were painted on the bases of EM II goblets from Knossos.

10 Grumach, *Die kretischen Schriftsysteme,* 1969, pp. 256 ff., discusses similarities between the Cretan scripts and Hittite hieroglyphic, suggesting that some early pictographic script in the region south and south-west of the Taurus mountains may have been the bridge between them. Cf. W. Brice, *LIMS,* Feb. 1, 1967, for the concept of a group of fundamentally *ideographic* scripts which once stretched from the Indus to the Aegean. M. Pope, *Antiquity* 40, 1966, pp. 17–23, offers a picture of linear and basically *syllabic* scripts around the cuneiform area, sharing a common origin but eventually diverging from one another.

11 Graffiti on walls, M. Cameron, *Kadmos* 4, 1965, pp. 7–15.

12 For the find-places of the Linear B tablets of Knossos see Palmer, *On the Knossos Tablets,* 1963, pp. 8 ff., and J.-P. Olivier, *Les Scribes de Knossos,* Rome 1967.

13 For inscriptions from western Crete see I. Tzedakis, *Kadmos* 6, 1967, pp. 106–9. Storage stirrup jars with painted inscriptions found at Thebes on the mainland may have been exported from eastern Crete according to H. W. Catling and A. Millett, A Study of the Inscribed Stirrup-jars from Thebes, *Archaeometry* 8, 1965, pp. 3–85, and *ibid.* 9, 1966, pp. 92–7; 11, 1969, pp. 3–20, for replies to critics.

14 Changes in the way of representing fractions between Linear A and B are described by E. L. Bennett, Fractional Quantities in Minoan Bookkeeping, *AJA* 54, 1950, pp. 204–22.

15 E. Grumach, Theben und das Alter von Linear B, *Kadmos* 4, 1965, pp. 45–57, suggested the possibility that the Linear B script was evolved at Knossos before the end of LM I B; although the few inscriptions from Knossos assignable with certainty to LM I B are more akin to Linear A. According to another theory the Linear B script developed in some region of the mainland where Linear A was already in use (e.g. J. T. Hooker, The Beginnings of Linear B, and S. Marinatos, The 'Volcanic' Origin of Linear B, in *Europa. Festschrift für Ernst Grumach,* Berlin 1967, pp. 132–42, and pp. 204–10). But no Linear A clay tablets have yet been recovered on the mainland, although short inscriptions akin to Linear A are known there (e.g. E. Grumach, Linear A auf dem Festland, *Kadmos* 1, 1962, pp. 85–6. E. Vermeule, *Greece in the Bronze Age,* Chicago 1964, p. 238).

16 Sceptics of the decipherment are listed by Grumach, *Die kretischen Schriftsysteme,* 1969, p. 264 note 1. Cf. **Epistimoniki Epetiris Filosofikis Skholis Thessalonikis* 1965, pp. 297–9. Among sceptics who originally accepted the decipherment is G. Klaffenbach, *Griechische Epigraphik* 2, Göttingen 1966, pp. 30–1. But like several others who are doubtful about the decipherment Klaffenbach believes the language of the Linear B tablets to be an early form of Greek.

17 In a remarkable article written before the Second World War Ventris suggested that the Linear B language was akin to Etruscan (*AJA* 44, 1940, pp. 494–520).

18 G. E. Mylonas, *Hesperia* 31, 1962, pp. 284–6, records the fact that even before the decipherment was announced in 1952 many archaeologists thought the language of the Linear B tablets was Greek. Mylonas himself had already urged Ventris to try for a Greek solution in the autumn of 1951 (*Archaeology* 9, 1956, p. 275).

19 Ventris published the first account of the decipherment in *The Listener* for 10 July, 1952, pp. 57–8.

20 The shift made by Ventris from assuming a non-Greek to trying for a Greek solution is investigated by Geiss, *Klio* 48, 1967, pp. 5–51, and in an important but technical article by F. R. Richards, Reflections on Ventris's Work Note 1, *Europa. Festschrift für Ernst Grumach,* Berlin 1967, pp. 257–76.

21 There has been much discussion among adherents of the decipherment as to how the 'Mycenaean' language obtained by it from the Linear B tablets relates to the historic Greek dialects. At one extreme it is regarded as an early form of East Greek (e.g. Chadwick, *CAH* rev. ed. Vol. II, Ch. XXXIX); at the other it is thought to have little or no connection with any later Greek dialect (e.g. F. Hampl, *Museum Helveticum* 17, 1960, pp. 57–86).

The decipherment assumes that all the signs of the Linear B script apart from the obvious ideograms are syllabic. Adherents of the decipherment have tended to believe that the earlier scripts were also essentially syllabic in character, while sceptics like E. Grumach and W. Brice have argued for a large measure of non-syllabic elements in them and even in Linear B.

Adherents of the decipherment have transferred the values postulated by it for the Linear B signs to what appear to be their equivalents in Linear A in an attempt to discover the language or languages of the Linear A tablets. One result of this study has been to suggest that many words or proper names are virtually identical in Linear A and B. The implication is that the language of the Linear A tablets, if not the same as that of the Linear B ones, may share elements of the same language with them (e.g. G. Nagy, Observations on the Sign-Grouping and Vocabulary of Linear A, *AJA* 69, 1965, pp. 295–330).

The Linear A language has also been deciphered as akin to Hittite (S. Davis, *Decipherment of the Minoan Linear A,* Johannesburg 1967), or as a variety of North West Semitic (C. H. Gordon, *Evidence for the Minoan Language,* Ventor 1966).

CHAPTER IX

1 For the palaces as centres of exchange see Schachermeyr, *Ägäis und Orient,* 1967. Shops in Bronze Age Crete: at Mallia, *Études*

Crétoises XI, 1959, p. 38, and Palaikastro, *BSA* 9, 1902–3, p. 292, Rooms 37–38. Royal control of foreign trade is emphasized by *S. Alexiou, *AE* 1953–54, pp. 135–45.

2 The existence of a council chamber at Mallia has been inferred by H. van Effenterre, Mallia 1956–65: Dix années de Nonconformisme, *Archeologia* 1966, pp. 60–5. Cf. *Études Crétoises* XVII, 1969. For councils in early Mesopotamia see C. J. Gadd, *CAH* rev. ed. Vol. I, Ch. XIII, p. 15.

3 For the throne at Knossos as that of Ariadne see H. Reusch, Zum Wandschmuck des Thronsaales in Knossos, in *Minoica: Festschrift zum 80 Geburtstag von J. Sundwall,* Berlin 1958, pp. 334–58.

4 Matriarchy in Crete is emphasized by J. Hawkes, *Dawn of the Gods,* 1958, and G. Thomson, *Studies in Ancient Greek Society: The Prehistoric Aegean,* London 1949.

5 Defence wall at Mallia, J. Deshayes and A. Dessenne, *Études Crétoises* XI, 1959, pp. 4–5. S. Hood, *Gnomon* 33, 1961, p. 827.

6 For the Siege Vase see J. H. Hooker, *AJA* 71, 1967, pp. 269–81.

7 Earlier Cretan weapons are listed by K. Branigan, *Copper and Bronze Working in Early Bronze Age Crete,* Lund 1968. Cf. *BSA* 62, 1967, pp. 211–39; 63, 1968, pp. 185–203. But the dating of most of these weapons is very uncertain except within wide limits. For later weapons see N. K. Sandars, The First Aegean Swords and Their Ancestry, and Later Aegean Swords, *AJA* 65, 1961, pp. 17–29; 67, 1963, pp. 117–53.

8 A northern origin for Type II slashing swords is strongly urged by J. D. Cowen, The Origin of the Flange-hilted Sword of Bronze in Continental Europe, *PPS* 32, 1966, pp. 262–312. But A. Snodgrass, *Early Greek Armour and Weapons,* Edinburgh 1964, pp. 93 ff., has reservations. Cf. H. W. Catling, *BSA* 63, 1968, pp. 95–104, and earlier articles in *PPS* 22, 1956, pp. 102 ff., and *Antiquity* 35, 1961, pp. 115 ff. Much depends on whether the beginning of phase D of the Bronze Age in Central Europe, when swords of this type first appear there, is dated *c.* 1300 BC or *c.* 1200 BC.

9 A man armed with a double axe and sword combats a centaur on an Archaic stamped pithos from Rhodes (*BCH* 74, 1950, p. 160, fig. 14).

10 For the Dendra armour see N. M. Verdelis, *AM* 82, 1967, pp. 1–53, and for the date of the tomb, P. Åström, *ibid,* pp. 54–67.

11 Helmets and remains of armour in Bronze Age Crete, *BSA* 47, 1952, pp. 256 ff.

12 Stone 'gaming tables' are discussed by H. van Effenterre, Cupules et Naumachie, *BCH* 79, 1955, pp. 541–8.

13 The men that seem to fit the Knossos draughtboard come from an earlier deposit, if Evans, *PM* I, p. 477, is right.

14 D. Levi, *Annuario* 14–16, 1952–54, p. 408.

15 *S. Alexiou, *Isterominoikoi Tafoi Limenos Knosou,* Athens 1967, pp. 39, 58.

16 Kantor, *The Aegean and the Orient,* 1947. Schachermeyr, *Ägäis und Orient,* 1967. P. Warren, *PPS* 33, 1967, pp. 37–56 for the export of Cretan stone vases.

17 K. Branigan, Prehistoric Relations between Italy and the Aegean, *Bull. di Paletnologia Italiana* 75, 1966, pp. 97–109; but the evidence seems inconclusive.

18 For the obsidian trade see C. Renfrew, J. R. Cann and J. E. Dixon, *BSA* 60, 1965, pp. 225–47.

19 *Études Crétoises* XI, 1959, pp. 76 ff. For sphinxes in general, A. Dessenne, *Le Sphinx,* Paris 1957.

20 Seager, Mochlos, 1912, pp. 22, 111, for the silver cylinder seal, which V. E. G. Kenna, *AJA* 72, 1968, pp. 322–4, suggests may be early Sargonid datable *c.* 2300 BC; but on the assumption that the context in which it was found was EM II, and that it cannot therefore be much later in date! As Kenna notes, this would be the only Mesopotamian cylinder seal of solid silver yet known!

21 Cypriot vases in Crete are listed by M. Popham, *BSA* 58, 1963, pp. 89–93. See H. Catling and V. Karageorghis, Minoica in Cyprus, *BSA* 55, 1960, pp. 109–27, for Cretan exports there. Some of the daggers are regarded as Syrian by K. Branigan, Byblite daggers in Cyprus and Crete, *AJA* 70, 1966, pp. 123–6.

22 S. Marinatos, La Marine créto-mycénienne, *BCH* 57, 1933, pp. 170–235, is still basic. For additions see C. Renfrew, *AJA* 71, 1967, p. 5. G. F. Bass, *Cape Gelidonya,* Philadelphia 1967, pp. 44–51, describes the scanty remains of an actual ship. J. S. Morrison and R. T. Williams, *Greek Oared Ships, 900–322* BC, Cambridge 1968, discuss mainland representations of Bronze Age vessels, but ignore Cretan ones as non-Greek!

23 For anchors, H. Frost, in *Ugaritica* VI, Paris 1969, pp. 235–45.

24 For some roads in Messenia and Crete assignable to the Bronze Age see W. A. McDonald and R. Hope Simpson, *AJA* 68, 1964, pp. 240–2.

25 Horse-like creatures on early Cretan seals, Kenna, *Cretan Seals,* 1960, p. 94 No. 50, and p. 28 note 5 for seals in the shape of horses' heads. J. Sakellarakis has shown me what seem to be well-drawn horses on the large ivory amulet found by him at Arkhanes (*Archaeology* 20, 1967, p. 277 fig. 6. *Corpus der min. und myk. Siegel* II. 1 Nr. 391). J. L. Caskey, *AJA* 72, 1968, p. 316, reports bones of horses from Middle Helladic levels at Lerna on the mainland.

26 For riding in the Bronze Age see S. Hood, A Mycenaean Cavalryman, *BSA* 48, 1953, pp. 84–93. J. Wiesner, Fahren und Reiten, *Archaeologia Homerica* Bd I, F, 1968, has a very full discussion with exhaustive references for both riding and chariots. For chariots see also H. W. Catling, *AJA* 72, 1968, pp. 41–9.

CHAPTER X

1 'Sheep-bells': N. Platon, *Revue archéologique* 31–32, 1948, pp. 833–46.

2 For the tomb of Zeus, A. B. Cook, *Zeus* I, Cambridge 1914, pp. 157 f. Cretans as liars, *N. T. Titus* 1. 12. Cf. Callimachus, *Hymn to Zeus,* lines 8–9.

3 F. Matz, *Göttererscheinung und Kultbild im minoischen Kreta,* Mainz 1958, argues against the existence of early cult statues in Crete, although gods and goddesses might be represented in human form. His views are criticized by D. Levi, *La Parola del Passato* 68, 1959, pp. 377–91; 73, 1960, pp. 297–300.

4 For Minoan 'genii' and dragons see M. A. V. Gill, *AJA* 79, 1964, pp. 1–21; *London Institute of Classical Studies Bulletin* No. 10, 1963, pp. 1–12.

5 Horns of Consecration are discussed by Nilsson, *The Minoan-Mycenaean Religion,* 1950, pp. 165 ff. A derivation from

Anatolian cooking hearths is suggested by S. Diamant and J. Rutter, *Anatolian Studies* 19, 1969, pp. 147–77.

6 For the shrine at Rousses see *BSA* 59, 1964, pp. 81–2, with references.

7 Peak sanctuaries: P. Faure, *BCH* 87, 1963, pp. 493–508; 91, 1967, pp. 114–50; 93, 1969, pp. 174–213. *N. Platon, *Kr Kh* 1951, pp. 96–160. B. Rutkowski, The Decline of the Minoan Peak Sanctuaries, *CIM* 1967, Vol. I, pp. 163–8.

8 Flag poles at shrines, *S. Alexiou, *Kr Kh* 17, 1963, pp. 339–51, and *AAA* 2, 1969, pp. 84–8.

9 Pillar crypts, mostly in palaces and houses, are treated by *N. Platon, *Kr Kh* 1954, pp. 428–83.

10 N. Coldstream, A Figured Geometric Oinochoe from Italy, *London Institute of Classical Studies Bulletin* No. 15, 1968, pp. 86–96, discusses what may be a representation of the sacred Crane Dance of Delos, said to be of Cretan origin, with women in a version of the old Minoan court dress.

11 For swinging see C. Delvoye, Rites de Fécondité dans les Religions préhelléniques, *BCH* 70, 1946, pp. 120–31, and S. Marinatos, *Journal of the Australian Society for Classical Studies* 2, 1968, pp. 1–14.

12 For clay coffins see B. Rutkowski, The Origin of the Minoan Coffin, *BSA* 63, 1968, pp. 219–27.

13 *A. Lebesis, *PAE* 1967, pp. 195–209.

14 Circular tombs: at Knossos, *AR 1957*, pp. 22–3; Krasi, *S. Marinatos, *A Delt* 12, 1929, pp. 102–41; Apesokari, Matz, *Forschungen auf Kreta,* 1951, pp. 13–22.

15 For the Arkhanes burial complex, J. A. Sakellarakis, Minoan Cemeteries at Arkhanes, *Archaeology* 20, 1967, pp. 276–81.

16 Evans, *PM* IV, pp. 962 ff.

17 P. Demargne, *Études Crétoises* VII, 1945.

18 The Kefala tholos tomb was published by R. W. Hutchinson, *BSA* 51, 1956, pp. 74–80. For a late re-use of the tomb, G. Cadogan, *BSA* 62, 1967, pp. 257–65.

The Isopata Royal Tomb was described by A. J. Evans, The *Prehistoric Tombs of Knossos,* London 1906, which also gives an account of a typical cemetery of the period after *c.* 1450 BC.

CHAPTER XI

1 For the end of the Bronze Age in the Aegean see V. Desborough, *The Last Mycenaeans and their Successors,* Oxford 1964. An acceptance of the decipherment of Linear B as Greek is here implicit, together with a belief that there were Greeks in Crete well before *c.* 1200 BC.

Bibliography

ABBREVIATIONS

**Titles in modern Greek marked with an asterisk*

AAA	*Athens Annals of Archaeology*
ADelt	**Arkhaiologikon Dheltion*
AE	**Arkhaiologiki Efimeris*
AJA	*American Journal of Archaeology*
AM	*Mitteilungen des deutschen archäologischen Instituts, Athenische Abteilung*
Annuario	*Annuario della Regia Scuola Archeologica di Atene*
AR	*Archaeological Reports*
BCH	*Bulletin de Correspondance Hellénique*
Bol. d'Arte	*Bollettino d'Arte*
BSA	*Annual of the British School of Archaeology at Athens*
CAH	*Cambridge Ancient History, revised edition*
CIM	*Atti e Memorie del Primo Congresso Internazionale di Micenologia, Roma 1967, Rome 1968*
Ergon	**To Ergon tis Arkhaiologikis Etairias*
ILN	*The Illustrated London News*
Jahrbuch	*Jahrbuch des deutschen archäologischen Instituts*
JHS	*Journal of Hellenic Studies*
Kr Kh	**Kritika Khronika*
LIMS	*Minutes of the Mycenaean Seminar of the London University Institute of Classical Studies*
PAE	**Praktika tis Arkhaiologikis Etairias*
PM	EVANS, A. J., *The Palace of Minos at Knossos*
PPS	*Proceedings of the Prehistoric Society*

A GENERAL WORKS

Basic for all aspects of the Cretan Bronze Age

EVANS, A. J., *The Palace of Minos at Knossos* I–IV with Index Volume, London 1921–36. Reprinted 1964. The Index Volume (1936) often clarifies the latest views of Evans.

Other general works in alphabetical order

ALEXIOU, S., *Minoan Civilisation,* Herakleion 1969.

ALEXIOU, S., PLATON, N., and GUANELLA, H., *Ancient Crete,* London 1968.

BRANIGAN, K., *The Foundations of Palatial Crete,* London 1969, deals with the Early Minoan period, but includes much of considerably later date.

FAURE, P., *Fonctions des Cavernes Crétoises,* Paris 1964, for the caves of Crete and their uses.

HUTCHINSON, R. W., *Prehistoric Crete,* Harmondsworth 1962. An excellent and comprehensive survey, continuing the story of Crete into the Early Iron Age.

HUXLEY, G. L., *Crete and the Luwians,* Oxford 1961, for the problem of a Luwian invasion of Crete.

MATZ, F., Minoan Civilization: Maturity and Zenith, *CAH* rev. ed., Vol. II, Ch. IV (*b*) and XII, Cambridge 1962.

— *Forschungen auf Kreta, 1942,* Berlin 1951, for excavations during the German occupation of Crete in the Second World War.

PENDLEBURY, J. D. S., *The Archaeology of Crete,* London 1939. Reprinted New York 1963. Still invaluable.

PLATON, N., *Crete,* London 1966, has many pictures of his discoveries at Zakro.

SCHACHERMEYR, F., *Die minoische Kultur des alten Kreta,* Stuttgart 1964. An exhaustive and very well documented survey of the Minoan civilization.

WILLETTS, R. F., *Everyday Life in Ancient Crete,* London 1969, also deals with Crete in later Greek times.

ZERVOS, C., *L'Art de la Crète néolithique et minoenne,* Paris 1956. A very full collection of pictures of the archaeological sites and the material recovered from them.

Dealing with other parts of the Aegean area as well as Crete

ALSOP, J., *From the Silent Earth. A Report on the Greek Bronze Age,* New York etc. 1962. Minoan and Mycenaean civilization as interpreted by a modern political journalist.

Archaeologia Homerica, appearing in separate fascicules by different authors, published at Göttingen from 1967 onwards. Basically concerned with the archaeology of the Homeric poems, like Lorimer, but with much useful information about the Bronze Age in Crete.

CASKEY, J. L., *Greece, Crete and the Aegean Islands in the Early Bronze Age, CAH* rev. ed., Vol. I, Ch. XXVI (*a*).

DEMARGNE, P., *Aegean Art. The Origins of Greek Art,* London 1964.

HAWKES, J., *Dawn of the Gods,* London 1968.

HIGGINS, R., *Minoan and Mycenaean Art,* London 1967.

HOOD, S., *The Home of the Heroes: the Aegean before the Greeks,* London 1967.

LORIMER, H. L., *Homer and the Monuments,* London 1950, is still basic. But see now *Archaeologia Homerica* above.

MARINATOS, S., and HIRMER, M., *Crete and Mycenae,* London 1960, with very fine illustrations.

MATZ, F., *Crete and Early Greece,* London 1962.

PALMER, L. R., *Mycenaeans and Minoans,* second ed., London 1965.

The following books deal with connections between the Aegean and the high civilizations of Egypt and the Near East

KANTOR, H. J., *The Aegean and the Orient in the Second Millenium B.C.,* Bloomington 1947.

SCHACHERMEYR, F., *Agäis und Orient,* Vienna 1967.

SMITH, W. S., *Interconnections in the Ancient Near East; a study of the relationships between the arts of Egypt, the Aegean, and Western Asia,* Newhaven 1965.

VERCOUTTER, J., *Essai sur les relations entre Égyptiens et Préhellènes,* Paris 1954.

— *L'Egypte et le Monde égéen préhellénique,* Cairo 1956.

B SPECIAL STUDIES

Architecture

GRAHAM, J. W., *The Palaces of Crete,* Princeton 1962.

The Minoans

Chronology

Sections in most of the books listed under General Works

WEINBERG, S. S., in EHRICH, R. W., *Relative Chronologies in Old World Archaeology,* and *Chronologies in Old World Archaeology,* Chicago 1954, 1965.

Final destruction of the palace at Knossos (see Appendix p. 149).

PALMER, L. R., and BOARDMAN, J., *On the Knossos Tablets,* Oxford 1963, with references to the earlier literature.

HOOD, S., 'Last Palace' and 'Reoccupation' at Knossos, *Kadmos* 4, 1965, pp. 16–44

— Date of the 'Reoccupation' Pottery from the Palace of Minos at Knossos, *Kadmos* 5, 1966, pp. 121–41.

— The Last Palace at Knossos and the Date of its Destruction, *Studi Micenei* 2, 1967, pp. 63–70.

PALMER, L. R., *A New Guide to the Palace of Knossos,* London 1969.

— *The Penultimate Palace of Knossos,* Rome 1969.

POPHAM, M. R., *The Last Days of the Palace at Knossos,* Lund 1964.

— The Destruction of the Palace at Knossos and its Pottery, *Antiquity* 40, 1966, pp. 24–8.

Jewellery

HIGGINS, R. A., *Greek and Roman Jewellery,* London 1961.

Pottery

EVANS, *PM* remains basic.

FURUMARK, A., *The Mycenaean Pottery,* and *The Chronology of Mycenaean Pottery,* Stockholm 1941.

POPHAM, M. R., Late Minoan Pottery, A Summary, *BSA* 62, 1967, pp. 337–51. It corrects many long current misconceptions.

ZOIS, A. A., *Der Kamaresstil, Werden und Wesen,* Tübingen 1968, deals with Middle Minoan pottery, but has no illustrations.

Religion

EVANS, A. J., *The Mycenaean Tree and Pillar Cult,* London 1901, is still basic.

FARNELL, L. R., Cretan Influence in Greek Religion, in *Essays in Aegean Archaeology, presented to Sir A. Evans,* Oxford 1927, pp. 8–26.

NILSSON, M. P., *The Minoan-Mycenaean Religion,* second ed., Lund 1950, remains the standard work.

PERSSON, A. W., *The Religion of Greece in Prehistoric Times* (Sather Classical Lectures 17), Berkeley and Los Angeles 1942, for the interpretation of cult scenes on seals.

PICARD, C., *Les Religions préhelléniques,* Paris 1948.

Seals

EVANS, *PM,* has much to say about seals that is still pertinent.

BIESANTZ, H., *Kretisch-mykenische Siegelbilder,* Marburg 1954, with suggested criteria for distinguishing Cretan seals from those of mainland origin.

KENNA, V. E. G., *Cretan Seals,* Oxford 1960, with a catalogue of the unique collection of Minoan seals in the Ashmolean Museum.

MATZ, F., and BIESANTZ, H., (eds.), *Corpus der minoischen und mykenischen Siegel.*

XENAKI-SAKELLARIOU, A., *Les Cachets minoens de la Collection Giamalakis,* Paris 1958.

Stone Vases

WARREN, P., *Minoan Stone Vases,* Cambridge 1969.

Tombs and Burial Customs

PINI, I., *Beiträge zur minoischen Gräberkunde,* Wiesbaden 1968, with lists and references.

Writing and the Decipherment of Linear B

GRUMACH, E., *Die kretischen Schriftsysteme,* in HAUSMANN, U., *Handbuch der Archäologie: Allgemeine Grundlagen der Archäologie,* Munich 1969, pp. 234–67, gives an excellent up-to-date account of the whole subject.

For the actual texts see:

BRICE, W. C., *Inscriptions in the Minoan Linear Script of Class A,* Oxford 1961.

EVANS, A. J., *Scripta Minoa* I and II, Oxford 1909, 1952, for inscriptions in the early 'Hieroglyphic' script and in Linear B.

For references to all the literature on the subject until 1965 consult:

GRUMACH, E., *Bibliographie der kretisch-mykenischen Epigraphik,* and Supplement I, Munich 1963, 1967.

In favour of the Decipherment of Linear B as Greek (in chronological order)

VENTRIS, M., and CHADWICK, J., Evidence for Greek Dialect in the Mycenaean Archives, *JHS* 73, 1953, pp. 84–103. The original statement of the case for the decipherment.

— *Documents in Mycenaean Greek,* Cambridge 1956.

CHADWICK, J., *The Decipherment of Linear B,* Cambridge 1958.

— The Prehistory of the Greek Language, *CAH* rev. ed., Vol. II, Ch. XXXIX, Cambridge 1964.

Against the Decipherment (in chronological order)

BEATTIE, A. J., Mr. Ventris' Decipherment of the Minoan Linear B Script, *JHS* 76, 1956, pp. 1–17.

GRUMACH, E., Bemerkungen zu M. Ventris—J. Chadwick, Evidence for Greek dialect in the Mycenaean archives, *Orientalische Literatur-Zeitung* 52, 1957, pp. 293–342.

BEATTIE, A. J., A Plain Guide to the Ventris Decipherment of the Mycenaean Linear B Script, *Mitt. des Instituts für Orientforschung* 6, 1958, pp. 33–104.

YOUNG, D., Is Linear B Deciphered?, *Arion* 1965, pp. 512–42. A witty and informative review of LEVIN, S., *The Linear B Controversy Re-examined,* New York 1965. Levin himself accepts the principle of the decipherment, but with many reservations.

GEISS, H., Untersuchungen zur Ventrisschen Entzifferung, *Klio* 48, 1967, pp. 5–51.

C TRAVELLERS

PENDLEBURY, *The Archaeology of Crete,* 1939, pp. 16–9.

LITHGOW, W., *The Totall Discourse of the Rare Adventures and Painefull Peregrinations of long Nineteene Yeares Travayles from Scotland to the most famous kingdomes in Europe, Asia and Affrica,* London 1640 etc. Reprinted Glasgow 1906.

PASHLEY, R., *Travels in Crete,* London 1837.

SPRATT, T. A. B., *Travels and Researches in Crete,* London 1865.

D SITES

PENDLEBURY, *The Archaeology of Crete,* 1939, has full lists of sites with references for the period before the Second World War.

For more recent work and new discoveries, see the accounts published each year in *Archaeological Reports,* and in *Chronique des Fouilles* in *BCH;* also those (for the most part in modern Greek) in *AAA, ADelt, Ergon, Kr Kh,* amd *PAE.*

Gournia

HAWES, H. B., *Gournia, Vasiliki, and other Prehistoric Sites on the Isthmus of Hierapetra,* Philadelphia 1908.

Knossos

EVANS, *PM,* and annual reports of the early excavations in *BSA* from 1900–1905. For definitive reports of later work, see *BSA* from 1952 onwards.

For the topography, HOOD, S., *Archaeological Survey of the Knossos Area,* Oxford 1958, with references for cemeteries and tombs.

Mallia

Études Crétoises I, Paris 1928, and later volumes, together with reports in *BCH.*

Mochlos

SEAGER, R. B., *Explorations in the Island of Mochlos,* Boston and New York 1912, for the cemeteries; *AJA* 13, 1909, pp. 273–303 for the town.

Palaikastro

Excavations from 1902–1906. Annual reports in *BSA*, together with *BSA Supplementary Paper* No. 1, London 1923, and *BSA* 40, 1939–40, pp. 38–56, for the pottery and other finds.

Excavations in 1962 and 1963. *BSA* 60, 1965, pp. 248–315.

Phaistos

PERNIER, L., *Il Palazzo minoico di Festòs,* I. *Gli Strati piu Antichi e il Primo Palazzo,* Rome 1935.

PERNIER, L., and BANTI, L., II *Il Secondo Palazzo,* Rome 1951.

LEVI, D., *The Recent Excavations at Phaistos,* Lund 1964, and annual reports in *Annuario* or *Bol. d'Arte,* for work since 1950.

Problems of the First Palace are discussed by FIANDRA, E., *Kr Kh* 1961–62, I pp. 112–26, *PLATON, N., *AE* 1968, pp. 1–58, and *ZOIS, A., *AE* 1965, pp. 27–109. The views adopted here are taken from E. Fiandra.

Sklavokampos

*MARINATOS, S., *AE* 1939–41, pp. 69–96.

Tylissos

HAZZIDAKIS, J., *Les Villas minoennes de Tylissos,* Paris 1934, with references to earlier reports.

Vasiliki

See under *Gournia,* and in *Transactions of the Dept. of Archaeology of the University of Pennsylvania* I, 1905, pp. 207 ff., and II, 1906, pp. 111 ff.

Vathipetro

Reports by S. MARINATOS in **PAE* from 1949–1956.

Zakro

The original British excavations were published by D. G. HOGARTH, *BSA* 7, 1900–01, pp. 121–55.

For the newly discovered palace see accounts with illustrations in PLATON, *Crete,* 1966, and HIGGINS, *Minoan and Mycenaean Art,* 1967, ALEXIOU, *Ancient Crete,* 1968, besides annual reports in **Ergon,* **PAE,* **A Delt* etc. from 1961 onwards.

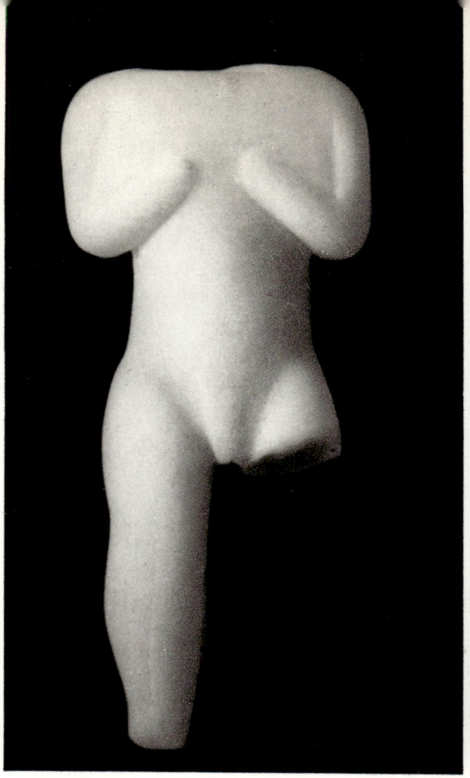
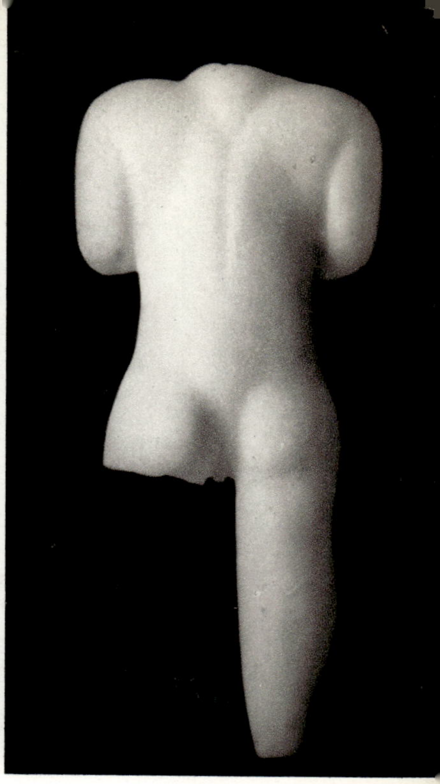

1, 2

3

4

5

6

7

8

9 , 10

12

11

13, 14

15

16

17

18

19

20

21

23

22

24

25, 26

27

28

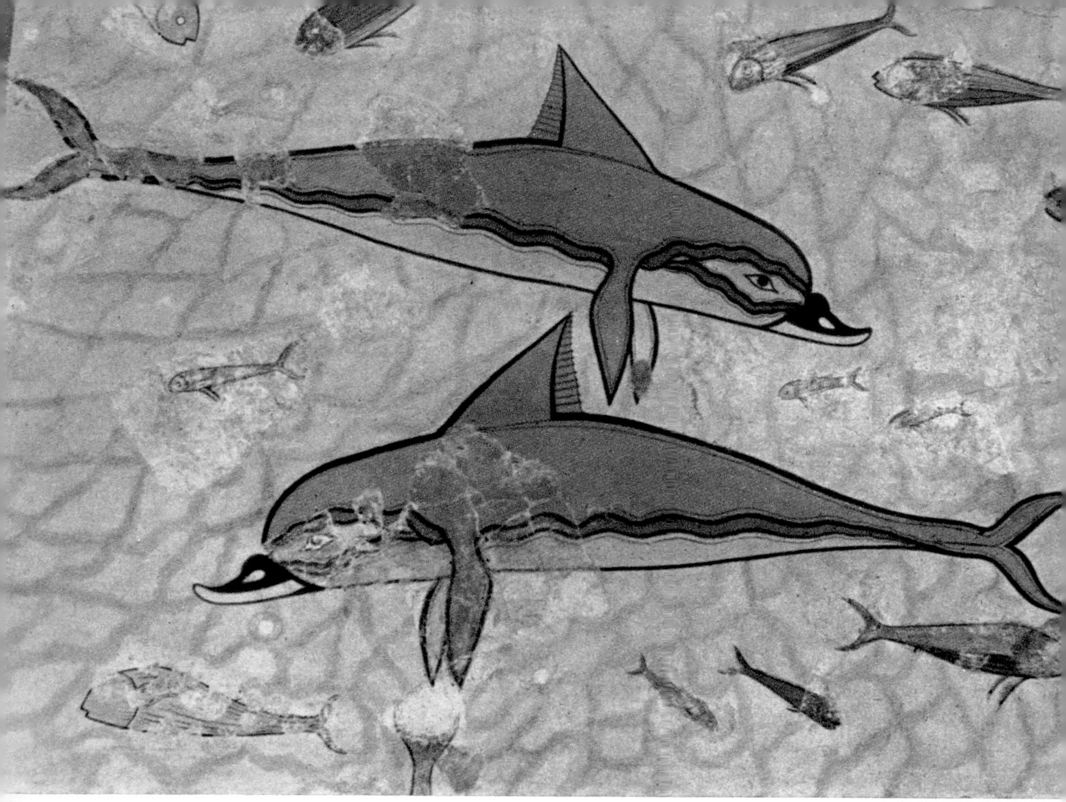

29

30

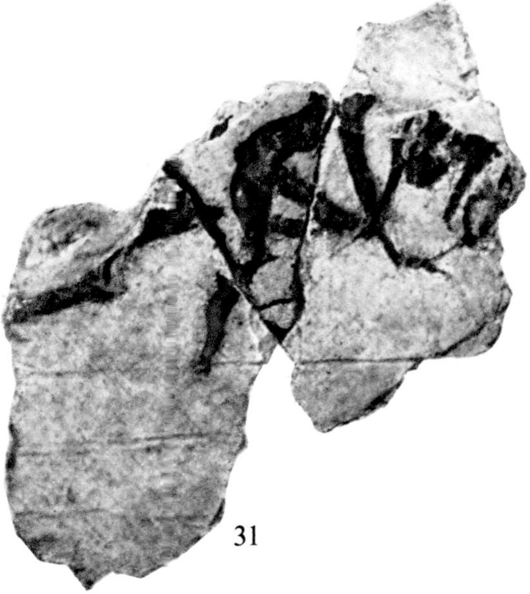

31

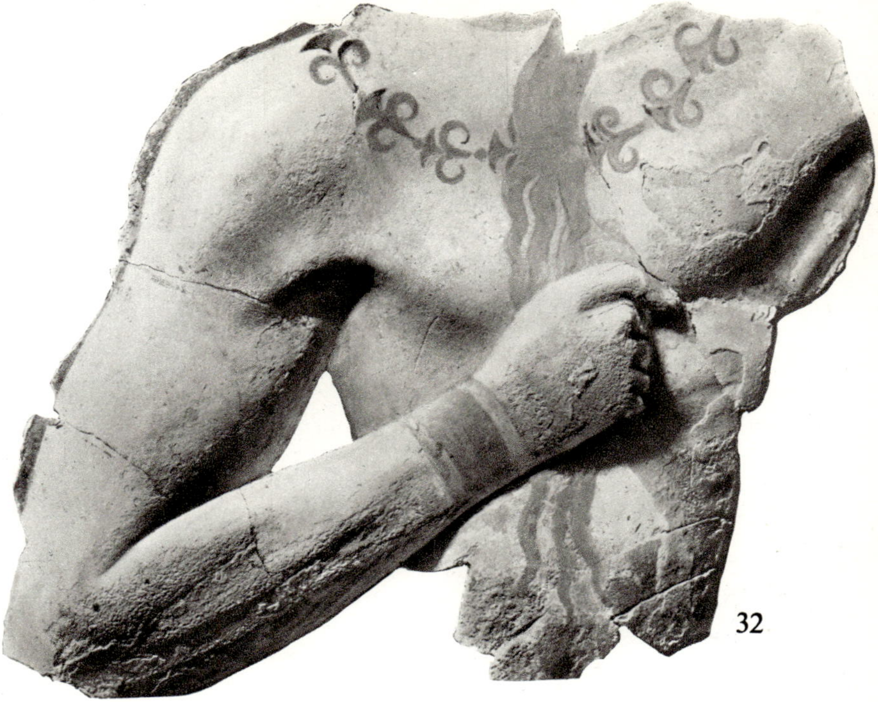
32

33

34

35

36

37

38

39

40

41

42

43

46

44

45

47

48

49

50

51

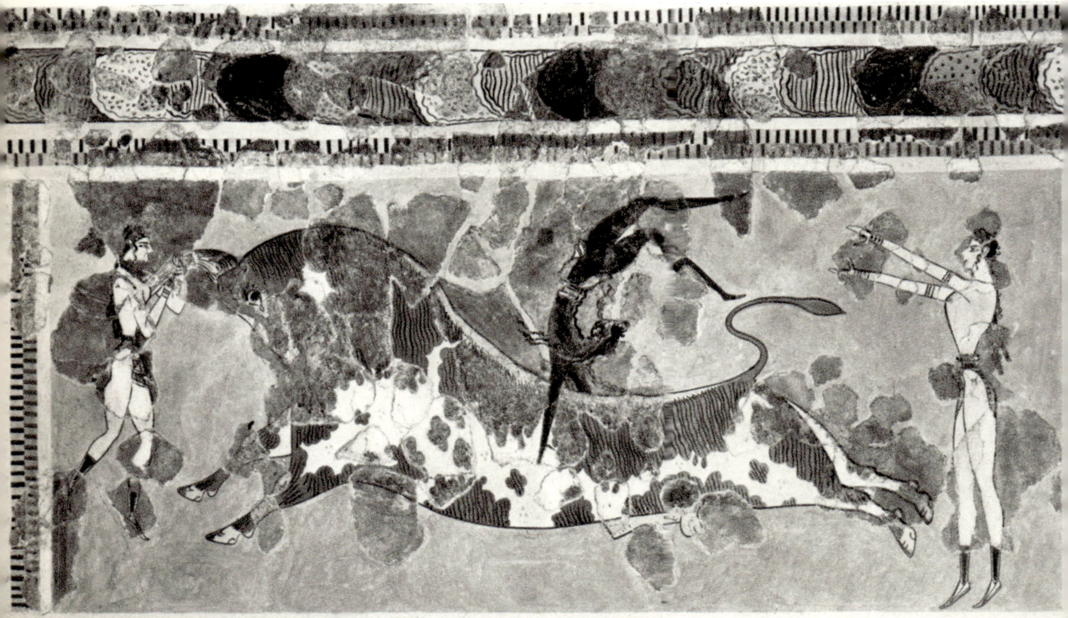

52

53

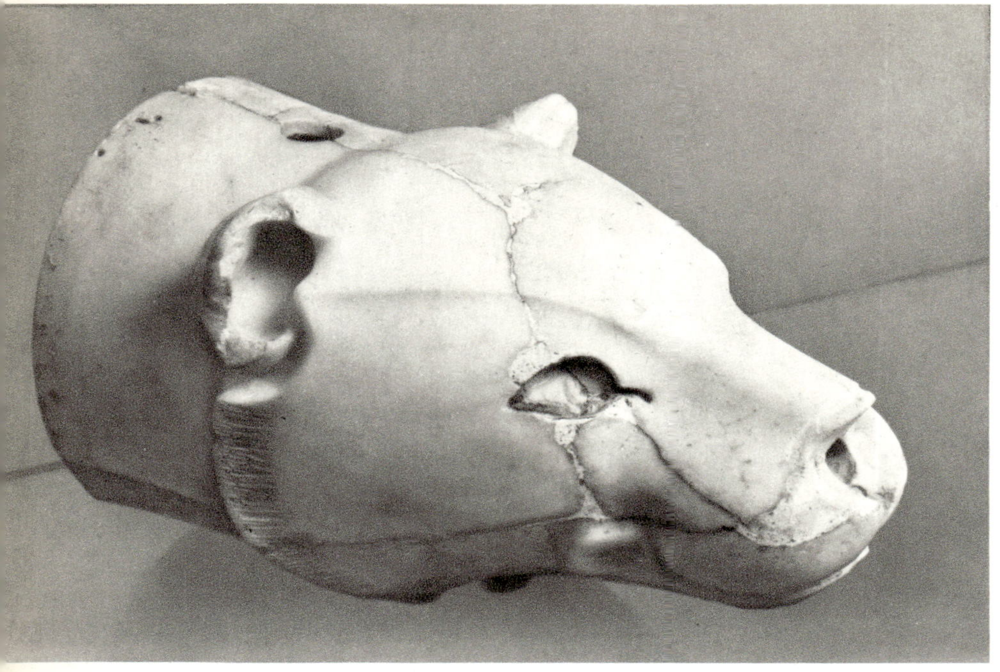

54

55, 56

57

58

59

60

61

62

63

64

65

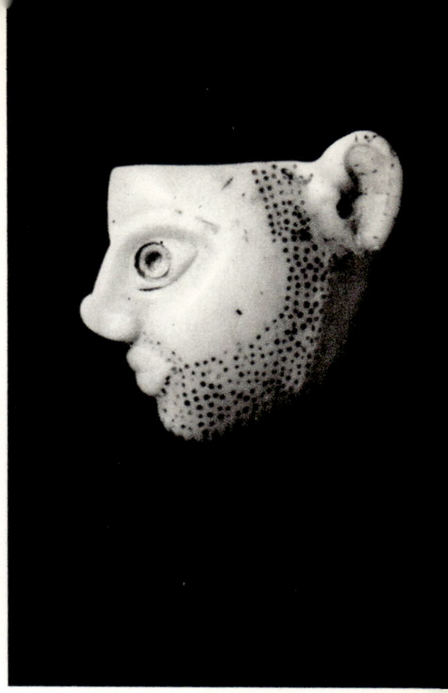

66

67

68

69

70

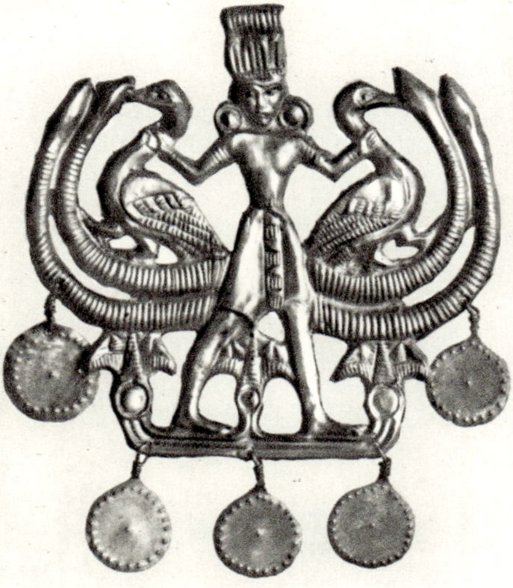

71

72

73

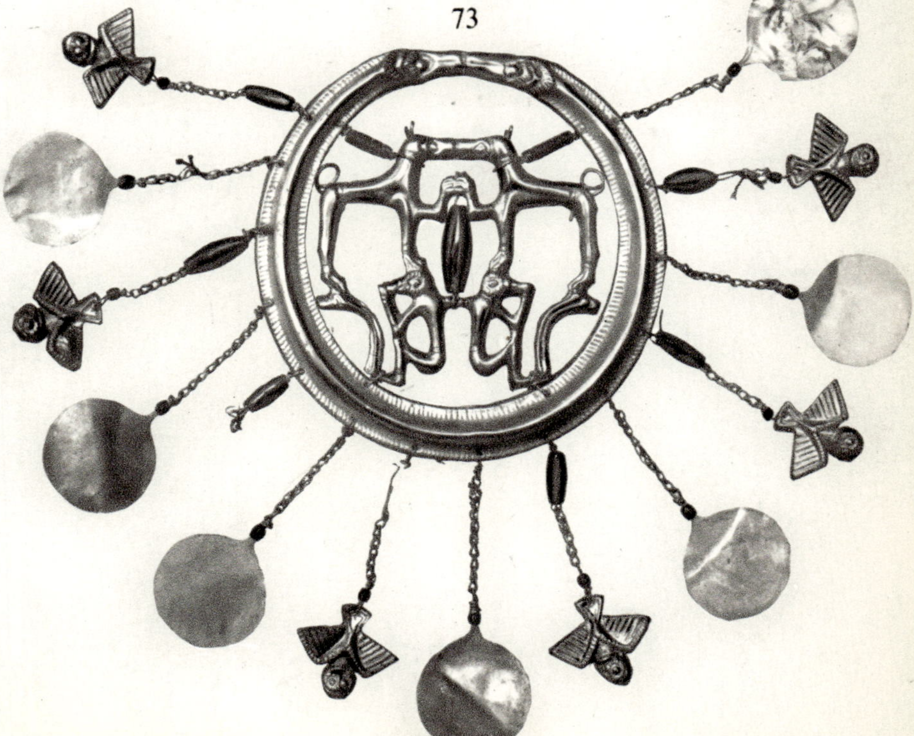

74

75

76

77

78

79

80

81

82

83

84

85

86

87

88

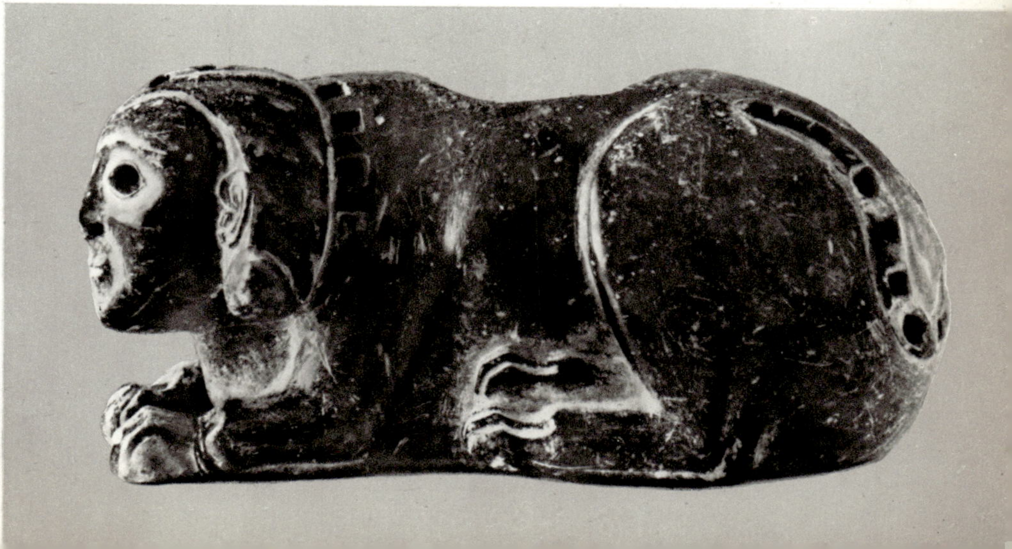
89

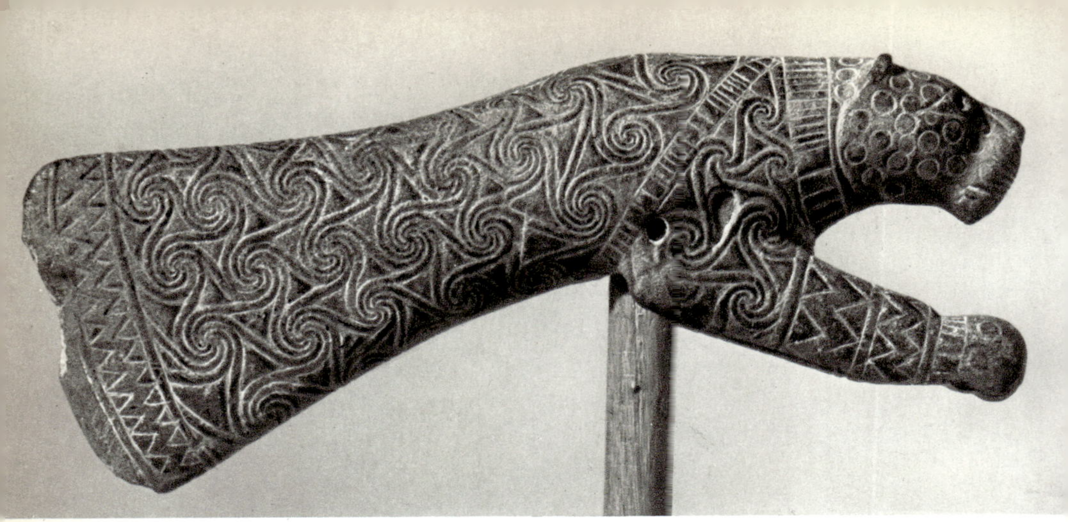

90

91

92

93

94

95

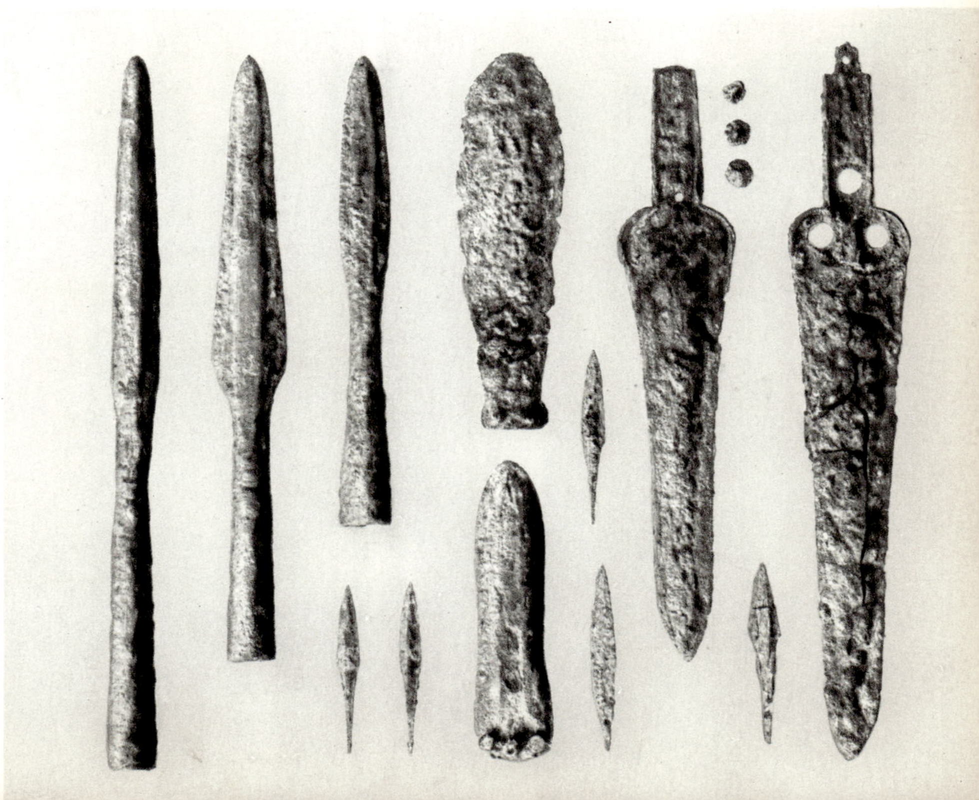

96

97

98

99, 100

101

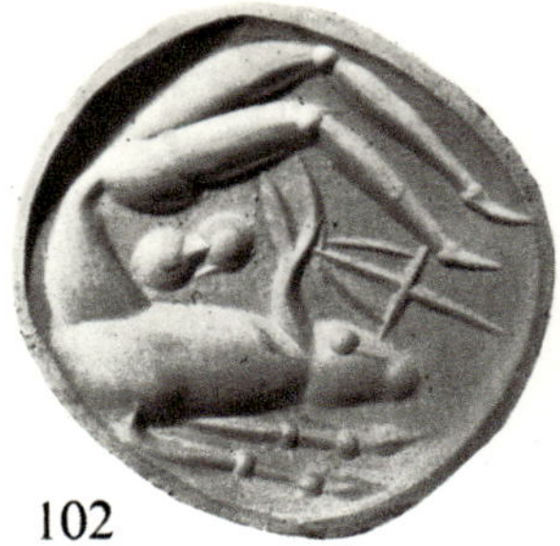

102

103

104

105

106

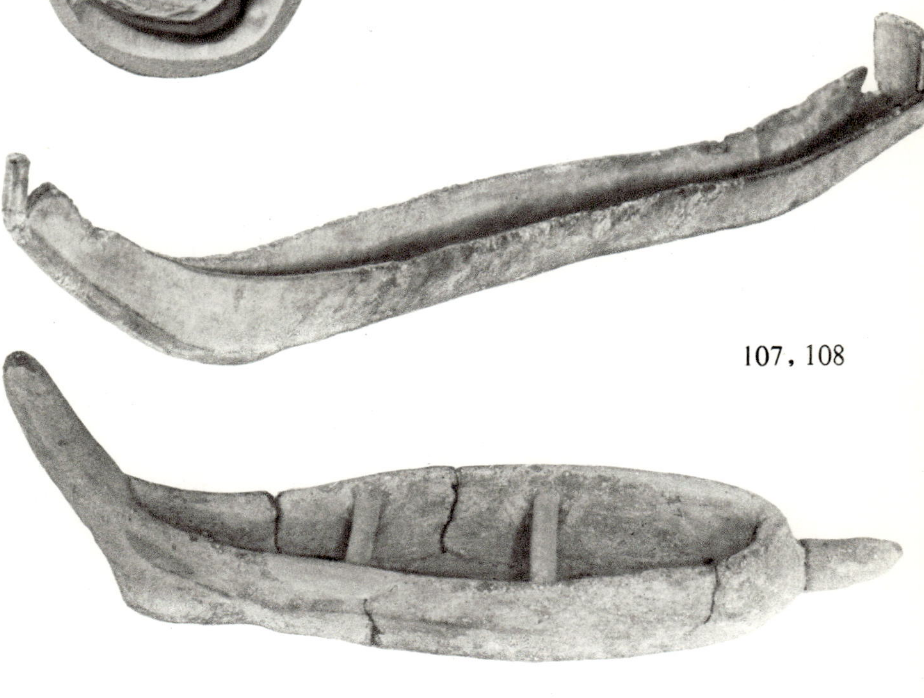

107, 108

109

110

112

113

114

116 ,117

115

118

119

Notes on the Plates

D = diameter, H = height, L = length, W = width

All objects are in Herakleion Museum, Crete, unless otherwise stated

AM = Ashmolean Museum, Oxford
BM = British Museum, London
NM Athens = National Museum, Athens
Kenna = Kenna, V. E. G., *Cretan Seals,* Oxford 1960

1, 2 Front and back views of male figurine (H 9 cm.) of polished white marble, found in the excavations of 1959 in the Early Neolithic I level 8 at Knossos (P. J. Ucko, *Anthropomorphic Figurines,* London 1968, No. 15). Both the head and feet are missing, but the body is very well finished, with a detailed rendering of the anatomy unique in Crete at the time. This and the material of which it is made suggests that the figure may have been brought from overseas; although some deposits of white marble exist in Crete.

3 Late Neolithic clay figurine (H 9 cm.) from Knossos (P. J. Ucko, *Anthropomorphic Figurines,* London 1968, No. 50). Grey-brown surface, burnished, and decorated with incisions originally filled with white paste; double zig-zag line running across the breast, seen here. There is a great variety in the Neolithic figurines of Crete; most of them are of clay, and highly stylised; where the sex can be distinguished they tend to be female, as in this instance.

4 Fine LM I A bridge-spouted jar (H 18 cm.) elaborately decorated in polychrome, combining brown to black and red paints with details added in white. Spirals with solid centres adorned with white spots are very characteristic of LM I A vase decoration. AM

5 Large jar (H 54.5 cm.) from the Loom-Weight Basement in the east wing of the palace at Knossos (Fig. 34; 34). Assigned by Evans to MM II B; but the naturalism of the palms is unique as early as this, and the vase may date from the beginning of MM III (pp. 43, 86). AM

6 Jar of Vasiliki ware (H 18.5 cm.) from the type site of Vasiliki itself. The long spout may be an Egyptian feature copied in Crete (p. 37). AM

7 Round-bottomed jug (H 20.5 cm.), found at Ayios Onouphrios near Phaistos together with the shell inlay on Plate 66. These objects may have come from a circular tomb of the type common in the Mesara region of southern Crete. The early 'dark-on-light' style of decoration is named 'Ayios Onouphrios' after this vase. The rounded base, reminiscent of original gourd vessels, is an early feature; but the jug may in fact date from EM II or later (p. 37).

8 Jug (H 29 cm.) decorated with reeds, from the ruins of the palace at Phaistos destroyed in LM I B *c.* 1450 BC. The exceptional quality of the decoration suggests that the jug may have been made in the royal workshops at Knossos from which during this period there seems to have been an active export of fine vases, most of them (unlike this jug) of a ritual character.

9 Vase of Minoan type (H to rim 7.5 cm.), found at Kahun in Egypt along with fragments of other vases from Crete assignable to MM I B—II A (p. 40). In view of the fabric this may be an Egyptian imitation of a Cretan vase rather than an import from Crete (*BM Catalogue of Vases* I Part 1, p. 93, A 562). BM

10 Cup of the Vafio shape (H 7.3 cm.) with tortoise-shell ripple decoration from the palace at Knossos, assigned by Evans to MM III (*PM* I, pp. 592 f., fig. 435). AM

11 Alabaster jar (H 29 cm.) engraved with the name of Thotmes III. This is one of three Egyptian stone vases found together in a tomb at Katsamba outside the Bronze Age harbour town of Knossos. The clay vases from the tomb are assignable to the beginning of LM III A about half a century after the reign of Thotmes III. An ancestor of one of the people buried in the tomb may have taken part in a Cretan embassy to Egypt where he was given the stone vases (*S. Alexiou, *Isterominoikoi Tafoi Limenos Knosou (Katsamba)*, Athens 1967, pp. 46, 76 ff.) (p. 47).

12 Egyptian scarab of glazed steatite found in the Royal Road area at Knossos in the top of a deposit assignable to MM II A. The scarab has been variously dated by experts to the end of Dynasty XII or Dynasty XIII, or to the Hyksos period.

13 LM I B clay jug (H 22 cm.) from the Royal Road area at Knossos like the scarab on the opposite page. Features such as the flat-topped rim and the 'rivet' on the handle are copied from contemporary metal vases. The design of spirals above arcades occurs on other clay vases of the period, and in repoussé on a gold cup found in a warrior's grave with the weapons on Plate 95.

14 Low-stemmed drinking cup (H 15.8 cm.) of the LM II period from the Royal Road area at Knossos like the scarab on the opposite page and the jug on the left. It is decorated on each side with a group of three stylised papyrus flowers. The design round the rim is a simplified version of the 'adder pattern' on the shoulder of the jug.

15 Large 'Palace Style' jar (H 72 cm.) assignable to the beginning of the LM III A period from the Tomb of the Double Axes north of Knossos. The octopuses are feeble and degenerate compared with those on the fine 'Marine Style' vases of LM I B.

16 The palace at Knossos as it is today, seen from the east. The Throne Room (Fig. 34; 5) lies behind the group of four doors with an upper storey above them at the far side of the Central Court. All the upper floors and roofs are modern restorations.

17 The Residential Quarter of the palace at Knossos, looking down from the Central

Court before the upper floors had been restored. In the left centre is the porch of the Hall of the Double Axes (Fig. 34; 20), with the private staircase (22) to the right of it, and at the bottom right the bedroom (23).

18 Grand Staircase leading from the West Court of the Later Palace at Phaistos to the *piano nobile* (Fig. 35; 3). The paving with a path across it belongs to the West Court of the earlier palace. The later West Court was at a higher level, and ran over the base of the façade of the earlier palace (Fig. 35; 2) beyond the paved area. The steps on the left date from the time of the earlier palace, but remained in use throughout the life of the Later Palace. They may have served as a stand for spectators at religious ceremonies and sports held in the West Court.

19 Part of the south-west corner of the earlier palace at Phaistos, showing the base of the outer façade with large slabs set on edge (orthostats) (Fig. 35; 17). In the background is a room with a bench against the wall in which a small cupboard is recessed (pp. 74, 81).

20 Fragment of a decorative relief frieze (H 18.5 cm.) which may have surrounded a monumental doorway approached by steps at the north-west corner of the Later Palace at Knossos. There was a stone frieze with half-rosettes like this above the doorway of the Treasury of Atreus at Mycenae, and similar friezes were used as dados in the palaces there and at Tiryns on the Greek mainland.

21 LM III clay bath tub (H 48 cm.) used as a coffin in a tomb at Pachyammos near Gournia in eastern Crete. Fish were commonly painted on the insides of bath tubs like this.

22 Selection of faience plaques (reproduced just over natural size) showing house façades, from the area of the Loom-Weight Basement of the palace at Knossos (Fig. 34; 34). The plaques were assigned by Evans to MM II B, although found in a deposit of MM III date. The house in the middle is built of squared masonry. That at the bottom may be of timber and mud-brick construction, the spots indicating the ends of logs of wood or painted imitations of them. The plaques, inlays it seems from a box or chest of some kind, evidently formed part of a scene of an attack upon a city. The helmeted head (Fig. 98) belonged to the same picture. If the houses were on the city wall, it would explain the absence of ground-floor doors and windows.

23 Ivory plaque (H 5.5 cm.) in the shape of a house façade built of squared masonry, from a LM deposit in the Royal Road area at Knossos. Unlike the earlier faience inlays on the left, this shows a door and slit-windows nearly at ground level.

24 The temple Tomb at Knossos, looking down from above the rock-cut burial chamber. The columns and roof of the loggia at the back, and the upper floor above the pillar crypt in the foreground, are modern restorations. The upper floor has been left half-open to show the huge wooden beams

(reproduced in concrete) which supported the ceiling (Fig. 129).

25 Fresco of lilies in what may be meant for a formal garden with a path or wall. This adorned a room in a mansion near the sea at Amnisos, one of the harbour towns close to Knossos, destroyed in LM I. The lilies are painted on especially fine plaster inserted into the plaster of the background (p. 79).

26 The so-called 'Saffron Gatherer' from the palace at Knossos may be the earliest wall picture that has survived in Crete. The flowers appear to be saffron crocuses from which yellow dye was extracted; but the figure which Evans restored like this as a blue boy was in fact one of a pair of monkeys (Fig. 39).

27 The Throne Room in the palace at Knossos (Fig. 34; 5) was evidently used for ritual, and the Queen as representative of the goddess may have sat upon the throne here. The paintings on the walls are modern restorations and inaccurate in detail. But the throne was probably flanked by wingless griffins as Evans inferred (p. 80).

28 Frieze of partridges and hoopoes from what Evans interpreted as a Caravanserai or hotel building south of the palace at Knossos. The frieze appears to have run around the top of the wall in what may have been the dining room.

29 The Dolphin Fresco from the palace at Knossos. The fragments of this were found scattered in the area of the bedroom in the Residential Quarter (Fig. 34; 23). Evans thought that the picture must have belonged to some earlier scheme of wall decoration in the bedroom itself. But it may have adorned the floor of an upper room in this part of the palace at the time of its final destruction in the fourteenth century BC.

30 Seal of flattened cylinder shape (L 1.6 cm.), made of black steatite and engraved with a pair of dolphins against a rocky background. Found at Palaikastro in eastern Crete, and datable to the end of the MM period *c.* 1600 BC. Like the stone ritual vase from Zakro on Plate 114 this seal was once covered with thin hammered gold, much of which has survived. AM (Kenna No. 203)

31 Miniature fresco (reproduced about actual size) from the palace at Knossos with a scene which Evans interpreted as boys playing a pavement game of some kind. Guide lines for the painter impressed with string while the plaster was still wet are visible at the bottom.

32 Fragment of a life-size figure in plaster relief from the southern quarter of the palace at Knossos. Possibly a god, or a priest-king as Evans thought; but the figure had an elaborate crown of a type worn by sphinxes, always female, and by a priestess on the Ayia Triadha sarcophagus (Plate 60, second from left); and in the opinion of M. Cameron the skin may have been painted white like that of a woman.

33 The fragment of miniature fresco known as the Captain of the Blacks from the area of the House of the Frescoes west of the palace at Knossos appears to represent a group of

negro soldiers led by a native officer at the double. Negro soldiers from the Sudan served in Egyptian armies, and these might be Sudanese mercenaries. Perhaps they served as Palace Guards as Evans suggested. Both officer and men wear goat's-skin caps with the horns attached, and the officer has a couple of throwing spears. On stylistic grounds this painting is assignable to LM II–III, well after the disasters of *c.* 1450 BC.

34 'La Parisienne', as this figure has been called, was part of the 'Camp Stool Fresco', a scene of men and women engaged in religious rites of some kind which adorned an upper room in the north-west corner of the palace at Knossos at the time of its destruction in the fourteenth century BC. M. Cameron has shown that 'La Parisienne' was one of a pair of twin figures considerably larger than the rest. They may have been a pair of goddesses presiding at the rites.

35 Restoration of part of a large picture from the House of the Frescoes west of the palace at Knossos. The picture decorated the walls of a room on the upper floor of the building at the time of its destruction by earthquake in LM I A *c.* 1500 BC. It incorporated birds, some in flight, and monkeys in a flowered landscape with streams and waterfalls (which Evans interpreted as artificial fountains!). One monkey was apparently engaged in eating an egg, and the theme of the picture may have been a raid by monkeys on a nesting area (M. Cameron, *BSA* 63, 1968, pp. 1–31).

36 Clay coffin (larnax) with a gabled lid, from Vasiliki Anoyia in the Mesara. During the LM III period clay chests like this appear to have been made as cheap imitations of wooden household chests especially for use as coffins. The more expensive wooden chests were also placed in the tombs on occasion.

37 Looking south along the Corridor of the West Magazines at Knossos (Fig. 34; 11), with storage jars and under-floor cists. This hitherto unpublished photograph was taken by a member of a Hellenic Cruise during the fourth season of the Knossos excavations in the spring of 1903.

38 The so-called Harvester Vase from the palace at Ayia Triadha near Phaistos destroyed in LM I B *c.* 1450 BC. The vase, of which only this top part has survived, was a libation vessel of a shape ultimately derived from ostrich-egg vessels like one found in the shaftgraves at Mycenae. It was made of black steatite or serpentine, and the surface was originally, perhaps, concealed by gold leaf as in the case of the vase from Zakro on Plate 114. The scene in relief appears to be a sowing festival rather than a harvest home; the men having bags of seed corn slung from their belts, and carrying what may be hoes with shoots of willow tied to them. They are led by the long-haired priest in the centre wearing a scaly ritual cloak or cuirass (J. Forsdyke, *Journal of the Warburg and Courtauld Institutes* 17, 1954, pp. 1–9).

39 Granaries in the south-west corner of the palace at Mallia. In the background is the hill of the Prophet Elias with a large building which may have been a sanctuary on its

summit. Circular granaries arranged in rows like these were usual in Egypt. A remarkable serpentine model of such a complex, evidently a ritual vase, was found many years ago in the island of Melos and is now in Munich.

40 Wine press (?) in the country villa at Vathipetro near Arkhanes south of Knossos. The grapes would have been placed in the spouted jar and trampled by a man or boy holding a rope fixed to the ceiling as in Egypt; the juice flowing through the spout into the lower vessel, from which it could be ladled into storage jars.

41 Lentoid seal of black haematite with a wild boar lurking in a thicket, from a deposit of LM I B date in the Royal Road area at Knossos.

42 Disc-shaped seal of black steatite (D 1.2 cm.) showing the head of an animal, apparently a lion, from a tomb of the MM period on the slopes of Ailias above the city of Knossos to the east. The irregular border of dots is unusual. One of these tombs is illustrated in Plate 113, and other objects from them on Plates 49, 65 and 67.

43 Lentoid seal of haematite from Knossos with a lioness leaping upon the back of a bull. Scenes like this suggest that Minoan artists were familiar with lions, which may have existed in Crete during the Bronze Age, although their bones have not yet been identified in settlement debris.

44 Impression of one face of an almond-shaped (amygdaloid) seal (L 2.8 cm.) of veined agate, assignable to the end of the MM period *c.* 1600 BC. The fish swimming in a pool with sea-weed was identified by Evans as a parrot wrasse (*scarus*). The other face of the seal is engraved with an owl-like bird. AM (Kenna No. 220)

45 Impression of a seal of flattened cylinder shape (L 1.5 cm.), showing a collared hound with a wild goat at bay on a rock above. This seal of pale blue chalcedony was dated by Evans to the end of the MM period like the seal on the left.

46 Clay head of a woman (H 8 cm.) with an elaborate coiffure held in place by a wide band or diadem. It belonged to a votive figurine placed in a MM sanctuary at Piskokefalo just south of Siteia in eastern Crete.

47 Clay statuettes of a woman (H 14. 3 cm.) and a man (H 17.5 cm.) from a sanctuary on top of the hill of Petsofa above Palaikastro in eastern Crete. These figurines may date from the beginning of the MM period (*c.* 2000 BC or earlier). They appear to represent worshippers, and are important for the light they throw on fashions of dress worn at the time (pp. 82, 95, 96, 98).

48 Impression from the bezel (L 2.8 cm.) of a signet ring of banded agate found at Avdhou east of Knossos. The style of the work suggests a date for the ring in LM I *c.* 1500 BC. The figures in the chariot may be divine, and the scene imaginary; but goats could have been trained to draw a chariot in this manner. AM (Kenna No. 308)

49 Small disc-shaped seal of silver with a bird, perhaps a hawk, above a spray. From the MM Ailias cemetery at Knossos like the seal on Plate 42. Other objects from this cemetery are the silver pendant on Plate 65 and the gold chain of Plate 67.

50 Lentoid seal (D 1.7 cm.) of green jasper, showing water birds against a background of papyrus flowers. Found at Knossos, and assignable to LM I–II. AM (Kenna No. 343)

51 Gold cup, one of a pair with relief scenes of bull-catching, from the burial pit of a princely tomb at Vafio near Sparta. Although found on the Greek mainland these cups were almost certainly made by a Cretan artist working in MM III or LM I (*c.* 1600–1500 BC). Here a bull has been caught in a net tied between two olive trees. Other bulls escape to left and right, tossing and trampling upon their would-be captors. NM Athens

52 Fresco panel with bull-leaping scene from the Court of the Stone Spout (Fig. 34; 35) in the palace at Knossos. The figures painted white appear to be women dressed as men. This picture, which was assigned by Evans to LM I A- LM II, may have been on the walls of the palace at the time of its destruction in the fourteenth century BC.

53 Libation vase (rhyton) of black serpentine in the shape of a bull's head (H 30.6 cm. excluding horns). From the 'Little Palace', a large city house north-west of the palace at Knossos. The horns, ears, left eye and part of the left cheek are modern restorations. The genuine right eye has a border of red jasper surrounding a crystal lens on the back of which the pupil and iris are painted in red and black. The white inlay round the nostrils is of shell. A hole in the tope of the neck was used to fill the vase, which was emptied by pouring through another hole in the mouth. This was one of a number of bull's-head rhytons made in Crete during MM III and LM I. It may have been lost when the 'Little Palace' suffered damage at the time of the disasters which afflicted Crete in LM I B, *c.* 1450 BC.

54 Libation vase (rhyton) in the shape of the head of a lioness (L 29 cm.). It is made of creamy white translucent marble-like limestone. There are holes for liquid in the top of the head and in the nose and mouth. This fine vase may date from MM III or LM I like the bull's head rhyton on Plate 53; but it was found together with other stone vases of the same period in a room in the west wing of the palace at Knossos that appears to have been in use at the time of the final destruction in the fourteenth century BC.

55 Inlaid dagger blade from the fourth shaft grave at Mycenae, showing a bowman and four men armed with spears and great body shields at odds with a troop of lions. One of the men has lost his shield and has fallen on his back as the lion rushes upon him. The men wear 'shorts' of a type found on contemporary Cretan representations, and the dagger may be the work of a Cretan artist. NM Athens

56 Another inlaid dagger blade from the fourth shaft grave at Mycenae, with lions

in a rocky landscape of conventional Minoan type. The technique of making these daggers was elaborate. A plaque of bronze or other metal was let into each side of the blade. But before this was done, the figures, cut from thin sheets of silver, gold (as here), electrum (an alloy of gold and silver), or copper, were set in hollows in the plaque and hammered into place; details being incised and afterwards filled with niello, whose shiny black surface contrasted with the silver and gold of the figures. No weapons or other objects decorated in this way have yet been found in Crete. But the technique may have been adopted in Crete from Syria, and afterwards spread from there to the Greek mainland. NM Athens

57 Wall painting from the palace of Ayia Triadha near Phaistos destroyed in LM I B *c.* 1450 BC. A cat stalks an elegant pheasant-like bird, with a red body and long black tail, against a background of rocks and flowers.

58 Dagger blade from shaft grave V at Mycenae, with cats hunting wild-fowl. The figures of cats, birds and flowers, are of silver, gold, and apparently copper. The plaque in which they were inlaid is of silver; but its surface is sunk, and it was originally concealed by niello, except for the stream which wound a silvery course through the shiny black niello background (Evans, *PM* III, pp. 113 ff.). NM Athens

59 Part of one side of the painted sarcophagus from an important tomb at Ayia Triadha near Phaistos. The style of the paintings suggests a date at the beginning of the LM III period before the final destruction of the palace at Knossos. The coffin was carved out of a single block of limestone, but was coated with plaster to form a surface for the paintings which depict funerary rites. Here on the left is a table-like altar with a calf tied for sacrifice upon it. A bucket on the ground below receives his blood, and two goats sit awaiting their turn. Three women in long robes (much damaged and not included here) approach from the left, while a man plays upon the double pipes. In front of him a woman clad in the skin of a sacrificed victim sets her hands upon an altar which may be reserved for offerings of fruit and libations to judge from the dish of fruit and the jug above it. Beyond is a tall pole surmounted by an elaborate double axe with a bird on it, and on the extreme right stands a shrine topped by horns of consecration with a sacred tree inside or behind.

60 The other side of the Ayia Triadha sarcophagus, with the dead prince (or his mummy) standing in front of his tomb to receive offerings—a boat and two bulls or models of them—from men clad in skins of sacrificed victims. On the left to the accompaniment of a seven-stringed lyre two women, one in a long robe and ornately crowned, the other wearing a skin, pour libations into a vase set between a pair of stepped bases which hold the poles for elaborate double axes with birds on them. On each short end of the sarcophagus there is a picture of a chariot with a pair of women, apparently goddesses, riding in it; one drawn by goats, like the chariot on Plate 48, the other by winged griffins.

61 Bronze figurine of a woman (H 19 cm.), apparently a worshipper or priestess, with her left hand covering her bared breasts and her right raised in adoration. At the back, if Evans is right, her hair is entwined with snakes. She is wearing a long flounced skirt with a V-shaped division in front as was fashionable at the beginning of the LM period. Berlin Museum

62 Bronze figurine of a male worshipper (H 22 cm. including stand) with right hand raised to forehead in a salute. He is wearing a codpiece of the exaggerated type with a wide belt and a kilt cut at the sides to expose the thighs but descending in front below the knees. This figure is stouter than the ideal Bronze Age Cretan, and may therefore be a portrait. BM

63 Faience figurine of a woman (H 29.5 cm.), apparently a goddess, from the Temple Repositories in the palace at Knossos (Fig. 34; 9) which were filled after an earthquake at the end of the MM period *c.* 1550 BC. In each hand she wields a snake, and upon her cap sits what Evans took to be a lioness (pp. 97, 132).

64 Impression of an almond-shaped (amygdaloid) seal (L 3.4 cm.) of green jasper from Knossos with a votary or priest, or perhaps a god, wearing a robe of Oriental type and carrying a bird with a long neck which may be intended for a dove. AM (Kenna No. 293)

65 Silver pendant (H 2.1 cm.) from a MM tomb in the Ailias cemetery at Knossos, like the seal on Plate 42. The babyish figure is reminiscent of the Egyptian Bes and may represent a god.

66 Inlay (L 4.5 cm. from chin to top of ear) of shell, thought by Evans to be *Tridacna* from the Red Sea. It was obtained by him in 1894 near Phaistos, and may have come from an early circular tomb at Ayios Onouphrios like the jug on Plate 7. The beard is unusual although by no means unknown in Bronze Age Crete. The face with its thick lips and snub nose, which Evans described as being of 'repugnant aspect', may reflect an element from Libya in the population of southern Crete (*PM* II, pp. 45 f., fig. 21 *a*). AM

67 Gold chain from a MM tomb in the Ailias cemetery at Knossos, like the seal on Plate 42. Similar chains made of gold wire were recovered from early tombs at Mochlos, and were incorporated in some of the jewellery of the 'Aigina Treasure' as seen on Plates 72 and 73.

68 Acrobat or bull-leaper in repoussé on the gold plate (D 7 cm.) which supported the large bone pommel of a long sword of the rapier type from the palace at Mallia. He is wearing an elaborately decorated kilt or pair of shorts held in place by a tasselled belt. The sword, which may have been made in MM III, was one of a pair found together in a deposit of a date before that of the final destruction of the palace in LM I B *c.* 1450 BC. These two swords may have been buried at the time of the eruption of Thera in LM I A, or in some earlier disaster.

69 Gold jewellery from three of the early tombs at Mochlos in eastern Crete. These were

probably hair ornaments, except for the object at the top with leaves hanging from a cap which may have tipped a staff or sceptre. The bulk of the material from the tombs in which these ornaments were found is conventionally assigned to the EM period; but the dating evidence is inconclusive, and much of the jewellery may in fact belong to the time of the early palaces at Knossos and Phaistos.

70 Gold pendant (W 4.6 cm.) in the shape of two bees (or wasps) heraldically placed each side of what may be meant for a honey-cake. Found in the great building at Chrysolakkos which appears to have been the sepulchre for the ruling house of Mallia. The jewel, datable on grounds of style to the later part of the MM period, shows a remarkable mastery of the arts of filigree and granulation (pp. 92, 101, 145).

71 Gold pendant (H 6 cm.), allegedly found in a Mycenaean tomb on the island of Aegina; but it may have been plundered in the mid-nineteenth century from the Chrysolakkos sepulchre at Mallia. It shows a god holding a pair of birds, apparently geese, and wearing a tall crown which may be made of feathers (p. 102). BM

72 Gold earring (L 8.5 cm.), part of the so-called 'Aigina Treasure' like the other jewellery reproduced on the same page. The lion's head at the top capped an object of some perishable material (ivory?) through which a pin ran to a gold plate enclosing its base. From the collar round the lion's neck hang chains like that on Plate 67, with eggs and birds (duck?) in flight on the end of them. More flying birds depend from the plate at the base of the missing object. BM

73 One of four ornaments (W 6.5 cm.), apparently earrings, made of gold with carnelian beads incorporated in them. Like the jewellery above it this formed part of the 'Aigina Treasure'. Inside an embossed ring in the form of a two-headed snake a pair of collared grey-hounds stand with muzzles joining; one of their forepaws rests upon the heads of a pair of monkeys seated back to back and engaged, it seems, in eating. From the ring hang chains like that on Plate 67, terminating in alternate gold discs and flying owls. BM

74 Vase (H 4.4 cm.) of grey and white dolomitic limestone; Minoan copy of an Egyptian type of stone vase fashionable during the First Intermediary Period and Dynasty XI. Found in the cemetery area at Mochlos, but not in a tomb.

75 Egyptian bowl (H 17.3 cm.) of porphyritic rock, with white crystals in a brown matrix; made during the Protodynastic period (Dynasties I–III), and later adapted by Minoan craftsmen who added a spout of a different stone with hollows for white inlays to match the crystals in the original. The Minoan adapters also cut away the Egyptian roll-handles, and drilled holes for the attachment of new handles of Cretan type, now missing. This adaptation probably dates from the LM period when the vase was already a thousand years old. Found in the palace of Zakro destroyed in the disasters of LM I B *c.* 1450 BC.

76 Pyxis lid (D 11 cm.) made of chlorite with the handle in the shape of a dog. From Tomb I at Mochlos, assigned to EM II. Incised hatched triangles like those on top of the lid are a characteristic motif of decoration on the earliest Cretan stone vases.

77 Pear-shaped libation vase (rhyton) of rock crystal. The neck-ring is made of separate pieces of crystal joined by gold bands. The handle consists of fourteen crystal beads threaded on a bronze wire. From the palace at Zakro destroyed in LM I B *c.* 1450 BC.

78 Mould in two pieces (L 16 cm.) for making a double axe with a circular shaft-hole. The numerous cuts through the sharp edges are for bindings which held the moulds together when an axe was being cast. Found with other debris of bronze- and stone-working in a deposit in the north-western quarter of the palace at Mallia assigned to the early part of the MM period.

79 Cauldron from House A at Tylissos, destroyed in the disasters of LM I B *c.* 1450 BC. With a diameter of *c.* 140 cm. and over 52 kilos in weight it is the largest of a group of four cauldrons which were all found together in one room. Each of these cauldrons was made of seven sheets of copper held together by rivets, and had three handles set on the rim.

80 Faience vase in the shape of an argonaut from the palace at Zakro destroyed in LM I B *c.* 1450 BC. The manufacture of faience may have been among the crafts practised in the block at the southern end of the palace (Fig. 33; 10), but such an exquisite object might be a product of the Palace workshops at Knossos.

81 Faience plaque (L 20 cm.) with a cow suckling her calf, found with the figurine on Plate 63 in the Temple Repositories of the palace at Knossos (Fig. 34; 9). Evans assigned it to MM III B.

82, 83 Ivory head (H 4.5 cm.), apparently from the figure of a bull-leaper, from a deposit below the floor of the Treasure Chamber in the palace at Knossos (Fig. 34; 27), assigned by Evans to the end of the MM III period like the objects from the Temple Repositories. The holes were for hair, which in the case of another head from the same deposit consisted of bronze wire plated with gold. The face may have been stained red or brown.

84 Bird (L 6.6 cm.), made from a thin piece of ivory, but carved in relief on both sides. It may be intended for a dove, and was evidently attached to some other object. Most of the surface of the ivory was polished, the rough patches being covered, it seems, with gold leaf which has not survived. Found in the Royal Road area at Knossos with debris of an ivory worker's shop destroyed in LM I B *c.* 1450 BC.

85 Ivory box (pyxis) (H 9.2 cm.), carved from a section of elephant tusk with reliefs showing an elaborate scene of bull acrobatics. In a rocky landscape a man balances on the horns of a bull which he clasps with crossed arms; he may have dropped from the palm tree behind. In front of the bull two men run, one (out of sight here) waving what

may be a net, the other with a spear levelled at the bull's head. Above the spear-man flies a long-necked bird. The box was found in a tomb of the LM III period at Katsamba by the harbour town of Bronze Age Knossos, but it appears to have been carved in LM I–II (*S. Alexiou, *Isterominoikoi Tafoi Limenos Knosou (Katsamba)*, Athens 1967, pp. 55 ff.).

86 Impression of one face of a three-sided seal (L 1.8 cm.) with hieroglyphic inscriptions, assignable to MM II. The signs round the cat are a door (below), leg, plant and snake. Evans suggested that the plant might be silphium, which flourished in North Africa in Classical times when its juice was used in food and medicine. This seal of reddish brown carnelian is of the highest quality, and could be a royal one, as Evans thought, containing the name and titles of a Minoan prince whose personal badge was a cat. AM (Kenna No. 174)

87 Impressions of three of the four sides of a fine hieroglyphic seal (L 1.7 cm.) of green jasper, assignable like that on Plate 86 to MM II. The fourth side has a row of cat-like faces. The others, seen here, display signs in the form of (above) a bird and goat; (centre) an eight-stringed lyre, calf's head, lily and mallet (?); (below) an arrow, rayed eye, and pair of razors of the early cutter-like type (Fig. 69a). The crosses on the right of the central and lower inscriptions may indicate where they begin. On the actual seal these crosses appear on the *left* of the sign-groups, which then read from left to right. AM (Kenna No. 170)

88 Part of a crystal plaque (L 5.5 cm.) with a bull-catching scene painted on it. From the area of the Lustral Basin attached to the Throne Room at Knossos (Fig. 34; 6). The plaque is shown here about twice natural size. The painting was done on the back so as to show through the crystal, the bull being in red-brown against a blue background. The hair of a leaper and part of a rope are visible above it. The rope may have been stretched between two trees to trip the bull, like the net on the Vafio cup on Plate 51. Evans called this plaque the '*ne plus ultra* of the Minoan miniaturist's art'. The detail of the painting is so fine as to suggest the use of a magnifier (PM III, pp. 108 ff.) (p. 110).

89 Serpentine sphinx (L 14 cm.) from a large tomb complex at Ayia Triadha near Phaistos. There is a hollow in the top of the back which Evans thought might have been an ink well. The rectangular cuttings in the neck and tail held inlays of some contrasting stone or shell. The eyes were also inlaid (p. 111).

90 Axe-head of brown schist (L 15 cm.) with the head of a leopard or lioness on the butt. From the palace of Mallia, destroyed in LM I B *c.* 1450 BC; but the axe-head may be older. The spiral-net design covering it was at home on clay vases at the beginning of the LM I period. The eyes of the animal were inlaid, and there were inlays in the drop-shaped hollows on the shoulders. The collar round the neck and the diagonal band running from it are reminiscent of the harness worn by the goats on the ring from Avdhou (Plate 48); the animal may have been conceived as drawing the chariot of

some god (J. Charbonneaux, *Monuments Piot* 28, 1925–26, pp. 6–18).

91 The Phaistos disc (D. *c.* 16 cm.), found on the northern edge of the Palace area (Fig. 35; 20) in a room that appears to have been destroyed towards the end of MM III. The script of the disc with picture-like signs is virtually unique among the surviving records of Bronze Age Crete. But it seems to be Cretan, and may have been confined to religious or magical uses (p. 112).

92 Clay tablet (H 15 cm.) with writing in the Linear B script, from the palace at Knossos. It was one of many recovered during the first year of the excavations in 1900 from burnt debris which had collapsed into the open passage leading into the Central Court on the north (Fig. 34, 3). Several of the Linear B signs still betray their origin in pictures; that at the end of the bottom four lines is an open hand, with next to it in two instances a conical libation vase like that from Ayia Triadha on Plate 96.

93 Reconstruction of a helmet plated with boar's tusks. The helmet had been placed at the feet of a warrior who was buried in the Zafer Papoura cemetery just north of the Bronze Age city of Knossos at the beginning of LM III A shortly before the final destruction of the palace (A. J. Evans, *The Prehistoric Tombs of Knossos,* London 1906, p. 67 Tomb 55).

94 Bronze casings for a helmet and cheek-pieces from a warrior-grave of LM II–III A date (*c.* 1400 BC) on the site of the new hospital just west of Zafer Papoura at Knossos. The knob which is rivetted to the top of the helmet has a hole for the attachment of a plume of some kind (*BSA* 47, 1952, pp. 243 ff., Tomb V) (p. 122).

95 Group of bronze weapons and razor from a warrior-grave of *c.* 1400 BC at Ayios Ioannis north of Knossos. The warrior was buried with a gold cup, two fine seal stones, a cruciform-hilted sword, a large spear-head, and these smaller spear-heads (the largest on the left is 35.7 cm. long), the leaf-shaped razor (top centre), two daggers, and arrow-heads. The smallest spear-heads may have tipped javelins.

96 Part of the Boxer Vase, a conical libation vessel (rhyton) of serpentine from the palace at Ayia Triadha destroyed in LM I B *c.* 1450 BC. It is decorated with four bands of reliefs; one of them with a scene of bull-leaping where a man has been impaled on a bull's horns. In the two lowest bands, seen here, men with long flowing hair, and wearing necklaces and short kilts that leave the thighs exposed, are engaged in boxing. They seem to be armed with knuckle-dusters, and those in the upper row have bronze helmets. The pillar at the back (top left) may be the base of a flag-pole like those on the vase from Zakro on Plate 114, indicating the religious character of the sports which take place in front of a shrine.

97 The Chieftain Cup (H 11.5 cm.) of serpentine, found in the palace at Ayia Triadha like the Boxer Vase on Plate 96 and the Harvester Vase on Plate 38. The reliefs on this show an officer before a king (or a king before a god). The 'king' holds a

staff; the 'officer' carries a long rapier-like sword at the slope, and in his left hand is what Evans interpreted as a lustral sprinkler; it is curiously like the holy water sprinkler used by priests in later Rome. Behind the 'officer' follows a troop of men with what may be hides of sacrificed oxen dedicated for the manufacture of great body shields like those on the contemporary Lion-Hunt Dagger from Mycenae (Plate 55).

98 Impression of a seal (L 2.1 cm.) of the flattened cylinder shape, made of translucent bluish chalcedony, with a pair of imps or acrobats wearing feathered caps doing handstands among flowers. The seal is said to have been found about half a mile north of the palace site at Knossos. Evans assigned it to the end of MM or beginning of LM times. AM (Kenna No. 204)

99 The 'Royal Draught-board' from the palace at Knossos. The large gaming board—it is nearly a metre (96.5 cm.) long and 55.3 cm. wide—was dated by Evans to the end of the MM period. Within a framework of gold-plated ivory were set transparent crystal plaques with backings of silver or blue paste. The board may have been mounted on wood to serve as the lid of a box containing the pieces (p. 122).

100 Circular stone table (D 87 cm.) of hard limestone, set in the floor of a loggia by the south-western corner of the Central Court of the palace at Mallia. Stone tables with a circle of hollows like this, but smaller and less elaborate, are commonly found on Bronze Age sites in Crete. They are sometimes called 'offering tables', but appear to have been used for some kind of game, although this may have had a religious or magical side to it (p. 122).

101 Mesopotamian cylinder seal (L 2.1 cm.) of black haematite from the smaller (Tholos B) of the two large circular tombs at Platanos in the Mesara. A goddess wearing a horned crown and long flounced robe lifts her hands in supplication before a mace-bearing god, if he is not a king. The seal is assignable to the period of the First Dynasty of Babylon, before rather than contemporary with the famous king Hammurabi (P. Robinson, *Studi micenei* 5, 1968, pp. 28 f.).

102 Impression of a lentoid seal (D 2.4 cm.) of *lapis lacedaemonius* (Spartan basalt), from the sacred cave near Psychro in Lasithi. The creature which combines the fore-part of a bull with a man from the waist down recalls the minotaur of later Greek legend. The figure-of-eight shield and the impaled triangle in the field are symbols which occur elsewhere with a religious value. AM (Kenna No. 322)

103 Impression from the face (D 1.3 cm.) of a signet-shaped seal of green jasper, assigned by Evans to MM II. The wingless sphinx with upright tail and coiling side-lock owes much to Egypt; but the signet shape of the seal may be of Anatolian derivation. AM (Kenna No. 122)

104 Impression of an almond-shaped (amygdaloid) seal (L 2.4 cm.) of carnelian, with a pair of Minoan genii holding libation jugs flanking a tree which is surmounted by a rayed orb. Behind the genii are other trees (p. 132). AM (Kenna No. 304)

105 Clay figure of a horse (?) laden with what appear to be water jars (H 17 cm.). Found on the site of the palace at Phaistos, but dating from the very end of the Bronze Age in LM III C. It may have been a libation vase, if it was not a toy; liquid poured into the jars came out through the animal's nose. The legs are modern restorations (p. 128).

106 Impressions of a three-sided seal (L 1.4 cm.) of white steatite, assigned by Evans to the end of the EM period. The animal at the top may be a horse (p. 129); below are two masted ships with high prows and projecting keels like the clay model on Plate 108. The three crouching men on the right may be meant for rowers, since these early ships had oars or paddles as well as sails. AM (Kenna No. 50)

107 Lead model of a boat (L 40.3 cm.); one of four said to have been found with marble figurines in a cist grave on the island of Naxos (C. Renfrew, *AJA* 71, 1967, p. 18 No. 12). AM

108 Clay model of a boat (L 19.5 cm.), from an EM ossuary at Palaikastro in eastern Crete. It has the high prow and projecting keel which appear in pictures of early boats and ships in Crete (e.g. the seal impression on Plate 106) and in the Cycladic islands (Fig. 104).

109 Model sedan chair or portable seat (H 10.5 cm.), found with other clay pieces belonging to a toy-sized shrine in the region of the Loom-Weight Basement of the earlier palace at Knossos (Fig. 34; 34). Assigned by Evans to MM II B like the jar with palm trees (Plate 5) and the faience house façades (Plate 22) from the same area.

110 Clay model of a cart (L 14.6 cm.) with four solid wheels, from the region of Palaikastro in eastern Crete. The style of the decoration suggests a date in MM I.

111 The 'Royal Road' at Knossos, looking east towards the 'Theatral Area' at the north-western corner of the palace, which lies to the right. A narrow raised pavement of squared slabs runs down the middle of the cobbled street. The excavations of 1957–61, from which came the objects illustrated on Plates 12–14, 23, 41 and 84, took place both sides of the road where it dips.

112 Shrine of the Double Axes in the palace at Knossos (Fig. 34; 33). This photograph was taken soon after the Shrine was excavated in 1902. The plaster front of the bench at the back has been repaired (p. 133).

113 Tomb in the cemetery of the MM period on the slopes of Ailias east of the palace at Knossos. The large circular chamber hollowed out of the kouskouras rock was divided into two compartments by a stone wall down the middle. This wall may have helped to support the roof, which appears to have been cut in the shape of a shallow dome. Most of the numerous burials were placed in storage jars.

114 Libation vase (rhyton) of chlorite from the palace at Zakro destroyed in LM I B *c.* 1450 BC. The surface of the vase was originally covered with gold leaf, of which some fragments still remain. The reliefs depict a peak sanctuary with wild goats (p. 136).

115 Clay statue of a goddess (H 79 cm.), from Gazi west of Knossos. Her bell-skirt is wheel-made. On the diadem round her head are three large poppies. Opium may have been used to induce ecstasy in the religion of Bronze Age Crete. These large clay goddess statues are usually assigned to LM III, but some may be earlier (p. 138).

116 Gold signet ring from a tomb at Isopata north of Knossos, showing women in long flounced dresses in a field of flowers engaged in some ritual dance. The little figure in the top left may be the goddess whom they are invoking to appear to them.

117 Bronze signet ring from the south edge of the city at Knossos, showing a shrine with what appears to be a mourning goddess and her attendant (p. 138).

118 Clay model from the large circular tomb at Kamilari near Phaistos. Within a columned building, perhaps a shrine, two figures bring offerings to place on altar-like tables in front of a pair of seated couples, who may be the dead receiving divine honours if they are not actually gods. (D. Levi, *Annuario* 39–40, 1962, pp. 123 ff.) (p. 139 f.)

119 Shell plaque (L 8 cm.) from the palace at Phaistos destroyed in LM I B *c.* 1450 BC, with a relief of four animal-headed figures wearing long tasselled robes and holding staffs. The plaque appears to have been fixed to some wooden object, perhaps a box with curved sides. Some details were incised and painted; traces of blue paint survive.

120 Entrance of the great circular tomb at Kamilari near Phaistos before the removal of the blocking slab which was found still in place. The comparatively large entrances of the later circular tombs in Crete needed slabs of considerable size like this to close them.

SOURCES OF THE PLATES

Professor John Evans (courtesy of the British School of Archaeology at Athens), 1, 2; Peter Clayton, 3, 21, 25, 27, 29, 36, 51, 59, 69, 76, 93, 96, 97, 100, 108, 110; courtesy of the Visitors of the Ashmolean Museum, 4, 5, 7, 10, 17, 30, 44, 45, 48, 50, 64, 66, 86, 87, 98, 102, 103, 104, 106, 107, 112; Josephine Powell, 6, 16, 18, 20, 38, 53, 60, 63, 79, 81, 111, 116; Professor Max Hirmer, 8, 40, 52, 55, 56, 58, 90, 92, 115; courtesy of the Trustees of the British Museum, 9, 62, 71, 72, 73; Dr S. Alexiou, 11, 68, 70, 85, 91, 105; the Author (courtesy of the British School of Archaeology at Athens), 12, 13, 14, 23, 41, 42, 49, 65, 67, 84, 94, 95, 113, 117; Professor D. Levi, 19, 118; John Carter, 24; *Palace of Minos,* 26, 28, 31, 32, 57, 88; Mark Cameron, 33, 34, 35; Lieutenant-Colonel C. R. C. Boyle, 37; the Author, 39, 82, 83, 120; Staatliche Museen zu Berlin, 61; Dr Peter Warren, 74; Professor N. Platon, 75, 80; Leonard von Matt, 77, 99, 114; from originals in Thames and Hudson archives, 15, 22, 43, 46, 47, 54, 78, 89, 101, 109, 119.

Index

Index

Index